CW01302010

# CLAUSEWITZ AND CONTEMPORARY WAR

# Clausewitz and Contemporary War

ANTULIO J. ECHEVARRIA II

**OXFORD**
UNIVERSITY PRESS

# OXFORD
**UNIVERSITY PRESS**

Great Clarendon Street, Oxford OX2 6DP

Oxford University Press is a department of the University of Oxford.
It furthers the University's objective of excellence in research, scholarship,
and education by publishing worldwide in

Oxford  New York

Auckland  Cape Town  Dar es Salaam  Hong Kong  Karachi
Kuala Lumpur  Madrid  Melbourne  Mexico City  Nairobi
New Delhi  Shanghai  Taipei  Toronto

With offices in

Argentina  Austria  Brazil  Chile  Czech Republic  France  Greece
Guatemala  Hungary  Italy  Japan  Poland  Portugal  Singapore
South Korea  Switzerland  Thailand  Turkey  Ukraine  Vietnam

Oxford is a registered trade mark of Oxford University Press
in the UK and in certain other countries

Published in the United States
by Oxford University Press Inc., New York

© Antulio J. Echevarria II, 2007

The moral rights of the author have been asserted
Database right Oxford University Press (maker)

First published 2007

All rights reserved. No part of this publication may be reproduced,
stored in a retrieval system, or transmitted, in any form or by any means,
without the prior permission in writing of Oxford University Press,
or as expressly permitted by law, or under terms agreed with the appropriate
reprographics rights organization. Enquiries concerning reproduction
outside the scope of the above should be sent to the Rights Department,
Oxford University Press, at the address above

You must not circulate this book in any other binding or cover
and you must impose the same condition on any acquirer

British Library Cataloguing in Publication Data

Data available

Library of Congress Cataloging in Publication Data

Data available

Typeset by SPI Publisher Services, Pondicherry, India
Printed in Great Britain
on acid-free paper by
Biddles, Ltd., King's Lynn, Norfolk

ISBN 978–0–19–923191–1

1 3 5 7 9 10 8 6 4 2

*To mom and dad. There has always been too much to say and not enough time to say it. I hope this says it all.*

# Contents

| | |
|---|---|
| *Acknowledgments* | viii |
| Introduction | 1 |

### PART I. *ON WAR*'S PURPOSE AND METHOD

| | |
|---|---|
| 1. A Search for Objective Knowledge | 21 |
| 2. Validating Concepts and Principles | 37 |

### PART II. THE NATURE AND UNIVERSE OF WAR

| | |
|---|---|
| 3. War Is More than a Chameleon | 61 |
| 4. Policy, Politics, and Political Determinism | 84 |
| 5. Genius, Giving the Rule to Art | 102 |

### PART III. STRATEGY, BALANCING PURPOSE, AND MEANS

| | |
|---|---|
| 6. Combat, War's only Means | 133 |
| 7. Principles of Strategy | 154 |
| 8. Center of Gravity | 177 |
| Conclusion | 191 |
| *Selected Bibliography* | 199 |
| *Index* | 209 |

# *Acknowledgments*

I would like to thank the growing community of Clausewitz scholars, as this work sought to incorporate as much of the existing literature as appropriate. In particular, I would like to thank Terence Holmes, Jan Willem Honig, Andreas Herberg-Rothe, Christopher Bassford, and Randy Papadopoulos for the fruitful discussions I have had with them. However, the 'other side of the hill'—those authors who reject Clausewitz's views—deserve credit as well; their critiques have inspired new research. I am also indebted to the able editors and publishing assistants at Oxford University Press; their reputation for excellence is well deserved. My deepest gratitude, however, must go to my wife and our four children. Without their loving support this book would simply not have come to be.

# Introduction

'Despite the manuscript's incomplete form, I believe an unbiased reader, who thirsts after truth and conviction, will not fail to recognize in the first six books the fruits of many years of considering and diligently studying war; perhaps he will even find in them the principal ideas from which a revolution in military theory might emerge.'

Clausewitz's prefatory note to *On War*, dated 10 July 1827[1]

Bernard Brodie, the renowned American scholar of strategic thinking, once claimed that *On War*'s ideas, 'though densely packed in, are generally simple and are for the most part clearly expressed in jargon-free language'.[2] Perhaps no other statement regarding Carl von Clausewitz's work has been so completely misleading. Understanding *On War* is a difficult and at times genuinely frustrating task. Most of its ideas are not simple, but complex; like a finely woven cloth, the significance of each thought depends on its relation to the others. At times the overall pattern is ambiguous, indicating that Clausewitz himself was not always sure where he stood. At other times, the pattern changes, sometimes abruptly and at others more subtly, leaving readers with conflicting impressions. The language he used to develop his thoughts, moreover, is at times sewn together with an outmoded philosophical jargon, all but impenetrable to modern readers. However, that jargon, like his frequent use of metaphor, serves important purposes, for he considered the form of an expression as essential as the content.[3] Overlooking form for substance thus runs the risk of misinterpreting *On War* altogether. In short, taking Clausewitz's ideas to be simple and jargon-free is a sure step toward misunderstanding them.

This is not to say that Clausewitz's masterwork is too difficult to grasp: it is not. However, Brodie's miscues underscore the need for an approach that offers readers an introductory knowledge of *On War*'s form, its purpose, and methodology. As Clausewitz himself warned, unless one's observations are rendered in the proper form, readers may understand the individual concepts, 'but the overall thought will remain incomprehensible'.[4] To be sure, several efforts to guide readers through *On War*'s concepts already exist.[5] However, none of them explains the book's form adequately. Brodie's own guide, which has the advantage of accompanying the justly celebrated English translation of *On War* by Sir Michael Howard and Peter Paret, is a chapter-by-chapter analysis all but bereft of any consideration for the form in which the ideas appear.[6]

This book has two goals: first, to shed light on the purpose of *On War* and the methodology Clausewitz employed to present his concepts; second, to use that knowledge as a basis for understanding his general theory of war, and his ideas concerning the relationship between war and politics, and his principles of strategy. We find many of these ideas being discussed in current debates over the nature of contemporary conflict, as well as in the instruction that prepares military and civilian leaders for their roles in the development and execution of strategy.[7] Thus, they warrant analysis. Studying *On War* can provide today's military practitioners and civilian analysts a foundational understanding of the primary elements of armed conflict.

Of course, understanding *On War* is no more a prerequisite for winning wars than knowledge is a requirement for exercising power. Still, Clausewitz's opus has become something of an authoritative reference for those desiring to expand their knowledge of war. The success of *On War* is, notably, both just what its author intended, and much more than he could have hoped.

Although this book considers Clausewitz's contributions to our knowledge of war, it is *not* an argument for *On War*'s relevance. Anything that stands or falls principally on the notion of relevance is likely to have a brief shelf life, especially in an era in which change appears ever more rapid. Instead, this study argues that Clausewitz's *On War* is as critical to our basic knowledge of war as Nicolas Copernicus' *On the Revolutions of the Heavenly Spheres* is to astronomy.[8] Ironically, neither work was fully appreciated when it first appeared; yet, each one eventually led to a revolution in its respective field, and in some cases beyond.[9] Clausewitz's revolution, though perhaps not fully understood, has yet to be undone.

Certainly, not all of Clausewitz's ideas contribute to our knowledge of war, or remain valid today. A number of scholars and analysts, in fact, contend that very little of what the Prussian theorist wrote so long ago applies to contemporary war. Many have argued, wrongly as we shall see, that his views were too subjective, too much a product of his own times, and that his concepts pertain only to the Western model of the nation-state, and thus overlook unconventional conflicts.[10] Nor did Clausewitz address every aspect of war. Careful readers will discover important gaps and inconsistencies in *On War*. He did not write about naval warfare, for instance, nor did he address the roles that economic power, diplomacy, or information play in war. Such shortcomings are only partially remedied by studying his many other works. In discussing *On War*'s content, therefore, this study will candidly reveal what he overlooked, where his logic fails, and where his arguments are unconvincing for other reasons.

## ON WAR'S PURPOSE

Clausewitz's masterwork is an attempt to capture what he called objective knowledge, observations that were universally valid and thus applicable to all wars. Ultimately, he desired to present this knowledge as a scientific theory, that is, as an organized body, not unlike Copernicus' heliocentric theory; hence, *On War* is also unavoidably a search for universal laws. While Clausewitz believed laws which prescribed action had no place in military theory, he also thought of laws in a different sense, as fundamental cause-and-effect relationships; discovering these would give his theory coherence. He used the term theory in several ways, one of which was to indicate an organized corpus of scientific observations. This, in brief, is what *On War* is.

Copernicus' *On the Revolutions* described the universe in terms of a heliocentric system, and offered that system as a replacement for Ptolemy's geocentric one. Similarly, Clausewitz introduced, through *On War*, a combat- or battle-centric theory of war, which he hoped would displace the other systems of his day, especially those advanced by leading Enlightenment thinkers such as Heinrich von Bülow.[11] Clausewitz referred to these theorists derisively as 'system builders', even though his own theory would have amounted to something of a system.[12] The difference is that Clausewitz believed his system, based on genuine laws rather than fashionable notions, would explain war's inner workings instead of dictating action. Still, as this study will show, Clausewitz struggled, and not always successfully, to keep his own subjective views from intruding into his objective analyses.

To arrive at objective laws, Clausewitz placed the principal elements of war, such as military genius and friction, under the microscope, so to speak, and examined them in detail. He used military history as a sort of crucible to test how each element functioned and influenced the others, if indeed it did so.[13] To validate his general concept of war, Clausewitz borrowed a method of proof from the German philosopher Immanuel Kant's system of logic; however, he did it indirectly, through the lectures and textbooks of Johann Kiesewetter, a professor of mathematics and logic, whom some in Berlin society referred to fondly as the 'national professor'.[14] This method required that Clausewitz conduct parallel lines of inquiry, one logical and one material, which were more comparative than dialectical in nature; as a third step, it also required that any valid concept be located within the established hierarchy of other known concepts.[15] Clausewitz's celebrated statement that war is the continuation of political activity by other means essentially satisfies that requirement: it situates war firmly and precisely within the field of politics (*Politik*), or what today might be called international relations. As we shall see, much of the philosophical terminology Clausewitz used in *On War* is defined in Kiesewetter's textbooks. Those definitions help shed light on Clausewitz's methodology, and enable us to resolve the time-honored complaint that *On War* is too theoretical or too wrapped in philosophical jargon to be deciphered by the general reader.[16]

Unfortunately, Clausewitz never finished the manuscript to his satisfaction despite more than a decade of effort. He began composing the work sometime after 1815, but died of cholera in 1831, before bringing the product of his long labor to final form.[17] Most scholars agree that the unfinished state of *On War* does not diminish its overall value. Nevertheless, it does raise important questions concerning how readers should approach the work. The prevailing view is that a dramatic shift took place in Clausewitz's thinking around the summer of 1827, when he was completing Book VI and while drafting several of the chapters for the final two of *On War*'s eight books. At that time, he penned a prefatory note indicating that he intended to revise the manuscript to bring out two ideas more clearly.[18] The first was that war can be of two kinds, based on two fundamentally different purposes—conquest or more limited aims—and that both types were valid. The second was that war was the mere continuation of political affairs by other means. His intention was to develop these ideas more fully in Books VII and VIII, then revise Books I through VI accordingly. It seems Clausewitz did, indeed, attempt to follow this plan, but several military postings and, ultimately, cholera intervened, preventing his revisions from progressing beyond Book I.

## APPROACHING *ON WAR*

The prevailing view concerning how to approach *On War*, therefore, is that readers should regard it as two different works superimposed on one another: a sort of Old and New Testament, to borrow the expression of one scholar.[19] Books II through VI (the Old Testament) are said to reflect the ideas of the younger Clausewitz, which are believed to stress the importance of battle, the imperative of destruction. Books VII, VIII, and the revised I (the New Testament) are held as representative of the ideas of the mature Clausewitz, which are said to emphasize the primacy of policy in the conduct of war.[20]

## Introduction

Another scholar put it somewhat differently, claiming the Prussian theorist was of two minds: Clausewitz the idealist, who saw fighting or combat as the essence of war; and Clausewitz the realist, who concluded war was the continuation of political activity by other means.[21] Clausewitz the realist took over the writing of *On War*, or attempted to, as the work was entering its final stages, though many of the ideas of Clausewitz the idealist remain evident throughout.

The problem with this approach is that it assumes Clausewitz's later ideas should take precedence over his earlier ones, that the New Testament should replace the Old one, and that the views of Clausewitz the realist should supersede those of Clausewitz the idealist. However, this assumption is not supported by what he actually said in the note of 1827, or by the revised portions of *On War*, or by the content of several of his earlier writings.

In Clausewitz's prefatory note of 1827, he indicated that incorporating the two ideas mentioned above would serve to clarify and simplify his earlier concepts, not nullify them. In fact, he stated that the ideas which appeared in the (then still unrevised) first six books—which include the all-important centrality of battle, and the concepts of friction, chance, uncertainty, danger, physical exertion, military genius, the interdependence of material and psychological forces, and the intrinsic superiority of the defense—would provide the groundwork for a revolution in military theory. It was the ideas of the young Clausewitz, or Clausewitz the idealist, in other words, which provided the basis for the revolution in military theory. In contrast, the revised portions of *On War* do, indeed, elaborate upon the vital importance of war's political purpose. However, they do so without ever diminishing the significance he had already attributed to war's means. Still, this so-called New Testament provides readers with an absolutely essential perspective by situating war within the larger framework of political affairs.

## A REVOLUTION IN MILITARY THEORY

As Clausewitz's earlier writings demonstrate, he clearly realized that all wars were driven by political purposes.[22] This idea, we know, did not actually originate with him, though he certainly examined it in greater detail than his contemporaries. In fact, the whole structure of *On War* is based on the relationship between purpose and means. For instance, strategy (Book III) establishes the purpose of an engagement (Book IV), which is also the means it uses to achieve the overall purpose of the conflict. Winning an engagement is, thus, the purpose of the armed forces (Book V), which employ one of two basic means: defense (Book VI) or attack (Book VII).

Clausewitz's revolutionary system, then, is an examination of a cause-and-effect relationship fundamental to the conduct of war. As with any relationship, the interplay between purpose and means works both ways: at times the purpose functions as the cause, influencing the selection of the means; at other times, alterations in the means force adjustments in the purpose. The idea that war is a continuation of political activity by other means certainly made Clausewitz's nascent scientific theory more complete; in a sense, it took the revolution full circle. However, except for the rigor of his analysis, this idea did not go much beyond some of the standard texts of the day or, the works of Machiavelli, with which Clausewitz was also familiar.[23] The idea is more of a finishing touch to his theory than a decisive turn.

Just as we describe Copernicus' system as heliocentric, so we should think of Clausewitz's system as combat-centric: he referred to combat or fighting as 'the highest *law* of war'.[24] Combat, or the threat of it, weaves 'its way through the whole fabric of military activity and holds it together'.[25] In fact, if we were to remove fighting or violence from Clausewitz's system, it would collapse; moreover, his other concepts, such as friction, danger, and uncertainty, would lose their significance.

Whereas Copernicus' revolution shifted astronomy away from a geocentric view of the universe, Clausewitz's revolution attempted to move military theory away from what he saw as artificial or geometric devices, toward the core of war, combat.[26] While other theories might acknowledge the many purposes war could serve, they failed to identify the correct means. Violence, or the threat of it, was the only proper means, though it might vary in degree as well as in kind. Indeed, as we shall see, Clausewitz's combat-centric theory still holds for conflicts in which violence plays only a minor role.

## AN UNFINISHED OPUS

The natural tendency in any act of interpretation is to render the subject as completely and coherently as possible. As Clausewitz himself observed, 'the human mind...has a universal thirst for clarity, and longs to feel itself part of an orderly scheme of things'.[27] Yet, while *On War*'s author indicated his opus was unfinished in terms of its form rather than its substance, we cannot know what other ideas might have occurred to him in the process of revising his manuscript. In a sense, *On War* resembles the classic unfinished symphony, like Franz Schubert's 'archetypal' unfinished eighth or Ludwig van Beethoven's 'hypothetical' tenth, for instance.[28]

While the temptation to finish such works may be great, the results are rarely satisfying. We always seem left with the nagging sense that the master would have done it differently. We ought, therefore, to resist the temptation to finish Clausewitz's opus for him, to privilege his so-called realist over his idealist views. Instead, we must take the work as it is, as a balanced blend of diverse and even conflicting ideas, unfinished and perhaps raw in parts, but not necessarily incomplete.

## STRUCTURE

This book consists of eight chapters arranged in three parts. Part I '*On War*'s Purpose and Method' is made up of two chapters, which describe what Clausewitz set out to do with his masterwork, and the method he used but only partially carried through. As mentioned earlier, what Clausewitz wrote cannot be separated from the way he presented it. Part II 'The Nature of War' consists of three chapters. The first chapter analyzes Clausewitz's general concept of war. The second examines the relationship he established between war and policy, and the secondary and often overlooked relationship between policy and politics. The third chapter discusses his views regarding friction and genius. Part II thus describes Clausewitz's universe of war. Part III 'Strategy, Linking Purpose and Means' discusses his concept of strategy, which was based on the dynamic relationship between purpose and means, and those strategic principles or concepts he unearthed through careful observation, many of which remain valid today. As Clausewitz pointed out, existing political conditions often determine what force can actually achieve in the service of policy. Yet, as the history of armed conflict shows, this fact is rarely appreciated. All wars end, it should be remembered, with at least one side disappointed, sometimes severely.[29] Part of the reason for such failures is the inability to recognize how existing political circumstances can limit the realization of policy goals.

Individuals as far apart on the political spectrum as Mao Zedong and Henry Kissinger have attested that, whatever its difficulties, studying *On War* is worth the effort.[30] This book endeavors to justify those views.

## NOTES

1. Carl von Clausewitz, *Vom Kriege. Hinterlassenes Werk des Generals Carl von Clausewitz*, 19th edn., Werner Hahlweg (ed.) (Bonn, Germany: Dümmlers, 1991), 181; hereafter, *Vom Kriege* (because Clausewitz's masterwork was still under revision at the time of his death, citations will include the work's book and chapter references). Compare: Carl von Clausewitz, *On War*, trans. Peter Paret and Michael Howard (Princeton, NJ: Princeton University Press, 1976), 71; hereafter, *On War*. Recent scholarship has raised concerns over the Howard–Paret translation; see Jan Willem Honig, 'Clausewitz's *On War*: Problems of Text and Translation', in Hew Strachan (ed.), *Clausewitz in the 21st Century*, (Oxford: Oxford University Press, 2007). Also, Howard and Paret have admitted their translation might be 'too clean'. Thus, the translations in this book are my own. However, since the Howard–Paret translation is the one most likely to be used by the general reader, relevant pages in *On War* are presented throughout for reference.
2. Bernard Brodie, 'The Continuing Relevance of *On War*', in *On War*, 45; Brodie qualified the statement on the next page, admitting Clausewitz's opus indeed poses some significant challenges.
3. 'Ueber den Zustand der Theorie der Kriegskunst', in Werner Hahlweg (ed.), *Carl von Clausewitz: Schrifte–Aufsätze–Studien–Briefe*, 2 vols. (Göttingen, Germany: Vandenhoeck, 1990), vol. 2, Part 1, 28–9.
4. Clausewitz, 'Ueber den Zustand der Theorie', 28.
5. Recent examples are: Beatrice Heuser, *Reading Clausewitz* (London: Pimlico, 2002); and Hugh Smith, *On Clausewitz: A Study of Political and Military Ideas* (New York: Palgrave, 2005), though this is more an analysis than a guide. Raymond Aron, *Penser la Guerre, Clausewitz*, 2 vols. (Paris: Gallimard, 1976), is a guide that provides some important introductory knowledge; however, the English translation: *Clausewitz: Philosopher of War*, trans. C. Booker and N. Stone (Englewood Cliffs, NJ: Prentice-Hall, 1985), is considered inadequate; see also *A Short Guide to Clausewitz's On War*, ed. and intro. Roger Ashley Leonard (New York: Putnam, 1967).
6. Bernard Brodie, 'A Guide to the Reading of *On War*', in *On War*, 641–711.
7. For recent contributions to those debates, see Jan Angstrom and Isabelle Duyvesteyn (eds.), *Rethinking the Nature of War* (London: Frank Cass, 2005); and *The Nature of Modern War: Clausewitz and His Critics Revisited* (Stockholm: Swedish National Defense College, 2003); David J. Lonsdale, *The Nature of War in the Information Age: Clausewitzian Future* (London: Frank Cass, 2004); Gert de Nooy (ed.), *The Clausewitzian Dictum and the Future of Western Military Strategy* (The Hague: Kluwer, 1997).
8. Nicholas Copernicus, *On the Revolutions of the Heavenly Spheres*, trans. Edmund Rosen (Baltimore, MD: Johns Hopkins University Press, 1992). Thomas S. Kuhn, *The Copernican Revolution: Planetary Astronomy in the Development of Western Thought* (Cambridge, MA: Harvard University Press, 1957).

*Introduction* 9

9. Hans Rothfels, 'Clausewitz', in Earle Meade (ed.), *Makers of Modern Strategy: Military Thought from Machiavelli to Hitler* (Princeton, NJ: Princeton University Press, 1943), 101, also makes the comparison, though only in passing. One would not want to carry the similarities between Clausewitz and Copernicus too far, but a comparison brings out several interesting parallels. First, each sought a better explanation for the universe: for Clausewitz it was the universe of war, for Copernicus, the cosmos. Second, each applied a scientific method of sorts to accomplish that aim: observations were made and collected, discrepancies with the prevailing views noted, and hypotheses or propositions developed, tested, more observations made, and so on. Third, neither observer was foremost a scientist: Clausewitz was a soldier, while Copernicus was a church canon, or lawyer. Each pursued his work as an avocational rather than a vocational interest (it is not necessary to be a theorist to be a soldier; in fact, the combination is a rare one).
10. Herfried Münkler, *The New Wars* (Malden, MA: Polity Press, 2005); Mary Kaldor, *New & Old Wars: Organized Violence in a Global Era* (Stanford, CA: Stanford University Press, 1999); Kalev J. Holsti, *War, the State, and the State of War* (Cambridge: Cambridge University Press, 1996); John Keegan, *A History of Warfare* (New York: Alfred Knopf, 1994); Martin van Creveld, *The Transformation of War* (New York: Free Press, 1991).
11. *Vom Kriege*, II/2, 281–4; *On War*, 134–6. Other such theorists include: Henry Lloyd and Antoine-Henri Jomini, whose theories are discussed briefly in the next chapter. See Martin van Creveld, *The Art of War: War and Military Thought* (London: Cassell, 2005); and Azar Gat, *The Origins of Military Thought from the Enlightenment to Clausewitz* (Oxford: Clarendon Press, 1989).
12. Carl von Clausewitz, 'On the Life and Character of Scharnhorst', in *Historical and Political Writings*, ed. and trans. Peter Paret and Daniel Moran (Princeton, NJ: Princeton University Press, 1992), 103.
13. Clausewitz, 'Strategic Critique of the Campaign of 1814 in France' (*c*. early 1820s), in *Historical and Political Writings*, 205–19, is an example of Clausewitz's use of military history as a crucible.
14. Johann G. K. Kiesewetter (1766–1819); his principal text was *Grundriss einer Allgemeinen Logik nach Kantischen Grundsätzen zum Gebrauch für Vorlesungen*, 2 vols., 3rd and 4th edn. (Leipzig, Germany: H. A. Kochly, 1824–25); vol. I deals with pure logic (or reason), while vol. II pertains to applied logic. Peter Paret, *Clausewitz and the State: The Man, His Theories, and His Times* (Princeton, NJ: Princeton University Press, 1985), 69; Hans Rothfels, *Carl von Clausewitz: Politik und Krieg* (Berlin, Germany: Dümmler, 1920), 23–4; and Werner Hahlweg, 'Philosophie und Theorie bei Clausewitz', in U. De Maizière (ed.), *Freiheit ohne Krieg? Beiträge zur Strategie-Diskussion der Gegenwart im Spiegel der Theorien von Carl von Clausewitz* (Bonn, Germany: Dümmler, 1980), 325–32, discuss Kiesewetter's value to Clausewitz. For the 'national professor' reference, see Roger Parkinson, *Clausewitz: A Biography* (New York: Stein & Day, 1971), 35.

15. Kiesewetter, *Grundriss* I (46–7), 109–11. Michael Handel, *Masters of War: Classical Strategic Thought*, 3rd edn. (London: Frank Cass, 2001), appendix C, 327–44; and Aron, *Philosopher of War*, esp. 89–175, overemphasize the use of the dialectical method in Clausewitz's approach.
16. For such complaints see General von Seeckt, *Gedanken eines Soldaten* (Leipzig, Germany: Hase & Kohler, 1935), 25; and Jehuda L. Wallach, 'Misperceptions of Clausewitz' *On War* by the German Military', and Williamson Murray, 'Clausewitz: Some Thoughts on What the Germans Got Right', in Michael I. Handel (ed.), *Clausewitz and Modern Strategy* (London: Frank Cass, 1989), 217, 270, respectively.
17. It is difficult, perhaps impossible, to pinpoint exactly when Clausewitz began writing *On War* proper. It is generally agreed that the work was started sometime after the defeat of Napoleon (1815), though some of its chapters clearly draw heavily from earlier essays. Eberhard Kessel, 'Zur Genesis der modernen Kriegslehre: Die Entstehungsgeschichte von Clausewitz' Buch 'Vom Kriege', *Wehrwissenschaftliche Rundschau*, 3/9 (1953), 405–23. Werner Hahlweg, 'Das Clausewitzbild Einst und Jetzt', *Vom Kriege*, esp. 34–40; Paret, 'The Genesis of *On War*', *On War*, 3–26.
18. *Vom Kriege*, 179; *On War*, 69.
19. Smith, *On Clausewitz*, 65; Hans Delbrück, 'Carl von Clausewitz', *Historische und Politische Aufsätze* (Berlin, Germany: Walther & Apolant, 1887) appears to have been the first to perceive this shift in emphasis within Clausewitz's work; see also Eberhard Kessel, 'Zur Genesis der modernen Kriegslehre: Die Entstehungsgeschichte von Clausewitz's Buch "Vom Kriege"', *Wehrwissenschaftliche Rundschau*, 3/9 (1953), 405–23; the idea was further developed in Aron, *Clausewitz: Philosopher of War*; see also Gat, *Origins of Military Thought*; and Heuser, *Reading Clausewitz*.
20. Gat, *Origins of Military Thought*; Aron, *Clausewitz: Philosopher of War*; see also the review essay by Jan Willem Honig, 'Interpreting Clausewitz', *Security Studies*, 3/3 (spring 1994), 571–80.
21. Heuser, *Reading Clausewitz*; see also Sir Michael Howard's review, in *The English Historical Review*, 117/474 (November 2002), 1537–58, which supports Heuser's interpretation.
22. Clausewitz, 'Observations on the Wars of the Austrian Succession' (early c.1820s), in *Historical and Political Writings*, 22; Gunther E. Rothenberg's review of Gat's *Origins of Military Thought* in *American Historical Review*, 96/3 (June 1991), 834, makes the same point.
23. Clausewitz, 'Notes on History and Politics' (c.1803–7), and 'Letter to Fichte' (1809), in *Historical and Political Writings*, 245, 279–84.
24. *Vom Kriege*, I/2, 229; *On War*, 99; emphasis added.
25. *Vom Kriege*, I/2, 225; *On War*, 97.
26. Andreas Herberg-Rothe, *Das Rätsel Clausewitz: Politische Theorie des Krieges im Widerstreit* (Munich, Germany: W. Fink, 2001) is a compelling analysis of how Clausewitz's views changed after his experience in, and subsequent

study of, three major Napoleonic battles: Jena-Auerstädt, Moscow, and Waterloo.
27. Clausewitz's undated prefatory note, *Vom Kriege*, 181–3; *On War*, 70–1.
28. Franz Schubert composed six symphonies between 1813 and 1818, but became dissatisfied with them due largely to the dramatic heights reached by Beethoven's symphonies. Schubert thus attempted to redefine the scope of his symphonic form with his eighth symphony, a feat he in fact accomplished; however, the work was still unfinished when he died in 1828, at the age of 31. Christopher H. Gibbs (ed.), *Cambridge Companion to Schubert* (Cambridge: Cambridge University Press, 1997). The consensus is that Beethoven intended to write a 10th symphony. Barry Cooper, *The Beethoven Compendium* (London: Thames & Hudson, 1991); Cooper attempted to assemble Beethoven's missing 10th symphony from several fragmentary sketches. However, the results failed to please Beethoven devotees.
29. David Kaiser, *Politics and War: European Conflict from Phillip II to Hitler* (Cambridge: Harvard University Press, 1990) provides four case studies where states failed to achieve their aims through war.
30. On Mao see Heuser, *Reading Clausewitz*, 138–42; on Kissinger see Christopher Bassford, *Clausewitz in English: The Reception of Clausewitz in Britain and America* (Oxford: Oxford University Press, 1992), 198–201.

# Part I

## *On War*'s Purpose and Method

Chapters 1 and 2 discuss the purpose Clausewitz pursued and the method he employed in writing *On War*. As the first chapter shows, his purpose was 'to dispel false and frail concepts' of war and to replace them with verifiable truths, arranged as a coherent body of knowledge, or theory.[1] Part of the reason for doing so, as he explained, was to determine whether universal laws govern the conflict of living forces that make up war, and, if so, whether those laws can provide a useful guide for action.[2] The second chapter examines how Clausewitz attempted to apply the Kantian doctrine of concepts both to validate the truths he set forth, and to order them appropriately.[3] *On War* is a compilation of a lifetime of personal experience and observation of war which its author captured in numerous essays, notes, and other writings. Without an accepted scientific or philosophical method to validate and arrange his reflections, Clausewitz realized, his theory would amount to little more than a memoir of his personal experiences or a loose collection of historical case studies. *On War* would, in other words, have been no better than the other profoundly dissatisfying military theories of his day.

A quick glance at a few of the most prominent military thinkers of the Enlightenment—such as Henry Lloyd (1729–83), Heinrich von Bülow (1757–1807), and Antoine-Henri Jomini (1779–1869)—will familiarize the reader with some of the theoretical works Clausewitz studied, and for various reasons found objectionable.[4] Lloyd, a highly educated English soldier of fortune, had a storied military career, serving in the armies of several European states, most notably the Austrian army during the Seven Years' War.[5] His major military writings include *The History of the Late War in Germany* (1766), a patently biased account of the Seven Years' War, and *Continuation of the History of the Late War in Germany between the King of Prussia and the Empress of Germany and Her Allies* (1781).[6]

In keeping with the Enlightenment tradition of distinguishing between art and science, Lloyd divided war into two parts: a mechanical branch, which was based on fixed principles and precepts which can be taught, such as the use of fortifications and artillery; and one that 'had no name, nor can it be defined, or taught'. The latter part 'consisted in the just application of the principles and precepts of war' to the countless situations that occur, and 'no rule, no study', and 'no experience', can teach it, for it was 'the effect of genius alone'.[7] Since this unnamed part of war was too difficult either to capture or to relate by scientific means, it tended to become a catch-all for everything the mechanical part of war could not explain. Lloyd is also credited with introducing the principle of 'the line of operations', the line connecting 'fixed and determined points' where provisions and munitions were stored and transported to the army; this principle is the forerunner of the modern-day concept of lines of communication and supply.[8] Although openly ridiculed by Napoleon, it would provide the basis for a number of subsequent theories, particularly those proposed by Bülow and Jomini.[9]

Bülow served in the Prussian army during most of the 1770s and 1780s, after which he became a world-traveler, writer, and commentator.[10] His most important military work was *The Spirit of the Modern System of War* (1799), which appeared in several editions and was translated into English and French.[11] In it, Bülow claimed to have discovered not only a geometric formula for strategy, but for the first time to have truly defined the difference between tactics and strategy. 'Strategy', he declared, was 'the science of the movements in war of two armies, out of the visual circle of each other', or beyond the range of artillery; tactics, in contrast, was 'the science of the movements made within sight of the enemy, and within reach of his artillery'.[12]

Bülow argued that the invention of firearms had revolutionized warfare by drastically and irreversibly increasing an army's logistical demands, which in turn made depots, bases of supply, and the principle of lines of operation essentially indispensable. One could now avoid pitched battles and instead achieve victory by attacking an opponent's lines of supply. To avoid losing the battle over supply lines, commanders must apply Bülow's principle of the base. This theory held that armies had to construct a fortified line of depots, a 'base', and that the lines of operations proceeding from the ends of that supply base must converge on the object of the attack at an angle of 90 degrees or greater; otherwise, the defender would hold the advantage. The formula was simple enough that anyone could apply it, which meant that superior talent and genius were no longer necessary; mass and firepower had essentially rendered courage and genius obsolete.

The art of war, in Bülow's view, had thus reached a state of 'perfection' where all that was art would continue to collapse into the realm of science, until it finally disappeared altogether. Henceforth, war would favor only those states with greater resources and larger armies. The conditions for 'perpetual peace' were at hand, at last, for smaller states would eventually be absorbed by larger ones, and larger states would no longer need to wage bloody battles to settle their differences.[13] Despite Bülow's dubious application of geometry, his theory became popular, particularly among the proponents of perpetual peace or those who saw bloodless victories as the acme of generalship.[14]

Jomini was a supremely confident and evidently irrepressible Swiss officer who served in Napoleon's army from 1805 to 1813, and then with the Russians from 1813 to 1814.[15] A highly prolific author, he is most noted for his *Treatise on Grand Tactics*(1804–5) and its successor *Treatise of Major Military Operations* (1807–9), and his *Summary of the Art of War* (1838).[16] The latter work, especially, went through several editions and became immensely popular in Europe and the United States the last half of the nineteenth century.[17] It benefited from its author's reading of *On War*, which caused him to make a number of accommodations for Clausewitz's views, such as introducing the term *politique* (politics), which parallels in meaning the Prussian's *Politik*.[18]

Jomini took Lloyd's theory of the line of operation as a start point, and developed a number of principles of maneuver, especially the concept of interior lines. This concept, drawn mainly from an analysis of the campaigns of Frederick the Great and Napoleon, held that one side might come to occupy a position between or 'inside' divided enemy armies; by the use of interior lines, then, a commander could defeat first one enemy army, then the other. In this way, a smaller army could defeat a larger one, as Frederick the Great had done on several occasions.

Jomini also wrote of discovering 'secrets' and 'keys' to victory and, indeed, to the whole science of war.[19] His most significant key to victory devolved to little more than bringing as much combat power as possible to bear against an opponent's decisive areas or points, especially his lines of communication and supply. Ironically, the twentieth-century military critic and theorist Liddell Hart would blame Clausewitz, whose *On War* was barely read, rather than Jomini, whose *Summary* was widely circulated throughout the last half of the nineteenth century, for the over-reliance on mass that characterized operations during World War I.[20]

As Clausewitz surveyed the condition of the military theory of his day he found it wanting in several respects. Contemporary military theory, he complained, was only 'of limited utility, was displeasing, and lacking entirely in nourishment for the mind'.[21] The underlying problem lay not with the difficulty of the subject matter, for he was sure war could be analyzed just as well as any other human activity. Instead, the 'blame lies in the incompleteness of the existing books and treatments themselves'. These works 'lacked the spirit of philosophical inquiry, were usually arranged in a defective manner, with principles and rules being drawn from insufficient bases, and with inconsequential views often being presented as if they were essential'.[22] These shortcomings, he determined, were partly due to the difficulty of finding military practitioners properly educated in scientific methodology, and partly due to the problem of acquiring the necessary range of experiences from which one could draw universal conclusions.

Clausewitz rejected the Enlightenment tradition of dividing war into an art or a science. The former, he explained, deals with skill and ability; the latter with knowledge. War may require the use of knowledge and skill, which are indeed inseparable in most individuals; however, war is a living force directed at another living force, not against inanimate matter, as in the mechanical sciences, nor against an animate but passive force, as in the arts. War was, therefore, neither an art nor a science.[23]

Clausewitz criticized Lloyd's theory of the line of operations for being based on assumptions about army organization that did not apply either before or after the Seven Years' War, and were thus not universal. He also took Bülow's theory of the base to task, not with respect to the concept itself, which he thought was of some use to strategy, but for the way its author recommended applying it as a formula for victory.[24] In a critical review published anonymously in 1805, Clausewitz also blasted Bülow for 'crawling around the truth' by means of a definition of strategy that was 'entirely mechanical (*mechanisch*) and completely un-philosophical'.[25] 'Strategy is *nothing* without combat (*Gefecht*)', Clausewitz insisted, 'for combat is the material that strategy makes use of, the means it employs. Just as tactics is the *employment of military forces in battle*, so strategy is the *use of battles . . . to achieve the ultimate purpose of the war*'.[26]

Clausewitz also made it a point to emphasize explicitly the importance of courage and genius in the opening chapter of *On War*: the very two human elements which Bülow argued had become obsolete. With respect to Jomini's principle of interior lines, Clausewitz maintained that it rested on a solid truth—namely, that combat was the only effective means in war—but he deemed it too limited and abstract to govern actions in the physical world. All three theorists, he added, failed to understand the importance of genius and of other psychological factors, and so simply ignored them.[27] Moreover, neither Bülow's principle of the base nor Jomini's principle of interior lines applied well to the defense when the aims were limited.[28] In short, military theory in Clausewitz's day needed a complete overhaul: what passed for theory was little more than a 'whirl of opinions, which had no firm point or discernable laws around which to revolve'.[29]

Although Clausewitz criticized these and many other theorists, he also borrowed ideas and historical examples from them when it suited him. For instance, his several references in book VIII to the Tartars and their ways of war parallel those found in the works of Lloyd, especially, and Bülow, though Clausewitz generally added his own twist.[30] There is some justification, therefore, for Jomini's complaint that Clausewitz plagiarized him, though hardly to the extent the Swiss theorist claimed.[31] Clausewitz used the historical examples of others as much to educate himself as to refute the points others made about them. One would certainly expect to find the theories of others incorporated in a work that endeavored to transcend subjective truths for objective ones. Like Copernicus, then, Clausewitz sought a better theory for explaining his universe, the universe of war, an explanation that accorded with the realities he observed, both in person and through the study of history.

## NOTES

1. Clausewitz, 'Zweck des Werkes', in *Schriften–Aufsätze–Studien–Briefe*, 24; the note is not dated, but Hahlweg believed it was written between 1807 and 1812.
2. *Vom Kriege*, II/3, 303–4; *On War*, 149–50.
3. The 'Doctrine of Concepts' is described by Kiesewetter in *Grundriss*, I, 46–7, 109–11.
4. Others include Georg H. von Berenhorst (1733–1814), whose ideas concerning the importance of morale and other psychological factors closely resemble, but also precede those of Clausewitz; Georg Friedrich von Tempelhoff (1737–1807) shared many of Clausewitz's ideas about the value of theory as a way of distinguishing between truth and preference; Gat, *Origins of Military Thought*, 150–5, 76–8, respectively; Creveld, *Art of War*, 88–115.
5. Patrick J. Speelman, *Henry Lloyd and the Military Enlightenment of Eighteenth-Century Europe* (Westport, CT: Greenwood, 2002); Gat, *Origins of Military Thought*, 67–78.
6. Both are reprinted along with Lloyd's other works in Patrick J. Speelman (ed.), *War, Society and Enlightenment: The Works of General Lloyd* (Boston, MA: Brill, 2005).
7. Lloyd, *Late War in Germany* (1766), in *War, Society, and Enlightenment*, 14.
8. Lloyd, *Continuation of the Late War in Germany* (1781), in *War, Society, and Enlightenment*, 484 ff.
9. Napoleon derided Lloyd's theorizing, referring to it as a pathetic joke; Smith, *On Clausewitz*, 57. Of course, Napoleon had, at least in part, been able to free himself of dependency on his own line of operations, while exploiting other armies' dependency, as in the Ulm campaign (1805).

10. Gat, *Origins of Military Thought*, 79–94; R. R. Palmer, 'Frederick the Great, Guibert, Bülow: From Dynastic to National War', in Meade (ed.), *Makers of Modern Strategy*, 49–74.
11. H.D. v. Bülow, *Geist des neuern Kriegssystems* (Berlin: Frölich, 1799); and *Lehrsätze des neuern Kriegs, oder reine und angewandte Strategie aus dem Geist des neurn Kriegssystems hergleitet von dem Verfasser desselben* (Berlin: Frölich, 1805); in English translation: H. Dietrich von Bülow, *The Spirit of Modern System of War* (London: C. Mercier & Co., 1806).
12. Bülow, *Modern System of War*, 86–7. Karl F. Weiland, 'Strategie und Taktik in der Theorie Carl von Clausewitz', http://www.carlvonclausewitz.de/weiland, compares Bülow's and Clausewitz's views of strategy and tactics.
13. Bülow, *Modern System of War*, 226–9.
14. Clausewitz took issue with this view from the outset: see *On War*, I/1, section 3.
15. John R. Elting, 'Jomini: Disciple of Napoleon', *Military Affairs*, 27 (1967), 17–26; Crane Brinton, Gordon A. Craig, and Felix Gilbert, 'Jomini', in Meade (ed.), *Makers of Modern Strategy*, 77–92; John Shy, 'Jomini', in Paret (ed.), *Makers of Modern Strategy*, 43–85; Gat, *Origins of Military Thought*, 106–35.
16. Antoine-Henri Jomini, *Traité des grandes opérations militaires*, 8 vols. (Paris: Michaud, 1811–16); *Précis de l'art de la guerre*, 2 vols. (Paris: Anselin, 1838); in English: *Summary of the Art of War or a New Analytical Compend of the Principal Combinations of Strategy, of Grand Tactics and of Military Policy*, trans. Winship and McClean (New York: Putnam Press, 1854); hereafter, *Summary*. Tracing Jomini's publications is difficult as separate volumes of the same works were sometimes published under different titles; the chronology of Jomini's writings is sorted out by John I. Alger, *Antoine Henri Jomini: A Bibliographical Survey* (West Point, NY: US Military Academy Library, 1975).
17. Michael Howard, 'Jomini and the Classical Tradition in Military Thought', in Michael Howard (ed.), The Theory and Practice of War (Bloomington, IN: Indiana University Press, 1965), 3–20.
18. Christopher Bassford, 'Jomini and Clausewitz: Their Interaction', paper presented to the 23rd meeting of the Consortium for Revolutionary Europe, at Georgia State University, February 26, 1993: http://www.clausewitz.com/CWZHOME/Jomini/JOMINIX.htm; see also Christoph M. V. Abegglen, 'The Influence of Clausewitz on Jomini's *Précis de l'art de la Guerre*', masters thesis, War Studies, King's College, London, 2003, who argues that Jomini and Clausewitz ought to be seen as 'complementary' and not 'mutually exclusive', 5; http://mypage.bluewin.ch/abegglen/papers/clausewitz_influence_on_jomini.pdf
19. Jomini, *Summary*, 12.
20. Liddell Hart, *Strategy*, 342.
21. 'Ueber den Zustand der Theorie der Kriegskunst', in *Schriften–Aufsätze–Studien–Briefe*, 25–6; as Hahlweg suggests, this essay could well have been the forerunner of *On War*'s Book II 'On the Theory of War'.

22. 'Ueber den Zustand der Theorie', 25.
23. *Vom Kriege*, II/3, 302–3; *On War*, 149.
24. *Vom Kriege*, II/2, 282–3; *On War*, 135.
25. [Clausewitz] 'Bemerkungen über die reine und angewandte Strategie des Herrn Bülow oder Kritik der darin enthaltenen Ansichten', *Neue Bellona*, 93 (1805), 252–87; reprinted in Carl von Clausewitz, in Werner Hahlweg (ed.), *Verstreute kleine Schriften* (Osnabrück: Biblio, 1979), 65–88.
26. 'Bemerkungen' 73, 77, emphasis original; see also 'Strategie aus dem Jahr 1804', *Verstreute Kleine Schriften*, 33, which offers virtually the same definition; and *Vom Kriege*, II/1, 277, III/1, 345; *On War*, 132, 177, where the variations are slight, indeed.
27. *Vom Kriege*, II/2, 283–8; *On War*, 135–40.
28. *Vom Kriege*, VI/30, 857–8; *On War*, 516.
29. *Vom Kriege*, II/2, 280–1; *On War*, 134.
30. Compare: Lloyd, *Continuation of the History of the Late War* (1781) in *War, Society, and Enlightenment*, 388, 452, 458, 484–5, 621, 624; Bülow, *Modern System of War*, 234; and *Vom Kriege*, VIII/3B, 962, 967, 969; *On War*, 586, 589, 591.
31. In the introduction to his *Summary*, Jomini wrote: '…as a critical historian, [Clausewitz] has been an unscrupulous plagiarist, pillaging his predecessors, copying their reflections, and saying evil afterwards of their works….' cf. Michael I. Handel, *Masters of War: Classical Strategic Thought*, 2nd edn. (London: Frank Cass, 1996), 244.

# 1

## A Search for Objective Knowledge

Readers might well expect any treatise comparable to the length and scope of *On War* to have an introduction that lays out the author's purpose and methodology. However, we do not discover the purpose of Clausewitz's opus until we arrive at the work's ninth and tenth chapters, that is, the first and second chapters of Book II 'On the Theory of War'. Even here, however, we learn little about the methodology he intended to employ, except that he aimed to use military history to extend his experiential base. In the first chapter of Book II, we learn that Clausewitz aimed to bring 'a spirit of scientific inquiry' to the subject of war, and thereby to clarify 'concepts and ideas that have been thrown together and entangled' and to eliminate, or at least expose, the 'confused and confusing', the 'trite', and the 'implausible'.[1]

More specifically, theory's primary task was 'to examine the main elements that comprise war, to make more distinct what at first glance seems merged, to describe in detail the unique characteristics of war's means, to demonstrate their probable effects, and to determine clearly the nature of war's purposes'.[2] His aim, in short, was to get at the truth about war: 'Not the vanity of having written something, but rather the desire to shed light and truth, to dispel false and frail concepts, is the reason for this book.'[3] These two themes—the desire to expose false theories, and to uncover and lay out war's truths—thus capture Clausewitz's motive for writing *On War*.[4]

In Clausewitz's terminology, *On War* is a search for objective knowledge, which he proposed to find through scientific observation and analysis.[5] In today's vernacular, the work is essentially an anatomy of war, a dissection of the inner workings of armed conflict, especially the multilevel, cause-and-effect relationships that exist between war's purposes and its means. In scholarly terms, *On War* is a phenomenology of armed conflict, an examination following the existing methods of scientific inquiry, of the laws and regularities that define war.[6] If principles emerged in the process of this inquiry, theory would highlight them, as it must all truths; in fact, verifiable truths in the form of governing laws, or cause-and-effect relationships, were the prerequisites for all principles.

## OBJECTIVE KNOWLEDGE

Clausewitz's understanding of objective knowledge derived from Kiesewetter's *Outline of General Logic*, an arrangement of lectures on the Kantian system of logic delivered at the Institute for Young Officers (later *Allgemeine Kriegsschule* or General War School) while Clausewitz was a student and later an instructor there.[7] Kiesewetter was, apparently, a perfect fit for the caliber of students at the Institute. He lectured without a salary through the school's first winter, and his pupils evidently described his lectures as 'lively', 'appealing', 'witty', and 'captivating', so much so, in fact, that one student wrote he made them forget they 'had to spend the cold winter mornings in an unheated classroom'.[8] As the late Clausewitz scholar Werner Hahlweg observed, by studying Kiesewetter's writings attentively one 'would not only be able to grasp the fundamentals of Kant's philosophy, but would also be able to acquire from them suggestions for the formulation of a practical military theory.'[9]

As already mentioned, many of the definitions and concepts found in *On War* are derived nearly verbatim from those established in this series of lectures. For instance, in his essay 'On the Condition of the Theory of the Art of War' Clausewitz wrote:

> Every educated person knows that a formal truth is the *conditio sine qua non* of all truth and that it can only exist in the correct form.... [By formal truth] we mean the agreement of a concept with respect to the laws of thought [logic]. These laws are the same for all humanity; consequently, logical truth must also be the same for all humanity.[10]

The similarities between this passage and what Kiesewetter wrote in the *Outline of General Logic* are too obvious to ignore:

> The formal truth of a concept is the subject of logic since logic concerns itself with the laws of thought.... We call a concept logically true if it accords with the formal laws of thought... logical truth is the necessary condition (*conditio sine qua non*) of the material truth of a concept.[11]

Other similarities exist, such as Clausewitz's and Kiesewetter's respective definitions of laws and principles, objective and subjective knowledge, and the concept of genius. These similarities suggest that Clausewitz did indeed use Kiesewetter's lectures and the *Outline of General Logic* itself as references for the development of his theory of war, as Hahlweg proposed.[12]

Kiesewetter defined knowledge as an observation or realization (*Wissen*) drawn either from a subjective or from an objective basis. A subjective basis is one that is valid only for an individual; an objective basis, by contrast, is valid for everyone. An example of the former is an individual's observation that 'snow is white', which is valid for that person, but not necessarily for all others. An instance of an objective basis is the realization that the sum of the three angles of a triangle (180°) always equal the sum of two right angles (90° + 90° = 180°), which is true no matter who observes it, or when. The primary difference between subjective and objective knowledge, therefore, is that the former is valid only in an individual case, while the latter possesses universal validity (*Allgemeingültigkeit*).[13] However, modern scholars, such as Karl Popper, have advanced the view that even objective knowledge is tentative, and thus any theory purporting to embody it is also of necessity tentative, that is, contingent on the discovery of new objective knowledge, which might expand or transform the original objective knowledge.[14] Put differently, under Popper's theory, the elimination of error that Clausewitz attempted to accomplish for military theory leads inevitably to the emergence of new problems, which in turn requires new theories, and so on. We can, in fact, see that this was the case as Clausewitz struggled to resolve certain difficulties, particularly in the last chapters of Book VI and parts of Book VIII. The first chapter of Book I, discussed in more detail in Chapter 3, shows his attempt to resolve some of these difficulties.

Clausewitz actually used the subjective–objective dualism several times in *On War*, which illustrates not only the further influence of Kiesewetter's *Outline of Logic*, but also the central importance the Prussian theorist ascribed to this construct as an analytical device. He employed it in his masterwork's introductory chapter, for instance, where he referred to the differences between the objective and subjective natures of war, though he appears to have conflated the former with the classical definition of the objective nature of probability.[15] He also used it in the fourth chapter of Book II, in which, among other things, he defined the properties of objective and subjective principles; again, the former were universally valid, while the latter were valid only for particular situations.[16] We find it again in the manuscript's second chapter where he described war as a series of engagements, each of which can be considered to possess a certain unity based on the level and type of military units (subjective aspects) involved and the purpose (objective aspect) of the particular engagement.[17]

It was also Clausewitz's intention to present this objective knowledge 'fully illuminated and in good order', so that others might use it as a basis for developing their own subjective knowledge or ability (*Können*).[18] As scholars have indicated, Clausewitz used the terms scientific (*wissenschaftlich*) and philosophical (*philosophisch*) almost interchangeably.[19] However, he also used the terms to refer to the desired end product, a body of verifiable knowledge arranged in an explanatory system. As Kiesewetter's *Outline of Logic* made clear, one could arrange observations in two ways: either in a 'rhapsodic' (*rhapsodistisch*) and fragmentary manner; or in a scientific (*wissenschaftlich*) one, that is, as a 'system of knowledge', where the individual elements are 'organized under a unifying concept (*Begriff*)'.[20]

Realizations form a system when they are organized according to the idea of a whole (*eines Ganzen*), and thus have unity. In a science, the place of every proposition is set; we can give a reason in every case as to why the proposition is where it is and nowhere else; every realization that occurs is in accord with the others that make up the system; we are quite sure that nothing is lacking, and nothing is superfluous. Thus, a recitation in mathematics, for example, is scientific: we can not arbitrarily alter the relationship of its propositions; rather, the whole is an elaborate structure, whose parts are subordinated in the most precise arrangement.[21]

As examples, Kiesewetter offered the Copernican planetary system, where the unifying concept is the distance from the sun, and the system the Swedish botanist Carl von Linné (Carolus Linnaeus) used for classifying plants, where the organizing concept is plant genitalia.[22] It is important to note that in neither example did the term system indicate a formal structure that prescribed action, though the laws of planetary motion certainly enable one to predict where a planet will be at any point in time. War, Clausewitz believed, did not allow for such predictions: one can apply one's knowledge of weapon technologies and predict the type of physical damage specific weapons will inflict. However, beyond such calculations, prediction in war was difficult, if not futile, due to the number of indeterminate variables involved, such as how one's opponent will react to physical harm. Instead, the approach defined by Kiesewetter was true to the spirit of scientific inquiry, that is, it was descriptive or explanatory rather than prescriptive, and Clausewitz embraced the same meaning.

Rhapsodic observations or realizations, in contrast, are those:

...that have a coincidental relationship rather than a necessary one, so that we can never be certain that they are complete. Accordingly, rhapsodic observations are like an explanation of nature that yesterday described the crocodile, today studies the volcano, and tomorrow learns about the frog and the bat. With each successive rhapsodic observation of nature we are never able to be certain whether the observation is complete, or whether and where something is lacking.[23]

Thus, in important respects, *On War* represents a scientific system as Kiesewetter defined it, that is, separate elements of knowledge organized under a unifying concept. Clausewitz rejected prescriptive and artificial systems, but he also valued system and order over rhapsodic impressions: 'My nature', he wrote, 'always drives me to develop and to systematize'.[24] As he remarked in an early essay on strategy and tactics:

Science is a collection of observations (in the broadest sense)....Theory is a collection of observations and it is scientific the instant it is systematically ordered; it is a rational science when its propositions are not merely ordered, but are deducible from one another.[25]

Just as Copernicus' system is defined by the distance of the planets from the sun, and von Linné's system is arranged according to plant genitalia, so Clausewitz's system is organized around the dynamic relationship between purpose (*Zweck*) and means (*Mittel*). This relationship, in fact, holds the eight books of *On War* together. He first established this relationship, or law, in the work's opening chapter 'What War Is' and then developed further in the second 'Purpose and Means in War'.[26] As we can see by some of *On War*'s preliminary essays, he kept the concept of purpose at the center of his work: 'War is the use of naked violence against others in order to force them to fulfill our will; in other words, it is the use of available means to fulfill that purpose.' The theory of the art of war is the 'doctrine of the use of the means at hand for the purpose of the war'. Consequently, 'the art of war is nothing but the rational combination of both [purpose and means]'. War itself is indeed only a means to an end; 'the end however can not exceed the means'.[27] 'The art of war teaches the use of the available armed forces for the purpose of the war.'[28]

*On War*'s eight books are essentially arranged in a descending hierarchy of purpose and means. Book I, 'The Nature of War', lays out the universe of war, which among other things revolves around the relationship between purpose and means. Book II 'On the Theory of War' describes the method (or means) to be used to analyze that relationship. Book III 'On Strategy in General' obviously discusses strategy, which is the means by which the purpose of war is attained. Book IV 'The Engagement' addresses combat or the engagement (*Gefecht*), as the means strategy uses to accomplish its purposes. Book V 'The Armed Forces' deals with military forces (armies actually), which are the means that do the fighting, and thus carryout the purposes of the engagements. Book VI 'Defense' and Book VII 'The Attack' examine the two basic means available to military forces when fighting engagements: defense or attack. All military missions essentially fall within the one or the other. Book VIII 'The Plan of War' was intended to provide guidelines or planning considerations appropriate to the two fundamentally different types of war he believed existed: those in which the purpose was to attain complete victory, and those involving more limited purposes.[29]

## A NEW PARADIGM?

*On War*'s emphasis on verifiable truths—objective knowledge—rather than process suggests that Clausewitz was less concerned with showing us how to think about war, as some have supposed, than with establishing a body of correct knowledge to serve as a foundation for our thinking, a platform from which to spring from objective to subjective knowledge. In a manner of speaking, he attempted to introduce a new paradigm of war, a grossly overused term popularized by the work of Thomas Kuhn, which means a basis for theorizing about or practicing something.[30] In fact, it may be more accurate to say Clausewitz endeavored to establish a paradigm where none yet existed.

However, his paradigm was to be a foundation for thinking, rather than a way of thinking. A way of thinking entails following a procedure, such as the scientific method, to arrive at the same truths the master theorist himself uncovered. While reproducing another's results to verify them is one of the hallmarks of science, Clausewitz never actually provided his readers with an explicit procedure for doing so. He did provide guidelines for conducting critical analysis and using historical examples. Yet, it is quite a stretch to conclude that the sum total of these guidelines amounts to a procedure. Rather, *On War* is an effort to spare readers the burden of recreating the universe of war, so to speak, whenever they needed to learn about war through books. Clausewitz performed that taxing and time-consuming labor for them.

The problem with the use of the term paradigm, as Kuhn's critics have pointed out, is that it connotes a level of satisfaction with the prevailing explanation that was rarely the case. As one critic remarked, in the era of Copernicus, 'astronomy had long been, not in a paradigmatic, but an unsettled state'. In fact, 'far from being placidly confident about the underpinnings and outcomes of their professional activities, they were at war with one another'.[31] Although military theorists in Clausewitz's day were also often 'at war with one another', few of them wrote about, or even appear to have considered, the underpinnings of their professional activities to the extent he did. Military theory was in an unsettled state before *On War* appeared, and for some time afterward. Indeed, the term paradigm hardly captures the dynamism of competing theories and schools of thought that exist in almost every field, whether art or science.

The classic first step in any paradigm shift, or revolution in theory, is of course to point out the inadequacy of existing explanations, and to begin demolishing them.[32] As we have seen, albeit briefly, Clausewitz endeavored to accomplish this step not only in *On War*, but through several of his other works. His major points were that existing theories did not reflect reality and that the principles they advanced were not universal. The second step is to introduce an adequate replacement paradigm or explanation. As we have said, *On War* is that, or rather an unfinished attempt at that.

It is not clear whether Clausewitz sought truth chiefly because he expected its discovery to validate his own firmly held convictions regarding war, or because, having read so many of the flawed theories of his day, he felt the need to conduct a thorough examination of war to satisfy himself as to what was true and what was not. Either way, we know he did not approach the writing of *On War* with a blank slate, but with many impressions concerning the essence and component parts of war already formed in his mind. As he admitted in 1809 in a letter to the German philosopher Johann Fichte:

I confess that I have a very elevated conception of the superiority of that form of war in which martial virtue animates every part of the army, and in which the main purpose of the art of war [strategy] is the fullest possible employment of this spirit. I believe this form of war will dominate any other, however intelligently conceived the latter might be, not to mention that, by its nature, it would most closely approach war in its most complete form.[33]

Again, in 1812, Clausewitz wrote an essay summarizing the main points of his military tutelage of the Prussian Crown Prince Frederick William.[34] In that essay, he laid down principles that resembled maxims more than guidelines. He argued, for example, that the principle of pursuing 'one great decisive aim with force and determination' was in reality a maxim that should rank first among all causes of victory.[35] These and other statements have led some scholars to claim Clausewitz was a doctrinaire thinker, holding fast to his own set of subjective preferences.[36] This may well be true, at least in part. After all, he did believe himself to be a man of conviction, who had spent some time developing clear ideas about the nature of things. Persons of conviction, by definition, need to be convinced of the correctness of another way of thinking before they will change their minds.

As we see later in this study, Clausewitz was willing to revise his ideas after subjecting them to critical analysis, and testing them against experience, his own as well as the more general experience reflected in history. In the process, he also developed several new concepts, such as the center of gravity, which we will explore in a later chapter. Whatever its source, his concern with uncovering verifiable truths remained prevalent throughout his theoretical works, and it is especially evident even in the early drafts of *On War*. The pursuit of truth, even if it cannot be fully attained, is of course the scholar's *raison d'être*.[37] The soldier, by necessity, is more concerned with deciding what actions to take in a given situation. Hence, the ends for each are different. Clausewitz, who had the practical experience of the soldier and the motives of the scholar, sought a scientific explanation for why certain actions were effective in war. In so doing, he hoped to bring military theory, which in his view had drifted into the realm of abstractions, closer to the reality of war.[38]

## FROM OBJECTIVE TO SUBJECTIVE KNOWLEDGE

Although *On War* is a search for objective knowledge, it is not an attempt to capture all knowledge of war. Clausewitz stressed that commanders need not master all that could be known of war. In fact, attempting to do so could prove detrimental, since in his view a preoccupation with trivialities would produce a trivial mind incapable of great thoughts, which all truly skilled commanders required.[39] Instead, commanders had but to understand those elements that affected the conduct of major operations or, in his words, the 'activities that empty directly into the ocean of war' rather than the 'many streams that come together to form the rivers'.[40] It was thus neither necessary nor desirable for commanders to become expert in every field of knowledge: they need not be political analysts or learned historians, just well versed in the higher affairs of state, current political issues, the interests at stake, and the key political figures involved; they need not be experts in psychology, but must understand the personalities and character of the officers and troops under them; they need not know how to drive artillery trains, just how to calculate march-rates under various conditions.[41]

The knowledge commanders required was, therefore, simple insofar as it involved relatively few subjects. However, the skill in judgment (*Takt*) they required when applying this knowledge was more difficult to acquire. Clausewitz complained that, heretofore, military theorists had failed to recognize the importance of the right kind of knowledge, or of knowledge in general. Their efforts to capture what commanders should know either included all kinds of extraneous matter or downplayed the value of knowledge altogether, attributing success to natural talent or genius, which according to prominent military theorists of the Enlightenment, such as Henry Lloyd, defied analysis. Clausewitz found both approaches unsatisfactory and believed instead that a genuine relationship existed between the knowledge that experienced commanders possessed, and the innate talent or skilled judgment they exercised. The former, if correct, would augment the latter in a favorable way.[42] History's greatest generals, according to Clausewitz, possessed a well-developed, or innate, talent for reducing war's many complexities to simple, yet accurate, expressions.[43] He saw this affinity for rapid simplification not as a negative trait, as it is commonly regarded today, but as evidence of genuine skill, even genius. This trait went hand in hand with the commander's *coup d'œil*, or 'the rapid recognition of a truth', which he clearly prized.[44] We find the expression *coup d'œil* in Lloyd's work as well. Indeed, Clausewitz might well have been inspired to explore the topic by Lloyd's comments.

In addition, Clausewitz also believed knowledge had a certain practical value in discussions and deliberations:

> When it is not a question of acting oneself, but of convincing another in the course of a discussion, then everything depends on clear ideas and proof of their inner connections. Because military education (*Ausbildung*) on such matters is not yet far enough advanced, most discussions are a simple back-and-forth of words, where each side either holds fast to its opinion or agrees to a superficial compromise, which in reality is of no value.[45]

To be successful in gathering knowledge, however, commanders needed an 'intellectual instinct' (*geistiger Instinkt*) of sorts that could extract the central truth, or essence, from phenomena as naturally as 'bees draw honey from flowers'.[46]

## JUDGMENT AND INSIGHT

Scholars typically refer to this quality, rather appropriately, as intuitive insight or understanding.[47] Recent work on the relationship between expert knowledge and decision-making, in fact, suggests a modern parallel. As contemporary experts explain, the predominant theory of a generation ago, where analysis and intuition were considered two different functions, 'on two different sides of the brain', has been replaced. The prevailing view now is that there is a single mode of thought that combines analysis and intuition: the brain takes in elements of information, stores them in short- or long-term memory, and then selects appropriate ones and combines them in flashes of insight. 'An expert's brain', in other words, 'stores cases from direct experience and the experience of others acquired through learning. Answers then come to the expert in flashes of insight, large and small' when needed.[48] In Clausewitz's terminology, then, internalizing objective knowledge—learning—about war can help nurture the judgment of commanders, which in turn can improve their decision-making.

*On War* complements the development of this affinity *not* by producing a facile system of rules that dictate action, but by explaining the complex cause-and-effect relationships from which the successful commander intuited his basic concepts. For this reason, *On War* proceeds, as its author explained, from the 'simple to the complex', that is, in the opposite direction in which skilled commanders think.[49] This style of intellectual reverse-engineering was intended to enlighten readers who might not have the benefit of practical experience, and who would therefore have to learn about war through books. By way of illustration, *On War*'s first chapter introduces a simple concept of war that Clausewitz claimed was typically used by experienced soldiers, namely, that war is 'nothing but personal combat (*Zweikampf*) on a larger scale'.[50] The chapter then moves toward a more complex definition—that war is 'an act of violence (*Gewalt*) to force an opponent to fulfill our will'.[51] It then discussed the individual components—violence, purpose, and effort— of this definition in some detail, eventually bringing them together in a sort of synthesis, described as a 'wondrous trinity', which we will examine in more detail later.[52]

Clausewitz's *On War*, thus, differs substantially from Jomini's *Summary of the Art of War* and standard military manuals in that it was not meant to prescribe action, but to provide a foundation of verifiable laws and principles for developing one's judgment. In keeping with the basic principles of the German concept of *Bildung*, or the enlightened cultivation of character and intellect, it was a tool to facilitate the military practitioner's self-education.[53] Prescribing action was, in Clausewitz's view, impossible for reasons related to the nature of war itself. As we have seen, he rejected the theories of Lloyd, Bülow, Jomini, and others, for overlooking or dismissing the importance of psychological forces, such as hostility and fear, as well as the intellectual and personality traits of the commander; these factors added to the overall diversity of outcomes, and combined with chance and probability, made war into modern scientific language might be described as a nonlinear phenomenon.[54] Second, such theories by their nature cannot account for unique cases; by necessity they deal in general possibilities, which require omitting the complex ways in which opposing forces interact. Finally, such theories fail to take into account the ever-present element of uncertainty; the information available in war is, for physical as well as psychological reasons, never sufficient for approaches that prescribe action.[55]

## THEORY AS OBSERVATION AND AS A BODY OF OBSERVATIONS

Hence, the role of theory was 'not to create an algebraic formula for the battlefield', or serve as a 'prescriptive body of doctrine' (*positive Lehrgebäude*) on which commanders could always rely when making decisions.[56] Instead, it should facilitate the development of individual judgment by providing readers with objective knowledge that they could internalize, or 'transfer completely into the mind', so that their understanding of war's major features would become second nature.[57] In other words, developing an 'intimate familiarity' (*genauen Bekanntschaft*) with knowledge meant that it would be readily available when decisions were needed, and could serve as a basis for constructing subjective theories.

Moreover, by casting his treatise, indeed his overall theory of war, as a work that both captured and conveyed verifiable observations, or knowledge, rather than as a manual that prescribed action, Clausewitz could realize his ambition of writing a book that would not soon fade into historical obscurity. We know from his many notes and letters that, for the greater part of his intellectual life, he desired to construct a theory of war capable of transcending the particularities of time and place and thus of serving as an authoritative source. As he stated in an introductory note written c.1818, 'It was my ambition to write a book that would not be forgotten after two or three years, and that possibly might be picked up more than once by those interested in the subject.'[58]

Clausewitz's chief criticism of the theories of von Bülow and Jomini, and others whom he referred to derogatorily as 'system builders', for instance, was that their concepts lacked universal validity.[59] Consequently, the theories themselves could not be considered valid beyond the specific period in which they were written, or indeed beyond the historical cases used to illustrate them. In other words, a scientifically valid theory would allow him to set the record straight, so to speak, regarding the many false theories and systems of his day. In several places in *On War*, in fact, he took these theories to task, which in turn contributed to the work's unmistakably combative tone, and certainly helps explain some of the rhetorical excess readers frequently encounter. *On War* is actually more explicitly combative, more a direct refutation of other theorists' points, than most readers realize.

Without a reliable foundation, commanders could only depend on 'talent or the mere favor of fortune'.[60] Yet Clausewitz provided little explicit advice in *On War* as to how readers were to internalize this knowledge. Rote memorization was in vogue in Clausewitz's day, not only in Europe but elsewhere; however, he did not think highly of it since it stifled the development of imaginative or conceptual thinking, an essential quality for any senior commander. Instead, he seems to have favored a form of what later became known as the applicatory method which, in short, was based on the idea of developing one's understanding of concepts through practical exercises.

According to assumptions underpinning Enlightenment theories regarding education and the 'perfectibility' of the individual, some of which evidently influenced Clausewitz at a young age, education should lead to independence of thought, among other things.[61] A program of instruction that was too rigid would not afford opportunities for reflection, and would thus not allow the student to develop a capacity for independent thinking.

However, a corpus of knowledge is a prerequisite for any form of education. Clausewitz believed he had captured most of the right ideas, even if he was not satisfied with the form in which he had presented them in *On War*.[62] Theory, in the sense Clausewitz used it, is thus both the act of observation or study (*Betrachtung*), as well as the corpus of collective observations (*Wissen*), appropriately arranged and ordered.

## CONCLUSIONS AND IMPLICATIONS

Clausewitz realized he could never capture all objective knowledge concerning war. Yet he believed it was possible to capture enough knowledge to help practitioners bring theory closer to reality. In this way, he could provide his readers something more than a rhapsodic assortment of subjective truths. Objective knowledge supplied a foundation for an individual's self-education, for the cultivation and development of subjective knowledge. Clausewitz frequently transitioned from objective to subjective knowledge in *On War*, from describing the parts of war to prescribing how we should act because of them. Readers unaware of this tendency are likely to find it confusing.

Of course, Clausewitz assumed objective knowledge existed, was attainable, and could be presented in a comprehensible form. Today, critics might challenge his assumption on grounds that objective knowledge, like objectivity itself, cannot be achieved. All perspectives, even those that lay claim to universality, inevitably dissolve into particular truths, subjective interpretations. However, the argument that all knowledge is inescapably subjective contradicts itself by making, or attempting to make, what is clearly an objective claim. The claim that all knowledge is universally subjective is itself subjective in nature and therefore only valid for the individual making it. Thus, it need not trouble the theorist or the practitioner. Our concern in this study, in any case, is not whether Clausewitz captured genuinely objective knowledge, but whether it remains valid, and thus makes meaningful contributions to our own invariably subjective observations of war. In other words, just because our views are subjective does not mean we can not broaden them.

## A Search for Objective Knowledge

We might do well to examine all our observations of war to determine how subjective they are. Much of the literature on contemporary war fails to establish any objective basis for the observations it wishes us to accept. Military doctrine, too, might benefit from first establishing an objective basis, however limited it may be, for the prescriptions it seeks to impose on practitioners.

### NOTES

1. *Vom Kriege*, II/1, 278; *On War*, 132.
2. *Vom Kriege*, II/2, 299; *On War*, 141.
3. 'Zweck des Werkes', in *Schriften–Aufsätze–Studien–Briefe*, 24.
4. They also run through the work's prefatory notes; see *Vom Kriege*, 181–2; *On War*, 61, 70–1. Four introductory notes appear in the Howard and Paret editions of *On War*: the 'Author's Preface', written between 1816 and 1818; the 'Author's Comment', written in 1818; the note of July 10, 1827; and the undated note presumably written in 1830. According to Paret, the 'Preface' belongs not to *On War* but to a lost collection of essays on the role and limits of theory. Paret, *Clausewitz and the State*, 360.
5. *Vom Kriege*, II/2, 298–300; *On War*, 146–7.
6. Martin van Creveld, 'The Eternal Clausewitz', in *Clausewitz and Modern Strategy*, 39–40, makes similar points; this essay differs greatly from van Creveld's later treatment of Clausewitz.
7. Kiesewetter's *Grundriss einer Allgemeinen Logik* appeared in four editions from 1791 to 1825. The name of the General War School would change again to War Academy or War College (*Kriegsakademie*); the latter name will be used hereafter for simplicity.
8. Cf. Charles E. White, *The Enlightened Soldier: Scharnhorst and the Militärische Gesellschaft in Berlin, 1801–1805* (Westport, CT: Praeger, 1989), 93.
9. Hahlweg, 'Entwürfe und Vorarbeiten zum Werk "Vom Kriege"', in *Schriften–Aufsätze–Studien–Briefe*, 18.
10. 'Ueber den Zustand der Theorie', in *Schriften–Aufsätze–Studien–Briefe*, 28, 34.
11. Kiesewetter, *Grundriss*, I, 110–11.
12. Hahlweg, 'Philosophie und Theorie bei Clausewitz', 327–8.
13. Kiesewetter, *Grundriss*, I (140), 463–4.
14. Karl R. Popper, *Objective Knowledge: An Evolutionary Approach* (Oxford: Clarendon Press, 1972); and *The Logic of Scientific Discovery* (London: Routledge, 2006), published in 1935 as *Logik der Forschung*.
15. The classic work: Marquis de Laplace, *Essai philosophique sur les probabilitiés* (Paris: Guthier-Villars, 1814); in English: *A Philosophical Essay on Probabilities*, trans. Frederick Truscott and Frederick Emory (New York: Dover, [1951] 1995), was popular at the time Clausewitz was writing *On War*; the similarities

between Clausewitz's use of the term probability and the definitions of classical probability theory are discussed below.
16. *Vom Kriege*, II/4 'Methodismus', 305; *On War*, 151.
17. *Vom Kriege*, I/2, 223; *On War*, 95. Paret, *Clausewitz*, 154, notes that Clausewitz used the same objective–subjective dualism in an earlier essay entitled 'Strategie und Taktik' (1804); Kessel, 'Genesis', esp. 410–17, suggests Clausewitz also viewed *Politik* in terms of objective (universal) and subjective (particular) qualities.
18. *Vom Kriege*, II/2, 291; *On War*, 141.
19. Paret and Moran, *Historical and Political Writings*, 3, n. 2; see also 'Vorrede des Verfassers', *Vom Kriege*, 184. Aron, *Clausewitz*, 229, incorrectly refers to this tendency as confusion on the part of Clausewitz.
20. Kiesewetter, *Grundriss*, I, 18.
21. Kiesewetter, *Grundriss*, I, 19.
22. Linnaeus (1707–78) was most noted for his study of plants, but he also founded the modern system of taxonomy. Under Linnaeus's system, genera were grouped into orders, orders into classes, and classes into kingdoms: the animal kingdom contained the class Vertebrata, which contained the order Primates, which contained the genus *Homo* with the species *sapiens*—humanity. This system is still in use today, though with modifications. L. Koerner, *Linnaeus: Nature and Nation* (Cambridge, MA: Harvard University Press, 1999).
23. Kiesewetter, *Grundriss*, I, 19.
24. *On War*, 'Author's Comment', 63; as Clausewitz's chief biographer, Paret, pointed out, the Prussian theorist had previously written a collection of tactical rhapsodies, a loose assortment of essays, which unfortunately is now lost. Paret, *Clausewitz*, 161; Rothfels, *Clausewitz*, 156, 162.
25. 'Rezension der Beyträge zur Taktik und Strategie. 1st Abteilung. Glogau 1803', in *Schriften–Aufsätze–Studien–Briefe*, 101.
26. *Vom Kriege*, I/1 'Was ist der Krieg' and I/2 'Zweck und Mittel im Kriege'; *On War*, 'What Is War?' and 'Purpose and Means in War'.
27. '2tes Kapitel. Von der Kriegskunst überhaupt und ihrer Einteilung', in *Schriften–Aufsätze–Studien–Briefe*, 78.
28. 'Einleitung in das Studium der Schlachten und Gefechte. Für den Kronprinzen', in *Schriften–Aufsätze–Studien–Briefe*, 107.
29. *Vom Kriege*, VIII/1, 951; *On War*, 577. See also Raymond Aron, 'Reason, Passion, and Power in the Thought of Clausewitz', *Social Research*, 39 (winter 1972), 601–2, who referred to this 'ends–means' relationship as *Zweckrationalität* (purpose-driven rationale), but made it prescriptive, whereas for Clausewitz its prescriptive aspects were overshadowed by its descriptive ones.
30. Thomas S. Kuhn, *The Structure of Scientific Revolutions*, 2nd edn. (Chicago, IL: University of Chicago Press, 1970), 6.
31. Edward Rosen, *Copernicus and the Scientific Revolution* (Malabar: Robert E. Krieger, 1984), 132.

32. I. Bernard Cohen, *The Newtonian Revolution with Illustrations of the Transforming of Scientific Ideas* (New York: Cambridge University Press, 1980), 8.
33. 'Letter to Fichte' (1809), in *Historical and Political Writings*, 284. Clausewitz's 1804 essay on strategy, 'Strategie', also reveals similar subjective preferences.
34. *Die wichtigsten Grundsätze des Kriegführens zur Ergänzung meines Unterrichts bei Sr. Königlichen Hoheit dem Kronprinzen*; reprinted in *Vom Kriege*, 1047–86. Hereafter, *Grundsätze*.
35. *Grundsätze*, 19; this maxim has often been taken as the essence of Clausewitz's theory.
36. Honig, 'Interpreting Clausewitz', 571–80.
37. J. H. Hexter, 'The Historian and His Day,' *Reappraisals in History* (Chicago, IL: Northwestern University Press, 1962), 4, refers to historians mainly, but it holds for other scholars as well.
38. *Vom Kriege*, II/2, 292; *On War*, 141–2.
39. *Vom Kriege*, II/2, 296; *On War*, 145.
40. *Vom Kriege*, II/2, 296; *On War*, 144.
41. *Vom Kriege*, II/2, 298–9; *On War*, 146.
42. *Vom Kriege*, II/2, 298–9; *On War*, 146–7.
43. *Vom Kriege*, VIII/1, 950–1; *On War*, 577.
44. *Vom Kriege*, I/3, 234, 237; *On War*, 102; English translations of *On War* also render *Überblick* (or comprehensive glance), which appears in Book VIII, chapter 1, as *coup d'œil*.
45. *Vom Kriege*, undated note, 182; *On War*, 71.
46. *Vom Kriege*, II/2, 298–9; *On War*, 146.
47. Katherine L. Herbig, 'Chance and Uncertainty in *On War*', *Clausewitz and Modern Strategy*, 95–116; Paret, *Clausewitz*, 55; Heuser, *Reading Clausewitz*, 73.
48. In 1981, Roger Sperry won the Nobel Prize for his work on the notion of the two-sided brain, where the right hemisphere was deemed to be more creative and holistic, and the left more analytical and sequential. In 2000, Erich Kandel won the Nobel Prize for overturning that work. See William Duggan, *Coup d'Oeil: Strategic Intuition in Army Planning*, (Carlisle, PA: Strategic Studies Institute, 2005) 1/42, n. 1; and *Napoleon's Glance: The Secret of Strategy* (New York: Nation, 2002); L. Squire and E. Kandel, *Memory: From Mind to Molecules* (New York: Freeman Press, 1999); Herbert A. Simon, *Models of Thought*, vol. II (New Haven, CT: Yale University Press, 1989).
49. For a parallel argument, see Yuan-Ling Zhang, 'Fortschreiten vom Einfachen zum Zusammengesetzten. Ein sonderbares methodisches Verfahren in Clausewitz' Werk "Vom Kriege"', in *Clausewitz-Studien*, Heft 1 (spring 1996), 37–45.
50. *Vom Kriege*, I/1, 191; *On War*, 75. The simplified concept of war as the expression of the skilled commander is also mentioned in the first chapter of Book VIII, *Vom Kriege*, 950; *On War*, 578, and the two references appear to relate to each other.
51. *Vom Kriege*, I/1, 191; *On War*, 75.
52. *Vom Kriege*, I/1, 213; *On War*, 89.

53. The concept of *Bildung* grew out of the German Enlightenment or *Aufklärung*, and was used in many contexts, and had many meanings. On the general concept, see Frederick C. Beiser, *Enlightenment, Revolution, & Romanticism: The Genesis of Modern German Political Thought, 1790–1800* (Cambridge, MA: Harvard University Press, 1992), 229–30; for its military context, see White, *Scharnhorst*, 2–3, and T. G. Otte, 'Educating Bellona: Carl von Clausewitz and Military Education', in Keith Nelson and Greg Kennedy (eds.), *Military Education: Past, Present, and Future* (New York: Praeger, 2002), 13–33; Paret, *Clausewitz*, 278.
54. Alan Beyerchen, 'Clausewitz, Nonlinearity, and the Unpredictability of War', *International Security*, 17/3 (winter 1992), 59–90.
55. *Vom Kriege*, II/2, 285–9; *On War*, 140.
56. *Vom Kriege*, II/2, 289, 291; *On War*, 140.
57. *Vom Kriege*, II/2, 299; *On War*, 141.
58. *On War*, 'Author's Comment', 63.
59. 'On the Life and Character of Scharnhorst', *Historical and Political Writings*, 104; and Paret, 'Genesis of *On War*', *On War*, 10.
60. *Vom Kriege*, II/2, 289; *On War*, 140.
61. Paret, *Clausewitz*, 46–7, 83–4.
62. See the note of 1827 and the undated note, *Vom Kriege*, 181; *On War*, 70–1.

# 2

# Validating Concepts and Principles

In this chapter, we examine the method Clausewitz sought to apply to his concept of war, 'an act of violence to compel an enemy to fulfill our will'.[1] As we have seen, he regarded form as at least as important as substance. As Kiesewetter's *Outline of Logic* explained, the 'form of an object is that which makes it what it is', while substance is that to which form gives shape. The form of a statue of Jupiter, for instance, is the statue's facial expression and attitude, and any other characteristics that distinguish it from other statues; the substance is the marble or other material from which the statue is made.[2] Clausewitz complained that many people considered 'form less useful than substance', and this belief was wrong. Only correct form could ensure the ideas were understood properly, that Mars was not mistaken for Jupiter, for instance.

Moreover, he believed correct form could ensure theory was more than a collection of individual experiences, that it was the product of disciplined observation rather than undisciplined imagination, and that it arranged observations and concepts appropriately. 'If this form is violated', Clausewitz warned, 'everyone will understand the individual concepts, but the body of thought as a whole will be incomprehensible'. 'Every educated person', he continued, 'knows that formal truth is the *conditio sine qua non* of all truth and that it only exists in the right form'.[3] If Clausewitz wished to construct a valid theory of war, therefore, he needed a method that would present knowledge in the right a form, and thus demonstrate the validity of his concepts. The form to which Clausewitz turned was the doctrine of concepts as described in the textbooks of Kiesewetter.

## LOGIC AS GRAMMAR

Clausewitz's use of logic was indeed rigorous and, because of its Kantian roots, sometimes torturously so. As a result, we find occasions throughout *On War*, particularly in its introductory chapter, where Clausewitz appears to have pushed his concepts to absurd extremes only to have to struggle later to modify or negate them.[4] This habit no doubt has caused practical-minded individuals to give up on the opus before they had gotten through the first chapter. However, a better understanding of his logical method will help shed light on the reason for this apparent inefficiency, and perhaps encourage readers to persevere.

Kiesewetter defined logic as the science of the rules of thought. 'Logic', he explained, 'is to thought what grammar is to speech'. 'It is a rule of thought', he went on to say, 'that we cannot think of affirming and denying a concept at the same time: as black and as not black, as a square and as a circle'.[5] He divided logic into two types: general, which pertains to rational thought overall; and special, which concerns specific subjects or fields of knowledge, such as history and jurisprudence. He further divided general logic into two types: pure (*rein*), which covers theoretical or abstract concepts; and applied (*angewandte*) logic, or practical reasoning, which concerns empirical data received through the senses.

Special logic establishes the 'ways and means' necessary for discovering and proving the validity of new ideas within specific subjects or fields of knowledge, while also uncovering any errors in existing ideas; it makes use of the rules of general logic, but defines them more precisely for the specific field of knowledge.[6] An example is the way in which lawyers use written law and precedent to build a case in jurisprudence.

As the *Outline of Logic* explained, applied logic was dialectical in nature since in contrasting opposites it went beyond appearances, and stripped away that which was false.[7] Clausewitz himself wrote that he used 'perfect contrasts', even extremes in some cases, to give his ideas greater 'clarity, definition, and persuasive force'.[8] As he said in the introductory chapter of Book VII, 'Attack', which followed directly after its opposite, 'Defense', the topic of Book VI: 'when two concepts form a logical contradiction, the one thus complements the other, and so the one brings to light the other'.[9] However, many forms of dialectic existed in Clausewitz's day, and still do, and it is easy to overstate Clausewitz's use of the dialectic in *On War*, and what it means. The style of dialectic associated with the German philosopher Georg Wilhelm Friedrich Hegel (1770–1831), for instance, pitted an idea against its contradiction, which raised the original idea to a higher plane. In today's terminology, this process is often described in terms of thesis, antithesis, and synthesis, but Hegel's use implied a certain perfect realization toward which thought, and indeed history itself, always moved. Moreover, as scholars have noted, Clausewitz's use of the dialectic rarely culminated in a Hegelian-style synthesis.[10] Instead, it underscored the need for skilled judgment in resolving ambiguities or contradictions. Actually, throughout *On War* Clausewitz worked with pairs of ideas, dualisms, which the term dialectics tends to obscure. Thus, readers would do well to consider his method more along the lines of a contrasting of opposites in order to penetrate appearances and explore the substance of concepts more closely.

## VERIFYING CONCEPTS

As mentioned earlier, the Kantian doctrine of concepts necessitated establishing the validity of a concept (*Begriff*) through parallel lines of inquiry, one logical and the other material, and then situating the concept correctly within or among other known concepts.[11] The first line of inquiry entailed examining the concept only according to the laws of logic to determine whether it contained any contradictions or inconsistencies that would render it logically invalid. A concept was logically true if it met any of following three conditions. First, if it contained no contradictory characteristics, that is, if it was conceivable; a 'round square' is inconceivable and would, therefore, be logically false. Second, if it was of a sufficient basis, that is, if it was derived from a true concept; the concept of a rectangle can be derived from a square, and so it has a sufficient conceptual basis. Third, if it emerged as a unified whole from two contradictory characteristics; the concept of 'four-cornered circle' combines the characteristics of a square and a circle, but does not emerge as valid unified whole, and is therefore false.[12] The color gray, however, emerges from black and white, and therefore is as true as black and white are.

The second line of inquiry necessitated investigating whether the concept actually could exist, or already existed, in the physical world and, if so, in what form. For this line of inquiry, Clausewitz relied heavily on military history, since he realized his own experience in war was too limited to provide a sufficient basis for drawing firm conclusions. A concept has material truth if it corresponded with an object in the physical world; a 'machine enabling one to fly', for example, could be conceived even in Clausewitz's day, and therefore would possess logical truth, but (aside from balloons) one did not exist in the physical world, so the concept lacked material truth.[13] In this case, our investigation would conclude that a flying machine could indeed exist, logically, but it was not clear if it could exist materially.

Finally, the doctrine of concepts also obliged arranging the concept within, or among, other known concepts in the same or a related field. This step amounted to a sort of finishing touch that completed the examination. The concept of a human, for instance, has demonstrable logical and material truth. Placing it within the larger concept of animal, rather than plant, completes the examination and helps establish its validity. At the same time, it reveals something more about the concept and its relation to other concepts.

Clausewitz applied this methodology to his concept of war, which he defined as 'an act of violence to force our opponent to fulfill our will'. Wherever he referred to the 'pure concept' (*blosse* or *reine Begriff*) of war, this is typically what he meant. While examining this concept from a strictly logical perspective, without physical conditions or constraints, he discovered that it contained no inherent contradictions.[14] However, there was also nothing about the concept to prevent the forces it described from escalating ad infinitum. Each side of the conflict would attempt to outdo the other in terms of the intensity of the violence and the amount of effort it would employ, as well as the aim it would pursue. In terms of pure logic, this limitless escalation would have to go on forever: there could be no conceivable end. Logic simply would not allow it. The moment one side relented it would give the advantage to the other, and be lost.

In the physical world, finite material resources would, of course, prevent limitless escalation. However, the physical world cannot come into play when one is considering a concept from a purely logical standpoint. Absolute war (*absolute Kriege*), as it appears *On War*'s opening chapter, was merely Clausewitz's term for the idea of limitless escalation, which was all but inconceivable. It is not the equivalent of the concept of total war, with which it is often confused, because it represents an impossible outcome, whereas total war could actually occur, and in many cases essentially has.[15] Moreover, as 'total' as real war might become, it would always do so because of, rather than in the absence of, political forces.

Clausewitz then examined his concept from a material standpoint. When he did so, he discovered that what kept his concept from escalating was something that came from outside war itself, policy, the trustee or custodian for the collective interests of the state.[16] Policy or the will of one's political leadership always existed prior to war, and thus was not part of war itself, but external to it. Policy decided the purpose for which the war would be fought, estimated how much effort should be expended, and how much violence should be used. It made these decisions based on the value of the purpose it wanted to pursue, and its estimate of how much its opponent would resist.

Accordingly, in the material world, the escalation of war was a matter of *probability* and not, as pure logic demanded, one of necessity. Whether escalation would occur was for judgment to estimate, and in so doing it would naturally have to take into account many factors. Interestingly, the concept of probability and the doctrine of chance were both rather nascent at the time, having appeared mainly in texts written in Latin until the late eighteenth century. Probability and chance were regarded by the educated elite as explanations for laws yet to be discovered; they were considered a scientific way of accounting for uncertainty with respect to outcomes as well as beliefs.[17] As we shall see, Clausewitz's references to the laws of probability have been largely overlooked, causing a great deal of confusion about his concept of the nature of war.

As the final step in the examination, Clausewitz determined that war was not a separate phenomenon, a thing-in-itself, as presupposed in the purely logical concept. Instead, it was a subordinate activity of policy, and was thus included within it as a secondary concept in much the same way as the concept of human belongs within the larger one of animal. Indeed, his perhaps most famous expression—that 'war is nothing but the continuation of political intercourse (*Politik*) by other means'—reflects his ordering of the concept of war within the hierarchy of other known concepts, in this case politics or international relations.[18] In Clausewitz's view, this was an objective observation. It gave the necessary *form* to the substance of his concept of war. His unfinished manuscript only partly touches on the implications of this ordering. One thing is certain, however: it did not upset his overall organization of *On War* itself, which as we have seen was founded on the hierarchical relationship between purpose and means. So, we should not expect that he would have carried out a complete overhaul of his opus, despite what some have claimed.

Clausewitz also used this method when examining other concepts, such as the engagement, defense, and attack. Of course, the principal danger with this method is that it is all too easy for readers to miss subtle but crucial turns in his argument and, thus, to mistake the observations or findings drawn from his theoretical analysis of a concept for more than they are. A point made at the beginning of a chapter based on a search for the logical truth of a concept might be contradicted later when its material truth was considered. In the case of absolute war, for instance, Clausewitz actually showed that this extreme of extremes possessed neither logical nor material truth.[19] Yet, some maintain he attempted to establish a theory of absolute war, whereby one waged war by going all out from the outset, regardless of the political purpose. Such misunderstandings can be avoided by first appreciating Clausewitz's method before reading *On War*.

Some scholars have characterized Clausewitz's methodology as setting ideal war in opposition to real war in a two-fold effort, first, to reveal the inadequacy of purely abstract thinking and, second, to tease out some of the more important characteristics of real war.[20] To a certain extent, this view is correct. However, it holds true mainly for concepts that are actual opposites, such as defense and attack, action and inaction. Clausewitz generally tended to set up the pure concept of war, then pick it apart piece by piece. It is best, therefore, to see his method as two parallel, but related, lines of inquiry into his concept of war. As mentioned earlier, Clausewitz might just as well have focused solely on examining real war. After all, that was how his contemporaries approached the subject. He was not compelled to use Kant's methodology, in other words, since the way the concept fares in a purely logical sense actually has little bearing on the validity of material war. Indeed, his use of this method only makes sense in the context of trying to prove a concept in route to arriving at objective, universally valid knowledge.

To be sure, Clausewitz was certainly capable of making his arguments in a more straightforward manner, as his contemporaries, especially Bülow and Jomini, had done, and as he himself had done in his many historical tracts.[21] Indeed, in some respects it is rather surprising that Clausewitz should have chosen this knotty system of logic, since he had little patience with purely abstract thinking, and since he clearly anticipated that the bulk of his readers would be practical-minded soldiers, and these would have little or no training in the Kantian style of logic. Moreover, he frequently warned against considering war solely from a theoretical standpoint, lest one arrive at false conclusions and logical absurdities. As he explained in one of his prefatory notes, 'examination and observation, philosophy and experience must never distain nor exclude one another; each supports and validates the other'.[22]

However, Clausewitz's opus can be seen as a contribution to what some scholars have described as the Second Scientific Revolution. This revolution took place in Europe from 1780 to 1850, and stressed two tendencies: 'formalization and temporalization'.[23] The former referred to the use of formal logic, or a priori reasoning, such as we find in Kant's critique and, perhaps somewhat surprisingly considering his fame as a man of letters rather than as a scientist, Goethe's studies of nature. The latter involved using historical examples or hypotheses to measure or appreciate how the object under study changed over time. It was also during this revolution that the term science finally 'crystallized', which may in part explain why Clausewitz tended to use the terms scientific and philosophical interchangeably.[24]

## PRACTICAL REASON AND EXPERIENCE

Practical reasoning balanced Clausewitz's application of pure logic. It came from two sources: his personal experience as a soldier, which he recognized as subjective, but valid; and military history. Subjectively valid observations or realizations were not necessarily inferior to objective ones, because subjective knowledge enabled individuals to take appropriate action in the here and now. These observations should not contradict objective knowledge, however. Subjective knowledge complemented objective knowledge, and was thus to be embraced, rather than shunned.[25]

Clausewitz's personal experience with war was considerable. He enlisted in Prussia's 34th Infantry Regiment (Prince Ferdinand) in Potsdam as an officer cadet at the age of 12, becoming a *Fahnenjunker* (officer candidate) and carrying the regimental standard. He saw his first action barely one year later in April 1793 during the siege of Mainz, where his regiment played a role in liberating the city from the French. He watched awe-struck as 'Mainz was being burned to the ground' after Prussian and Austrian troops bombarded the city, and added his shouts of triumph to those of the others.[26] In 1795, the French and Prussians signed a separate peace, and Clausewitz spent the following six years with his regiment in the small garrison town of Neuruppin outside Berlin. There he was exposed to the drill and routine that, regardless of the era, seems to make up the bulk of military life, even in wartime; like every young officer who is unaware of the importance of politics even in peacetime maneuvers, he was dismayed with the prescribed nature of the regiment's annual maneuvers as well as the apparent willingness of senior commanders to regard them as serious affairs.[27] However, he also found time to experiment with the new skirmishing tactics employed by the French and, even more important for his later pursuits, took classes in history, French, and mathematics, thereby expanding his intellectual abilities, though some feelings of inadequacy evidently remained.[28]

In 1801, Clausewitz was admitted into the three-year course of instruction at the War College. There he met Gerhard von Scharnhorst, a former Hanoverian artillery officer now in Prussian service, who would become something of mentor and father figure for the young Prussian. Clausewitz's time at the War College afforded him opportunities to expand his intellectual horizons still farther; he attended lectures in philosophy, history, and military science and theory. In 1802, he became a member of the elite *Militärische Gesellschaft* (Military Society), which held presentations and discussions on all types of military topics, particularly Napoleon's apparent revolution in the methods of war, and was attended by luminaries, royalty, and officers of all ranks. As Article 1 of the Society's bylaws explained:

The purpose of the Society is to instruct its members through the exchange of ideas in all areas of the art of war, in a manner that would encourage them to seek out truth, that would avoid the difficulties of private study with its tendency to one-sidedness, and that would seem best suited to place theory and practice in proper relationship.[29]

Clearly, Clausewitz's *On War* can be seen as an effort to carry on the Society's, and Scharnhorst's, ideal of seeking out truth. The work's formal system of logic and its use of historical examples were measures that would aid in overcoming the one-sidedness that tended to characterize individual study.

In 1803, on Scharnhorst's recommendation, Clausewitz became aide-de-camp to Prince August, nephew of King Frederick William III. The young captain graduated from the Institute at the top of his class of forty students the following year. Two years later (October 1806), Clausewitz accompanied Prince August, who had become his friend and confidant, to the battle of Auerstädt, where the main Prussian army would suffer a crushing defeat at the hands of a veteran French corps under Marshal Davout. At the same time, the rest of the Prussian army was routed by Napoleon at the battle of Jena.[30]

While Clausewitz had serious misgivings about the Prussian campaign plan overall, he had been optimistic about the ultimate outcome of the impending battle. As he wrote in a series of letters to his wife, Marie, in the weeks leading up to the dual battles of Jena-Auerstädt:

26 September:

If one considers all the intelligence we get, brought by those who have recently been in France and have gone through the French theater of war, it would seem that Fate offers us at this moment a revenge, which will cover all faces in France with a pale horror, and will topple the arrogant Emperor into a precipice, where his bones will dissolve to nothing...

12 October:

The day after tomorrow...there will be a great battle, for which the entire Army is longing. I myself look forward to this day with joy as I would to my own wedding day.

14 October:

If I were to forecast a result, there is still the probability we will be victors in the next great battle.[31]

Clausewitz acquitted himself well, participating in a counterattack and bloody hand-to-hand fighting, but the battle was lost before it began. Key Prussian leaders became casualties early on, not that it would have made much difference, as the overconfident heirs of Frederick the Great's army had been outmaneuvered on both fields of battle.[32] Clausewitz and Prince August became prisoners of war during the ensuing Prussian retreat, and they were held in what might be described as gentlemanly captivity in France until the Peace of Tilsit (1807) allowed their repatriation. Like many other Prussian officers of his generation, Clausewitz had to endure the humiliation of military defeat and foreign occupation. His ensuing animosity toward the French apparently never abated.

In the spring of 1808, Clausewitz traveled to Königsberg to rejoin Scharnhorst, who was heading the Military Reorganization Commission, which had been established by the Prussian crown to assess the reasons for the army's poor performance in the war. While there, he made the acquaintance of another important soldier and reformer, August von Gneisenau. In August 1810, Clausewitz was promoted to major and assigned to the War College as an instructor of tactics. Some of his lectures are still extant, particularly those on *Kleinkrieg*, or small war, which address the importance of partisan warfare and the use of minor detachments independently, or in conjunction with larger formations; these particular lectures, which number well over 300 pages in the annotated German edition, were in part a response to the Prussian army's failure to adapt to such flexible tactics in the campaigns of 1806–7.[33] From October 1810 to March 1812, Clausewitz also served as military tutor to the young crown prince (later Frederick William IV). In the spring of 1812, Clausewitz penned a short monograph summarizing the key elements of that instruction.[34]

Clausewitz, convinced that Prussia should continue to resist Napoleon for the sake of honor, resigned his commission and transferred his services to the Russian army in the spring of 1812, against the wishes of King Frederick William III. This action would cause him to be regarded with suspicion and disdain throughout the remainder of his career. Clausewitz had no facility with the Russian language, but attempted to serve as a staff officer and military advisor nonetheless. However, his most important role, at least as far as history is concerned, appears to have been that of military observer because the campaign added immeasurably to his ideas of war. Clausewitz saw the colossal battle of Borodino on September 7, 1812, first hand; he also witnessed Napoleon's long and agonizing retreat from Moscow during the following winter, especially the horrific crossing of the Berezina river. As he confessed to Marie, the 'ghastly scenes' he observed would have driven him 'mad' had his sensibilities not already been hardened by war; as he wrote later:

I felt as if I could never be released from the terrible impressions of the spectacle. I only saw a small fraction of the famous retreat, but in this fraction of some three days' march, all the horrors of the movement were accumulated.[35]

Clausewitz was later instrumental in negotiating the Convention of Tauroggen in December 1812, which resulted in a favorable outcome for Russia: General York pulled his corps of some 20,000 Prussian troops, who had been forced into fighting on the side of Napoleon, out of the conflict, though this was against the king's wishes.[36] Clausewitz participated in the Wars of Liberation from 1813 to 1814, first as an advisor on the staff of Marshal Gebhard von Blücher, then as a staff officer in the Army of the North. His mentor

Scharnhorst died in 1813, the result of a wound incurred at the battle of Gross Görschen, and Clausewitz took the loss hard.

Much to Clausewitz's dismay, the Army of the North performed only observation duties in northern Europe, and so he missed the decisive fighting in France, which culminated in Napoleon's abdication and exile to Elba in May 1814. Clausewitz remained in a Russian uniform until April 14, 1814, when he was finally readmitted into the Prussian army; even then, he was placed in command of only a brigade of the Russo-German Legion, a unit comprised of German officers and men who had fought against Napoleon—and by extension Frederick William III—in Russia and, thus, considered to be of dubious loyalty.[37] When Napoleon returned from exile in 1815, Clausewitz served as chief of staff of the III Prussian Corps under General Johann von Thielmann and fought at the battles of Ligny on June 16, 1815, and Wavre on June 18, 1815. At the latter battle, the III Corps defeated a superior French force under Marshal Emmanuel de Grouchy, which denied Bonaparte the reinforcements he so desperately needed at the battle of Waterloo. The corps to which Clausewitz was assigned thus played a key, if little recognized, role in the final overthrow of Napoleon. For his part, however, Clausewitz felt slighted by the evident injustice of the official report, which emphasized Blücher's triumph and minimized the vital contribution of the III Corps.[38] Yet, as a mature officer, he seemed no longer surprised by such orchestrations.

After the successful conclusion of the wars against Napoleon, the quality and quantity of Clausewitz's historical and theoretical works increased. In 1818, he was appointed head of the War College, and promoted to *Generalmajor* (brigadier general). Within the first few months of his arrival, he assessed the program of instruction at the College, and found it wanting in both form and content. He submitted a formal memorandum to General Hermann von Boyen, then Minister of War, with recommendations for reshaping the War College along the lines of a school of application similar to the French Polytechnique, instead of the more academically oriented German universities.[39] However, for a number of reasons, Boyen took no action on the recommendations. Clausewitz did not pursue the matter farther and, instead, turned to his research and writing to the extent that his administrative duties would allow. From 1820 to 1831, he produced numerous political and historical writings, as well as his masterwork, *On War*, which remained unfinished at the time of his death.

Clausewitz's military career thus spanned four decades, almost one fourth of which was wartime service, though, as usual, only a fraction of that was actually spent under fire. He had seen war from a variety of perspectives—from that of the rank and file, as well as from that of a senior staff officer responsible for planning and coordinating large-scale marches and deployments. He participated in minor engagements, as well as major encounters, in deliberate advances as well as desperate retreats, in prolonged sieges as well as fast-paced battles of maneuver; he knew the bitterness of defeat as well as the elation of victory. Perhaps more important, he saw first hand the consequences of the dramatic changes in warfare brought about by the social and political effects of the French revolution and the operational methods of Napoleon.[40] The critical battles of Jena-Auerstädt, Moscow, and Waterloo, all of which he studied in some detail, helped refine his own military theories, particularly with respect to the qualities of courage and judgment so essential for the successful military commander, and the relative strength of the defense compared to the attack.[41] Clausewitz, thus, had a wealth of combat experience, which he augmented considerably through his study of military history, as a basis on which to rely in developing his theory of war.

## PRACTICAL REASON AND HISTORY

Clausewitz's chapter entitled *Kritik* (Critical Inquiry) in *On War* lays out guidelines for the use of history in the study of war. Kiesewetter's *Outline of Logic* defines *Kritik* as a collection or set of 'rules for judgment', and that definition describes the purpose of Clausewitz's chapter more completely than any brief title could.[42] Indeed, his chapter lays out general rules for learning about war through military history, for conducting what military practitioners today might recognize as campaign analyses. The guidelines the master theorist offered covered three primary activities: (*a*) the unearthing and weighing of the pertinent facts, (*b*) the tracing of effects to their causes, and (*c*) the investigation and assessment of all available means.[43] The chapter also offers several key considerations readers ought to keep in mind while conducting such analyses: every effect has more than one cause, no theory should be considered sacred, war involves a real rather than an abstract enemy, and one always had to conduct analysis thoroughly. Clausewitz also cautioned against the three principal errors that critics make, namely, using one-sided analytical systems as laws; using jargon, technicalities, and metaphors; showing off their erudition, and misusing historical examples.[44]

This chapter in *On War* shows that, for Clausewitz, history played an important role in military education. It could, among other things, help exercise and develop the judgment of officers through the analysis and critique of past battles and campaigns.[45] Clausewitz considered history an expansion of practical experience.[46] He saw both history and its more immediate counterpart, experience, as genuine reflections of reality.

However, using history in these ways posed some problems that neither Clausewitz nor Scharnhorst fully appreciated. As the distinguished historian Sir Michael Howard once wrote, the past could be used to 'prove anything or its contrary'.[47] The past has indeed been used to validate or discredit practically every major theory, precept, or principle. The past, simply put, is what happened. History, in contrast, is the historian's interpretation of what happened. Accordingly, history is a body of knowledge that is incomplete, deeply flawed in places, and essentially and inescapably dynamic. One reason for this is that the available evidence concerning the past is rarely sufficient, or is often too abundant to permit of only one interpretation. Thus, the historian's views are not necessarily universal and might not hold up under close scrutiny.

A second reason is that history has nothing resembling the scientific method to aid it in determining whether what is written about the past is at least a reasonable approximation of it. While historians may begin their research with a question or hypothesis, they cannot conduct the various experiments necessary to determine whether the main conclusions they have drawn about what happened are in fact valid.[48] Subjective measures, such as peer review and critique, can help to a degree, but can also reinforce a veritable Cartesian circle of interpretation: historians write what they do based in part on the fragments of the past, but how they see those fragments is largely influenced by knowledge they have gained in the present, including the works of other historians who may indeed only be offering their best guesses as to what those fragments mean. In other words, the problem is not so much that history is a 'fable agreed upon', as Napoleon reportedly said, but that, except for those accounts that blatantly contradict or disregard the available facts, the reader cannot determine objectively which historical interpretation is more accurate than another. Ultimately, historical truth, like beauty, remains in the eye of the beholder.[49] The foundation history offers for an objective theory of war is, therefore, a dubious one.

History's shortcomings notwithstanding, as a discipline, it can facilitate critical thinking and evaluation and, therefore, critical analysis. It can, in other words, move students along a progression from simple knowledge of facts to higher levels comprehension, to include acknowledging when something cannot be fully known, and why. It can help build a habit of rigorously scrutinizing facts and sources, of detecting biases and specious arguments, and of developing an eye for penetrating the myths of interpretation that surround the past. As scholars have pointed out, however, while Clausewitz appears to have read his sources critically and compared them to one another, he nonetheless assumed that history was more or less an accurate representation of the past. In other words, with respect to history he was 'an amateur scholar, not an academic'.[50]

## CONCLUSIONS AND IMPLICATIONS

To arrive at a valid theory of war, something more than a rhapsody of observations, Clausewitz needed a formal system of inquiry. Kant's system of logic was regarded as authoritative at the time. The combination of logical and material analyses, pure logic and practical reason, embodied in the doctrine of concepts served much like checks-and-balances. Each, when pursued rigorously acted as a check against false or empty concepts or catchwords. He was well aware that his own personal experience, though considerable, was too narrow to form the basis for a valid theory of war; hence, he sought to overcome that limitation via the use of history. Yet a string of historical examples was hardly sufficient for a sound military theory either. The doctrine of concepts solved the riddle by bringing pure logic and practical reason together.

It also seemed to capture the principle of formalization that characterized the Second Scientific Revolution, a principle that had direct, albeit vague, ties to Clausewitz's understanding of the importance of formal truth. While he considered it necessary to prune his conclusions close to the soil of experience, he also realized that experience alone was an insufficient basis for objective knowledge. His choice came at a price, however, for those readers he most desired to reach were (and still are) also the least equipped to understand him.

Unfortunately, the way in which *On War* shifts between logical demonstrations and their material counterparts—or between pure logic and practical reason—while perhaps familiar to some of Clausewitz's contemporaries, tended to confuse later generations. Ironically, his effort to develop a valid theory of war made *On War* enduring, but less accessible. He believed the doctrine of concepts would enable him to establish the objective truths. Yet he was also aware that hardly any soldiers were educated enough to identify even the basics of logic, as he pointed out in several of his letters.[51] Military practitioners who passed through the War College would acquire those basics, but those individuals were relatively few in number.[52]

In selecting this Kantian framework, therefore, Clausewitz had to know he was putting *On War* beyond the reach of the general reader. Only members of the educated elite, such as Countess Sophie Schwerin, who wrote that Clausewitz 'makes it impossible, even for a weak head like mine that is otherwise no good for studying, not to follow him', were likely to follow his competing lines of inquiry.[53] Whatever didactic purposes his opus had, therefore, they came second to his intention to establish the correct ideas about war. He had also placed a great deal of weight on a system that might eventually prove to be flawed, or might fall out of fashion.

As his manuscript took shape over the decade and a half he labored on it, Clausewitz's struggle to finish it owed as much to the complexity of the ideas as to his search for an appropriate form in which to express them. His note of 1827 was prescient, indeed, since it accurately predicted *On War* would suffer endless criticism and misunderstanding due less to the substance of the ideas, than to the form in which they were expressed.

### NOTES

1. *Vom Kriege*, I/1, 191; *On War*, 75.
2. Kiesewetter, *Grundriss*, I, 8.
3. 'Ueber den Zustand der Theorie', in *Schriften–Aufsätze–Studien–Briefe*, I, 27–8.
4. Gallie, *Philosophers of Peace and War*, 52, makes this point as well.
5. Kiesewetter, *Grundriss*, I, 3, 5; and *Darstellung der Wichtigsten Wahrheiten der neueren Philosophie*, 4th edn. 2 vols. (Berlin: Flittner, 1824), II, 29.
6. Kiesewetter, *Grundriss*, I, (1), 6.
7. Kiesewetter, *Grundriss*, I, 13.
8. *Vom Kriege*, VI/30, 859; *On War*, 517.
9. *Vom Kriege*, VII/1, 869; *On War*, 523.
10. Paret, *Clausewitz*, 84, points out that Clausewitz's dialectical method did not insist on resolution, and was primarily used to clarify concepts. See also Uwe Hartmann, 'Dialektik bei Carl von Clausewitz', *Clausewitz-Studien* Heft, 3 (winter 1996), 152–75; and *Carl von Clausewitz and the Making of Modern Strategy* (Potsdam: Miles, 2002), 30–2; Werner Hahlweg, 'Das Clausewitzbild einst und jetzt', in *Vom Kriege*, 38–41; and Aron, *Clausewitz*, 225–30. Most of the leading thinkers and writers of Clausewitz's day used some form of dialectic; compare the works of the German poet Friedrich von Schiller (1759–1805) and those of the theologian Friedrich Schleiermacher (1768–1834). Andreas Herberg-Rothe, 'Clausewitz und Hegel: Ein Heuristischer Vergleich', *Forschungen zur Brandenburgischen und Preußischen Geschichte*, 10/1 (2000), 49–84, maintains that Hegel's influence in *On War* was greater than typically believed.
11. Kiesewetter, *Grundriss*, I (44), 109.
12. Kiesewetter, *Grundriss*, I (45–7), 111–13.
13. Kiesewetter, *Grundriss*, I, 115.
14. *Vom Kriege*, I/1, sections 3–5, pp. 192–5; *On War*, 75–7.

15. Kaldor, *New and Old Wars*, 25, is an example of this confusion. For the development and realization of the concept of total war, see Manfred F. Boemeke, Roger Chickering, and Stig Förster (eds.), *Anticipating Total War: The German and American Experiences, 1871–1914* (New York: Cambridge University Press, 1999); Roger Chickering and Stig Förster (eds.), *Great War, Total War: Combat and Mobilization on the Western Front, 1914–1918* (New York: Cambridge University Press, 2000); Roger Chickering and Stig Förster (eds.), *The Shadows of Total War: Europe, East Asia, and the United States, 1919–1939* (New York: Cambridge University Press, 2003); Roger Chickering, Stig Förster, and Bernd Greiner (eds.), *A World at Total War: Global Conflict and the Politics of Destruction, 1937–1945* (Cambridge: Cambridge University Press, 2005).
16. *Vom Kriege*, VIII/6B, 993; *On War*, 606.
17. Ian Hacking, *The Taming of Chance* (Cambridge: Cambridge University Press, 2002), 11–13.
18. *Vom Kriege*, I/1, 210; *On War*, 87.
19. Gary Wills, 'Critical Inquiry (*Kritik*) in Clausewitz', *Critical Inquiry*, 9 (December 1982), 281–302, overlooks this vital point in an otherwise brilliant analysis.
20. Michael I. Handel, *Masters of War: Classical Strategic Thought*, 3rd edn. (London: Frank Cass, 2001), 328–31, is an example of this misunderstanding; Handel is correct, however, in stating that Clausewitz was not advocating absolute war. See also Raymond Aron, 'Clausewitz's Conceptual System', *Armed Forces and Society*, 1/1 (November 1974), 49–59.
21. See Clausewitz's *Nachrichten über Preussen in seiner Grossen Katastrophe: Kriegsgeschichtliche Einzelschriften* (Berlin: Mittler, 1888) and 'Feldzug von 1812 in Rußland', in *Hinterlassene Werke des Carl von Clausewitz über Krieg und Kriegführung*, vol. VII (Berlin: Dümmler's, 1834); major parts of the texts have been retranslated by Moran and Paret as 'Observations on Prussia and Her Great Catastrophe', and 'The Campaign of 1812 in Russia', in *Historical and Political Writings*, 30–84 and 110–204, respectively.
22. *Vom Kriege*, 'Vorrede des Verfassers', 184; *On War*, 61.
23. Daniel Steuer, 'In Defense of Experience: Goethe's Natural Investigations and Scientific Culture', in Lesley Sharpe (ed.), *The Cambridge Companion to Goethe* (Cambridge: Cambridge University Press, 2002), 163–4; these tendencies clearly parallel the Kantian sense of a priori and a posteriori reasoning.
24. Steuer, 'Defense of Experience', 163; as noted by historian Ernst Cassirer, *The Philosophy of the Enlightenment* (Princeton, NJ: Princeton University Press, 1952), vii, philosophy, not unlike science, was 'the all-comprehensive medium in which principles are formulated, developed, and founded'.
25. According to some scholars, German historians deliberately rejected the more empirically based methods of their French and British counterparts which they considered insufficient. They believed it was possible to arrive at a more 'complete Truth' by insinuating the historian's own intellect or spirit (*Geist*) into

historical writing. H. Stuart Hughes, *Consciousness and Society: The Reorientation of European Social Thought, 1890–1930* (New York: Octagon, 1976), 183–91; and George G. Iggers, *The German Conception of History: The National Tradition of Historical Thought from Herder to the Present* (Middletown, CT: Wesleyan University Press, 1983), 63–89. Leopold von Ranke said that the historian's spirit needed to become one with the historical spirit that 'dwells within the sources'. Leopold von Ranke, in Roger Wines (ed.) *The Secret of World History: Selected Writings on the Art and Science of History* (New York: Fordham University Press, 1981), 21; and Leonard Krieger, *Ranke: The Meaning of History* (Chicago, IL: University of Chicago, 1977), esp. 10–11.
26. Cf. Parkinson, *Clausewitz*, 25.
27. 'Observations on Prussia and her Great Catastrophe', in *Historical and Political Writings*, 40–1.
28. Parkinson, *Clausewitz*, 30–2.
29. Cf. White, *Scharnhorst*, 40.
30. Holger Nowack, 'Die Schlacht bei Jena und Auerstadt (1806)', in Eckardt Opitz (ed.), *Gerhard von Scharnhorst: Vom Wesen und Wirken der Preußischen Heeresreform* (Bremen, Germany: Temmen, 1998), 49–65.
31. Cf. Parkinson, *Clausewitz*, 56–8.
32. Prussian casualties numbered about 25,000 of 50,000 troops engaged at Jena, while the French lost about 5,000; at Auerstädt, the Prussians lost another 13,000 of 60,000 soldiers, while the French suffered about 10,000. David G. Chandler, *The Campaigns of Napoleon* (New York: Macmillan, 1966), 479–501.
33. For Clausewitz's lectures on small wars, see 'Meine Vorlesungen über den kleinem Krieg, gehalten auf der Kriegs-Schule 1810 und 1811', in *Schriften–Aufsätze–Studien–Briefe*, I, 205–588.
34. Paret, *Clausewitz*, 193–5. 'Die wichtigsten Grundsätze des Kriegführens', in *Vom Kriege*, 1047–87; in English translation as Clausewitz's *Principles of War*, trans. Hans W. Gatzke (Harrisburg, PA: Stackpole, 1942).
35. Parkinson, *Clausewitz*, 194.
36. Peter Paret, *York and the Era of Prussian Reform, 1807–1815* (Princeton, NJ: Princeton University Press, 1966), 191–5.
37. Paret, *Clausewitz*, 243–6.
38. Paret, *Clausewitz*, 250.
39. Paret, *Clausewitz*, 272–80.
40. However, the extent to which Napoleon's wars influenced Clausewitz's theories or merely confirmed them is debatable. Philip Windsor, 'The Clock, the Context and Clausewitz', *Millennium: Journal of International Studies*, 6/2 (autumn 1977), 190–6, exemplifies the view that the Napoleonic experience shaped Clausewitz's theories; see also Gerhard Ritter, 'Revolution der Kriegführung und der Kriegspolitik. Napoleon und Clausewitz', in Günther Dill (ed.), *Clausewitz in Perspektive* (Frankfurt, Germany: Ullstein, 1980), 291–333; John Tashjean, 'The Transatlantic Clausewitz, 1952–1982', *Naval*

*War College Review* (November–December 1982), 69–86, holds that the Napoleonic experience confirmed Clausewitz in his theories; Daniel Moran, 'Clausewitz and the Revolution', *Central European History*, 22/2 (June 1989), 183–99, rightly contends that it was not just Napoleon, but the entire experience of the French Revolution that contributed to shaping Clausewitz's views.

41. Herberg-Rothe, *Rätsel Clausewitz*, 27–49, discusses the effect that Clausewitz's analyses of the Jena, Moscow, and Waterloo campaigns, on which he labored between 1823 and 1827, had on his theories of war. Herberg-Rothe maintains that Jena convinced Clausewitz that wars should be waged offensively, with the utmost concentration, and with the aim of achieving a decision by battle. In contrast, the Moscow campaign shows Clausewitz the superiority of the defense over the attack, and the Waterloo campaign demonstrates that political circumstances can trump military considerations.
42. Kiesewetter, *Grundriss*, I/11.
43. *Vom Kriege*, II/5, 'Kritik', 312–13; *On War*, 156.
44. *Vom Kriege*, II/5, 332–4; *On War*, 168–9.
45. 'Ueber Militär-Bildung und Wissenschaft', *Beiheft zum Militär-Wochenblatt*, 1 (1873), 1–37, demonstrates that history was still used in this way at the Berlin *Kriegsakademie* many years later; this is also true today in other military schools.
46. *Vom Kriege*, II/2, 290–1; *On War*, 147; Jon Tetsuro Sumida, 'The Relationship of History and Theory in *On War*: The Clausewitzian Ideal and Its Implications', *Journal of Military History*, 65 (2001), 333–54, attempts to add a provocative twist to this logical extension, but his experiment is ultimately too anachronistic, removing Clausewitz from his Prussian intellectual context; Col. Richard Swain, ' "The Hedgehog and the Fox": Jomini, Clausewitz, and History', *Naval War College Review*, 43/4 (autumn 1990), 98–109, compares the approaches of Clausewitz and Jomini.
47. Sir Michael Howard, ' "The Lessons of History": An Inaugural Lecture given at the University of Oxford, March 1981', in *The Lessons of History* (New Haven, CT: Yale University Press, 1991), 11.
48. Siegfried Kracauer, *History: The Last Things before the Last* (Princeton, NJ: Marcus Wiener, 1994), 47–8, discusses the differences between the scientific method and the method of the historian.
49. Antulio J. Echevarria II, 'The Trouble with History', *Parameters*, 35/2 (summer 2005), 78–90.
50. He did not fully appreciated the difference between published texts and unpublished manuscripts or archival sources, for instance. Paret and Moran, 'Introduction', *Historical and Political Writings*, 12–13.
51. See also Gordon A. Craig, *The Politics of the Prussian Army, 1640–1945* (New York: Oxford University Press, 1955), 25, for the lack of education among Prussian officers throughout most of the eighteenth to the beginning of the nineteenth century.

52. In 1810, for instance, each class was limited to only fifty individuals. Dennis E. Showalter, ' "No Officer Rather than a Bad Officer": Officer Selection and Education in the Prussian/German Army, 1715–1945', in *Military Education*, 38.
53. Cf. Heuser, *Reading Clausewitz*, x. To what extent Countess Schwerin is to be believed is debatable; Clausewitz was a personal acquaintance of the Countess. Paret, *Clausewitz*, 316–17.

# Part II

# The Nature and Universe of War

The next three chapters examine Clausewitz's understanding of war's nature, the complex relationship he perceived between war and political activity, and his theories of friction and military genius. He spent the first book of *On War*, nearly 10 percent of his masterwork, explaining the nature of war, the principal forces that shape it—hostility, chance, and purpose. In that book, he also put forth his definition of war, and introduced the dynamic relationship between purpose and means.

Just as Copernicus described the nature of the celestial universe in the first part of his treatise, so Clausewitz portrayed the universe of war in the opening of his masterwork. The nature of this universe was 'complex' (*zusammengesetzte*) and 'variable' (*veränderliche*), and it was governed by the laws of probability, rather than those of logical necessity.[1] It was within this dynamic and multidimensional universe, then, that theory and practice must do their work.

War, Clausewitz explained, is more than a 'simple chameleon' that can alter its external appearance according to its environment.[2] A chameleon can change its color, but not its internal composition. War, on the other hand, can alter in its internal composition as well, both in kind as well as a matter of degree. The purposes for which wars are fought range in kind from overthrowing an opponent to achieving a negotiated settlement. One might begin a war pursuing the former, but end it seeking the latter, or vice versa. An intrinsic force such as hostility, moreover, could vary in intensity from one war to the next, or even multiple times within the same war. Clausewitz even described violence as a 'pulsation' (*Pulsieren*), increasing here diminishing there.[3]

Conceivably, a change in degree in any one of these, if severe enough, could amount to a virtual change in kind. The wars of Napoleon, for instance, in which hostility reached new levels, differed substantially from those of Frederick.[4] If the Napoleonic Wars represent any kind of revolution in warfare, it was, as he pointed out, due to the changes that occurred in the realm of social and political conditions, the realm of hostility. Thus, war, according to Clausewitz, varied not only in terms of the means used to wage it, but also because of the external forces which influenced it. In other words, contrary to what many of the old soldiers claimed through the centuries, war's nature was dynamic, rather than constant or immutable.

To be sure, Clausewitz believed all wars were things of the same nature. However, that nature was, like the nature of the weather, dynamic, and its principal elements, even if always present, were constantly in flux. Like war, the weather consists of a few common and inescapable elements, such as barometric pressure, heat index, dew point, wind velocity, and so on. Nevertheless, the difference between a brief summer shower and a hurricane is significant, so much so, in fact, that we prepare for each quite differently. Indeed, the difference in degree is so great, the danger to our lives and property so much higher in the latter, that we might do well to consider showers and hurricanes different in kind, though both are certainly stormy weather. We might apply some of the same rules of thumb for each kind of weather, but also many different ones.

As we see, Clausewitz found the principles governing major wars easier to discern than for other types. His fundamental purpose in discussing the nature of war was, therefore, to identify not only the elements common to all wars, but also how changes in one or more of those elements might influence what we perceive to be the nature of any given war.

CONFLICTING VIEWS

Perhaps the most common misreading of Clausewitz's description of war's nature is that he believed it to be merely political. This interpretation seems to agree, on the surface at least, with what is probably his most famous statement: 'War is the mere continuation of political intercourse by other means'.[5] However, it is unidimensional, whereas Clausewitz's depiction was ultimately trinitarian. A contrasting, but equally flawed, opinion holds that war's true nature is more or less captured in his concept of absolute war, which is taken as being akin to total war; we discussed this error in the previous chapter.[6]

A third argument, advanced by the late historian Russell Weigley, takes issue with each of these views; Weigley insisted that politics tends to become an instrument of war rather than the other way around: 'War once begun has always tended to generate a politics of its own: to create its own momentum, to render obsolete the political purposes for which it was undertaken, and to erect its own political purposes'.[7] In other words, the dynamics of war are such that policy is likely to exchange places with its instrument as the fighting intensifies. For this view, the question becomes how to make war safe for policy.[8] Or, put differently, how to keep the grammar of war from dictating the logic. However, part of Clausewitz's point in his discussion of war's nature is precisely that the use of violence for the ends of policy entails risk, and just because some wars involve more violence than others does not make them less political.

Other writers take a more considered approach to Clausewitz's description of the nature of war, reducing the term nature to its modern definition, that is, a set of 'essential qualities', and identifying those qualities as political purpose, violence, friction, chance, and uncertainty.[9] Advocates of this view distinguish between the nature of war (the above qualities) and the character of war (its means); they are wont to say that the former is constant, and thus the nature of war is immutable, while the latter changes over time, giving rise to different forms or styles. Many discussions of the nature of war, however, fail to distinguish between *war*, as an act of violence, and *warfare*, as the technique of applying that violence, thus adding to the confusion.[10] These approaches, however, tend to overlook just how intimate and dynamic the relationship is between war and warfare; the two are clearly not the same, but the violence of war comes from war's means, from warfare.

Finally, in an interpretation nearer to Clausewitz's than might appear at first glance, other scholars, notably historians John Keegan and Martin van Creveld, contend that war itself has no specific nature.[11] Instead, it takes on the forms and motives that societies and cultures give it. Accordingly, the search for war's nature leads everywhere and nowhere. This interpretation insists, moreover, that Clausewitz's concept of war was limited to state-on-state conflict, and thus did not account for nonstate wars.[12] The logical flaw in this argument, however, is that variety precludes pattern. No two wars are exactly alike. Yet, that does not mean that underlying laws, cause-and-effect relationships, do not exist. In fact, the history of war reveals discernable patterns, which are evidence that such laws do exist. These laws are what Clausewitz attempted to discover and explain in his description of war's nature.

Interestingly, the above interpretations capture aspects of Clausewitz's views. They are incomplete, in part, because his method was not as straightforward as it needed to be for so complex a topic. Another reason is that understanding the nature of war is often thought of as a philosophical rather than a practical problem. In fact, works claiming contemporary wars are new often avoid the question of war's nature altogether. Hence, the topic receives little serious consideration.

Yet the debate over contemporary war actually demonstrates the need for a clear and defensible understanding of war's nature. Otherwise, vague impressions and unexamined assumptions are as likely as not to influence policy-makers and practitioners. Our understanding of war's nature, or whether we believe it has one, influences how we approach the conduct of war—how we develop military strategy, doctrine and concepts, and train and equip combat forces. If we view war primarily as an act of violence with a tendency to spiral out of control, we may use it sparingly, or not at all. If, on the other hand, we see war largely as an obedient instrument of policy, we may try to use it to achieve a great deal, perhaps too much. Since our understanding of war's nature will influence, even if only indirectly, the way we approach armed conflict, we would do well to take the question seriously, and try to answer it, so as to move beyond the vague impressions that would otherwise inform our choices. Clausewitz's description of the nature of war can facilitate that endeavor by challenging our impressions and assumptions.

Far less controversy than confusion surrounds Clausewitz's concept of politics, though perhaps it would be better if the opposite were the case. Chapter 4 addresses and sheds light on some of that confusion. There are issues also with Clausewitz's concept of genius, and those are covered in Chapter 5.

## NOTES

1. *Vom Kriege*, I/2, 214; *On War*, 90.
2. *Vom Kriege*, I/1, 212–13; *On War*, 89.
3. *Vom Kriege*, I/1, 210; *On War*, 87.
4. *Vom Kriege*, VIII/3B, 970–4; *On War*, 592–3.
5. *Vom Kriege*, I/1, 210; *On War*, 87. For example, see Angstrom, 'Debating the Nature of Modern War', 5; Eliot Cohen, 'Strategy: Causes, Conduct, and Termination of War', in Richard H. Shultz, Jr, Roy Godson, and George H. Quester (eds.), *Security Studies for the 21st Century* (Washington, DC: Brassey's, 1997), 364–6, refers to 'politics' as the defining element in war; and Brodie, 'A Guide', in *On War*, 641–6.
6. For works making this error, see: Col. J. K. Greer, 'Operational Art for the Objective Force', *Military Review* (September–October 2002), 22–9; Christopher Coker, 'Post-Modern War', *Royal United Services Institute Journal*, 143/3 (June 1998), 7–14; Stephen J. Cimbala, *Clausewitz and Escalation: Classical Perspective on Nuclear Strategy* (London: Frank Cass, 1991); G. F. Freudenberg, 'A Conversation with General Clausewitz', *Military Review*, 57/10 (October 1977), 68–71; Col. Joseph I. Greene, 'Foreword' to Karl von Clausewitz, *On War*, trans. O. J. Matthijs Jolles (New York: Modern Library, 1943), xiii.

7. Russell Weigley, 'The Political and Strategic Dimensions of Military Effectiveness', in Williamson Murray and Allan R. Millett (eds.), *Military Effectiveness* (Boston, MA: Allen & Unwin, 1988), vol. 3, *The Second World War*, 341.
8. Wendell J. Coats, 'Clausewitz's Theory of War: An Alternative View', *Comparative Strategy*, 5/4 (1988), 351–73.
9. Lonsdale, *Nature of War in the Information Age*, 19–22; James M. Dubik, 'Has Warfare Changed? Sorting Apples from Oranges', Landpower Essay, no. 02–3, July 2002, Institute of Land Warfare.
10. Lonsdale, *Nature of War in the Information Age*, uses war and warfare interchangeably; Martin van Creveld, 'Through a Glass Darkly: Some Reflections on the Future of War', *Naval War College Review*, 53/4 (autumn 2000), 25–44, discusses changing *forms* of war rather than changes in the nature of war; The Cantigny Conference Series, *The Changing Nature of Conflict* (Chicago, IL: Robert R. McCormick Tribune Foundation, 1995), 32, actually only discusses changes in war's root causes; William E. Odom, *America's Military Revolution: Strategy and Structure after the Cold War* (Washington, DC: American University Press, 1993) purports to discuss the changing nature of war, but only addresses changes in weaponry.
11. Keegan, *History of Warfare*, 24, 46; van Creveld, *Transformation of War*, 33–62, 124–26; and '*The Transformation of War* Revisited', *Small Wars and Insurgencies*, 13/2 (summer 2002), 3–15; Philip Wilkinson, 'The Changing Nature of War: New Wine in Old Bottles—A New Paradigm or Paradigm Shift?', *The Royal Swedish Academy of War Sciences: Proceedings and Journal*, 207/1 (2003), 25–35, argues that the nature of war is in the eye of the beholder. For a rejoinder, see Andreas Herberg-Rothe, 'The Primacy of "Culture" over War in a Modern World? John Keegan's Critique Demands a Sophisticated Interpretation of Clausewitz'. http://www.clausewitz.com/cwzhome/herberg-rothe/keegan2.htm. Originally printed in *Defense Analysis*, 2 (August 2001).
12. See Kaldor, *New & Old Wars*, 25–7; for a counterargument: Isabelle Duyvesteyn, *Clausewitz and African War: Politics and Strategy in Liberia and Somalia* (London: Routledge, 2004).

# 3

# War Is More than a Chameleon

Of all Western military works, *On War* offers by far the most cogent, and surely the most complex, articulation of war's nature. Whether theorists and practitioners agree or disagree with Clausewitz's views, they tend to invoke the authority of his masterwork in their discussions of the nature of war.[1] As a result, *On War* occupies at the center of the ongoing debates over the nature of contemporary war, and warfare.[2] Nonetheless, readers will find little agreement regarding what Clausewitz said about the nature of war. His articulation of that nature is far too complex for most analyses, which merely want to use it to make a point. And grabbing a key phrase or sentence from the work on the assumption that it captures the essence of what he had to say is generally misleading. This chapter takes readers through the opening sections of *On War*, where Clausewitz laid out his initial concept of armed conflict, examined it from the purely logical and material standpoints, and in the process identified the principal forces that influence the waging of war itself.

## WAR'S NATURE

When Clausewitz referred to the nature of war he meant the sum of the fundamental cause-and-effect relationships, or laws, which defined it.[3] By definition, any such laws and associated principles must be universal, applicable to all wars. Conversely, if war had no unifying nature, it could have no fundamental laws or principles.

Clausewitz's study of history revealed that wars did not conform to a single pattern: 'Each era had its own kinds of war, its own limiting conditions, its own biases. Each would also, therefore, have had its own theory of war.'[4] Hence, history seemed to suggest that war did not have a single nature. If true, his desire to construct a universally valid theory was in jeopardy. We find his concerns expressed in the following working note, which was probably penned during the writing of Books VIII and I:

Is one war of the same nature as another? Is the aim (*Ziel*) of a war distinguishable from its political purpose (*Zweck*)?

What size force must be brought forth in war?

What amount of energy must be applied in the conduct of war?

What causes the many pauses that occur in fighting; are they essential parts of it, or actual anomalies?

Are the wars of the 17th and 18th centuries where force was constrained, or the raiding parties of half-civilized Tartars, or the ruinous wars of the 19th century representative of the phenomenon of war itself?

Or is the nature of war determined by the nature of the relationships of the warring parties, and what exactly are these relationships and conditions?

The subjects of these questions do not appear in any book written on war, and least of all in those which have been written recently about the conduct of war in general, and about strategy. Yet, these subjects are the foundation of all observations, all principles, all guidelines and rules, which could be made about strategy....

Without knowing what war is, what war should be, what war can do, no theory of the conduct of war is possible, and all attempts made in the realm of strategy are futile.[5]

Clausewitz presented his answers to these questions, and more, in Book VIII and the first two chapters of Book I. Most scholars still believe the first chapter of *On War* was the only one he considered finished, and that he wanted it to serve as the model for the others.

## WAR'S ESSENCE

As mentioned earlier, *On War* proceeds from the simple to the complex. It begins, as its author said, by going directly to the heart or core (*das Element*) of the war:

War is nothing but personal combat (*Zweikampf*) on a larger scale. Conceiving the countless individual combats of which war consists as a single unity is best done by imagining a pair of wrestlers. Each attempts, through the use of physical force, to compel the other to do his will; his *immediate* purpose is *to lay low* (*niederzuwerfen*) his opponent and thereby to render him incapable of further resistance.[6]

The metaphor of the duel, or of personal combat, captures the essence of war, which for Clausewitz was more than a unilateral use of violence.[7] It is the bilateral use of violence: violence met by violence. As he explained later in *On War*:

... it is at the heart of the matter that the side that first brings the element of war into question, from whose perspective it is first possible to think of opposing wills, and also establishes the initial contours of the conflict—is the defense.[8]

In other words, it is not the action of the saber, but that of crossed sabers that makes up war. He reiterated the theme again in Book IV, where he reminded the reader that 'the essence (*Wesen*) of war is fighting (*Kampf*)'.[9] The violent clash of opposing wills is, thus, the essence of war.

The term *Zweikampf* is usually translated as duel, a meaning common in Clausewitz's day. However, it can also mean personal or individual combat, a broader interpretation, which in many ways is more appropriate.[10] A duel (*ein Duell*) in late eighteenth- and early nineteenth-century Prussia was a rigidly structured and, ultimately, proscribed affair.[11] In a typical duel, adversaries would meet at an appointed time and place, choose their weapons, agree to certain conventions for executing the fight, such as the use of seconds, and then try to inflict harm on one another for the specific purpose of satisfying their honor.

However, the activity itself was frowned on by Frederick the Great as an unnecessary wastage of noble lives 'from whom the Fatherland had expected the greatest service'.[12] It was finally made illegal in 1794 by Frederick's successor, Friedrich Wilhelm II. Moreover, the custom of dueling was limited to the privileged classes, usually military officers and members of the nobility, in other words, those capable of giving satisfaction. Typically, one did not engage in a duel with an individual of a lower social rank because killing a person of inferior status could not, by the accepted codes of the day, provide satisfaction to one of higher standing. The term duel thus lacks the universal quality necessary to serve as a microcosm of war.

As Clausewitz stated in Book IV, 'The engagement is a vastly modified form of duel', for it is driven not only by the desire to fight, but also by the larger situation of which it is a part, and by overarching political purposes.[13]

The idea of personal combat is, thus, more flexible. We can engage in personal combat with any manner of opponent regardless of social rank. Personal combat can occur with or without weapons, and can end in one party's destruction, or a less severe outcome. Whether we choose to think of war as a duel or as personal combat, therefore, the central point is that it is essentially a collision of violent forces, with each party pursuing its purposes, while reacting to the actions of the other.

## THE CONCEPT OF WAR

Clausewitz then introduced his concept (*Begriff*) of war, which was somewhat more complex: '*War is thus an act of violence (Gewalt) to force an opponent to fulfill our will.*'[14] The word *Gewalt* can mean force or violence, which are virtually synonymous in English. Little difference exists between a violent act and a forceful one, for instance. The term force has become something of a euphemism for violence in contemporary strategic literature, and rendering *Gewalt* as violence accords better with Clausewitz's implicit and explicit references to the violent aspect of war's nature elsewhere in *On War*. War, he insisted, is essentially an act of violence, despite whatever trappings it might assume as the result of developments in the arts and sciences, or whatever restrictions it must abide by for the sake of international conventions.[15]

Clausewitz's concept consists of three principal parts: the act of violence; the purpose (*Zweck*) of making our opponent do our will, which requires rendering him 'defenseless' (*wehrlos*)—the real aim (*Ziel*) of all military activity; and the physical and psychological effort required to accomplish that aim. The aim of rendering one's opponent defenseless, Clausewitz pointed out, *typically takes the place of the purpose*, and 'treats it as something that does not belong to war itself'.[16]

The distinction he made between the overall purpose (*Zweck*) of war and its military aim (*Ziel*) is an important one, and he maintained it throughout *On War*. The discussion that takes place in the first chapter examines his concept of war with the military aim (*Ziel*) displacing the overall purpose (*Zweck*), and actually ends up proving that purpose is inseparable from war; otherwise, escalation would always occur, which history shows is not the case. If it were, Clausewitz could have offered posterity a simple formula for success—always apply the maximum possible violence, aim, and effort in war.

### From a Purely Logical Standpoint

Examining his concept from the standpoint of pure logic, Clausewitz demonstrated that, without the overarching influence of purpose, the elements of violence, aim, and effort have no inherent logical limits. Unlike a square-circle or a round-square, it was not self-contradictory, or logically false, though he clearly implied that the idea of limitless escalation, however necessary by the rules of logic, was itself absurd.

By way of illustration, in section 3 'The Utmost Use of Violence', he determined that the amount of violence one could employ in war had no conceivable theoretical limit.[17] He began with the premise that combatants who were willing to use more violence than their opponents would have an inherent advantage over them. The logical tendency for each side, therefore, would be to escalate toward ever higher levels of violence. In other words, if one side employed a certain amount of violence, the other would be compelled to respond with yet more violence in order to avoid giving the advantage to its opponent. That response, in turn, would compel the first to raise the level of violence yet again, and so on.

From a purely logical standpoint, then, this escalatory cycle or reciprocal action (*Wechselwirkung*) must continue ad infinitum, because neither side would want to give the other an advantage, and because there are no logical (only material) limits as to how much violence either side could employ. In other words, if we think of the amount of violence one side wishes to apply against its opponent as $n$, it is always possible to conceive of the other side responding with $n + 1$.

The same logic holds true for aim and effort. In section 4 'The Aim Is to Render the Enemy Defenseless', Clausewitz began with the premise that as long as our adversary is not completely defenseless, he has at least the possibility of rendering us defenseless.[18] Logic dictates, therefore, that each side must raise its aim higher than its opponent's, that is, it must ever escalate. Similarly, in section 5 'Utmost Exertion of Effort', Clausewitz began with the premise that rendering an opponent defenseless required putting forth enough effort, both physical and psychological, to overcome his capacities to resist.[19]

While we can reasonably determine our adversary's physical capabilities through intelligence, he continued, we can only estimate his psychological capacity, his will, to resist based on how much value we think he will place on the purpose at stake. Since neither side knows for sure how much the other might resist, logic dictates that each must increase its physical and psychological effort to ensure it exceeds that of the other. This dynamic, in turn, generates yet another form of endless escalation.

## From a Material Standpoint

Turning to the examination of the concept from a material standpoint, Clausewitz noted that escalation was not inevitable in the material world, but is rather an outcome explainable by the laws of probability

(*Wahrscheinlichkeitgesetzten*).[20] Some wars, as he observed, are fought merely to fulfill treaty obligations, and participants put forth only the minimum effort necessary to satisfy those obligations, while looking for the first opportunity to withdraw from the conflict honorably.[21] In those cases, escalation is neither sought nor welcome. In sections 6 through 8, in fact, he stressed that the elements of violence, aim, and effort have historically never reached the extremes required by pure logic.[22]

The idea that escalation was not determined by the laws of necessity, but by the laws of probability was truly a revolutionary one in the military theory of Clausewitz's day. Interestingly, classical probability theory held that probabilities were objective, that is, they were inherent in nature.[23] As the French mathematician and probability theorist, Simon de Laplace, wrote in 1814: 'All events, even those which on account of their insignificance do not seem to follow the great laws of nature, are the result of it just as surely as the revolutions of the sun'.[24] In other words, probability was a way to account for the unpredictability, or apparent randomness, of some events until science or philosophy could properly explain the laws that determine those events. It would be some time yet before scientists and philosophers would admit that some events are not determined by laws inherent in nature.

Accordingly, Clausewitz's references to the objective nature of war in sections 19 through 21 of the first chapter of *On War* appear to be a conflation of two ideas.[25] The first is that the apparent variance of the purposes for which wars are fought is explainable by the laws of probability, which are inherent in nature and thus universal. And, second, this realization is true of all wars, not just those of his day, and is therefore objective. Escalation is a potential outcome rather than a necessary one. All things being equal, war would either escalate or it would not: the probability would thus be 1 in 2.

However, other factors such as the value of the object being sought, the resources available, and the propensity of one's leadership to escalate come into play as well. Intelligence might provide other information that could alter the odds, perhaps to 3 in 5 or 9 in 10, but intelligence, as Clausewitz also believed, was itself based on uncertainties. Without getting into the details of an involved mathematical proof, we can see that estimating how our opponent will react is akin to calculating compound probabilities.

Clausewitz did not advocate the development of a calculus for decision-making, though 'game theory' evolved as an attempt to do just that.[26] Rather, his point was that strict laws of necessity did not apply to the nature of war. Ultimately, determining whether escalation will occur was a matter for skilled judgment, an invaluable quality for soldiers and statesmen.[27] Again, if escalation were a certainty, we could reduce the waging of war to a formula: use the utmost violence, strive for the maximum aim, and spare no effort.

Clausewitz's examination of war from a purely logical standpoint is *not* an argument that war has an inner logic, an inherent tendency to escalate. Real war has no such tendency: it follows the laws of probability, not the laws of necessity. Its grammar is its own, but not its logic. When war escalates, it is because policy, which is essentially external to war, decided to raise the ante. Many of Clausewitz's interpreters have misunderstood this point. They see absolute war, correctly, as a strictly philosophical or logical concept, but then, quite incongruously, take it to represent an 'ideal type of war, never found in reality, which all real wars approximate but never attain'.[28] However, what Clausewitz actually said was that war had no inner tendency pushing it to approximate an ideal. Put differently, absolute war is *not* Clausewitz's warning of what would happen, should war occur without the controlling influence of policy. It is simply a rejection of the notion that war follows the laws of logical necessity.

To reemphasize, the term absolute war captures the idea of limitless escalation, but this idea is *not* associated with real war; again, it was barely conceivable even in the purely logical sense. If it were a part of real war, every war in history would have shown the same general pattern of escalation. Since that is not the case, absolute war—the idea that escalation is intrinsic to war—is not valid. An earlier draft of Clausewitz's manuscript used the term 'total concept' (*Total-Begriff*) of war rather than absolute war to refer to the idea of escalation proceeding to its logical and thus unlimited extreme.[29] Nonetheless, absolute war should not be construed as total war, as it has come to be known in contemporary literature. From the standpoint of pure logic, it has no inherent contradictions, but it is still problematic since it lacks conceptual boundaries; in short, the problem with limitless war is essentially that it is limitless.

Although Clausewitz admitted in Book VIII that Napoleon's wars came about as close to 'perfection in violence' as was possible, he repeatedly pointed out in the first chapter of *On War* that the absolute extreme required by pure logic had no material existence, no direct correspondence with reality.[30] War under Napoleon reached its point because of the political purpose it served and because the political conditions brought about in part by the French Revolution enabled it to do so, not because of any inherent tendency in war. In section 6 of *On War*'s first chapter, he stated that the absolute form of war could only exist if (*a*) it was an entirely isolated act that arose suddenly and without any connection to the political conditions which preceded it; (*b*) it consisted of a single decisive act, or several simultaneous ones; and (*c*) that the decisive act was complete in itself, and did not require any consideration of the political conditions that would follow it.[31]

However, in sections 7 through 9, Clausewitz stressed that these three conditions never obtain in reality: war is never an isolated act; it never consists of a single, instantaneous blow without duration; and in its results, it is never final, since vanquished parties sometimes rise like a phoenix from the ashes to take revenge, as Prussia and her allies eventually did in the Napoleonic Wars.[32] These points have led some scholars to define absolute war as 'war "absolved", loosened, set free from reality'.[33] Thus, the escalatory tendencies of the pure concept do not reflect the tendencies of real war. Far from showing escalation as a natural tendency in war, Clausewitz's concept of absolute war actually reveals the fallacy of thinking that war has any inherent tendency. Put simply, he demonstrated that the view that war will escalate of its own accord does not correspond with reality.

Clausewitz thus removed the law of necessity from war, and replaced it with the law of probability, that is, the need to make uncertain judgments based on imperfect information and unclear situations. The governing purpose, which he had removed in section 2, represents the sum or outcome of that judgment. Accordingly, in section 11 he restored the political purpose (*Zweck*), to his original concept of war: 'war is an act of violence to compel our opponent to do our will'.[34] He then considered this restored concept from a purely logical standpoint once again, and identified yet another problem: the influence of the political purpose does not account for the suspension of activity in war. Logically, time should only favor one side or the other. If it is an advantage to one, it must be a disadvantage to the other. Therefore, the side which time does not favor, usually the attacker, should always push aggressively to shorten the duration of the conflict; thus, pauses in activity should never occur.

Yet, when Clausewitz viewed war from a material sense, he saw that such pauses do occur, and rather frequently. The reason, he concluded, was twofold. First, the defense is inherently stronger than the attack, and at times the attacker does not have enough strength to overcome the defense. Thus, pauses in activity occur, and they continue until either (*a*) the attacker builds up enough strength to overcome the defense, or (*b*) the defender builds up enough strength to switch to the offensive and to counterattack.[35]

Second, in material war, neither side has perfect knowledge of the other.[36] Each estimates the strength of the other based on imperfect reports or intelligence. Imperfect knowledge can lead to an acceleration of activity as well as a suspension of it, Clausewitz admitted; however, he also pointed out that human nature tends to err on the side of caution, to exaggerate or worse-case the enemy's strength.[37] In general, then, uncertainty acts to decelerate activity in war, though it can also accelerate it. One way to look at his reasoning is to say that the friction of uncertainty prevented nuclear war from happening during the Cold War, despite an obvious arms race. In summation, if the attack was equal to or stronger than the defense and if both sides had perfect intelligence of the other, pauses in activity would never occur. The suspension of activity in war thus further substantiated Clausewitz's conviction that war followed the laws of probability rather than the laws of necessity.

## Subsumed under Politics

In terms of war's proper place among other known concepts, Clausewitz determined that war was a subconcept of politics—which he defined as 'the interaction (*Verkehr*) of governments and peoples'—or what today might be referred to as internal and external relations.[38] In sections 24 through 26 of the first chapter, he made it clear that war itself did not interrupt this interaction, but rather continued it, albeit with violent means.[39] As he insisted, 'War is a Mere Continuation of Political Intercourse by Other Means'; it was not just a 'political act', but a true 'political instrument'. It did not exist independently, but sprang from motives, or hostile intentions, which were essentially political in nature; those motives established the purpose or purposes of the conflict, which in turn flowed through each of the levels of war—from strategy to combat to military forces to the subsequent selection of defense or attack. The resultant clash of opposing forces at the lowest level of war was thus also a clash of opposing purposes at the highest. The fact that war was not an independent thing, but a subconcept of politics also helped explain why its nature was so variable: war took on different forms over time to serve the diverse political purposes that call it into being.

### THE CONSEQUENCES FOR THEORY

Clausewitz then summarized his analysis thus far, and set forth the implications for the formulation of a valid theory of war. His discussion to this point had centered on three principal tendencies or forces, all essentially extrinsic, which seemed to shape how wars unfolded: hostility, chance, and purpose. In the final section of *On War*'s first chapter, he pulled these forces together into a single, unifying concept, a synthetic metaphor of sorts, which he referred to as a 'wondrous trinity' (*wunderliche Dreifaltigkeit*):

War is thus not only a genuine chameleon, since it alters its nature somewhat in each particular case, it is also, in its overall manifestations, a wondrous trinity with regard to its predominant tendencies, which consist of the original violence of its nature, namely, hatred and hostility, which can be viewed as a *blind natural force*; of the play of probabilities and of chance, which make it into an *unpredictable activity*; and of the subordinating nature of a political instrument whenever it submits to *mere reason*.[40]

As he indicated in *On War*'s introductory paragraph, after examining the various parts of war he intended to discuss '*the whole* in terms of its internal relationships'.[41] This approach parallels the modern definition of a synthetic dialectic, which is an analysis of 'the ways in which a whole depends upon, because it interdepends with, its parts and how a new whole emerges from a synthesis of opposing parts'.[42] The key difference between the two, however, is that Clausewitz's synthesis does not produce a new whole, but rather shows how the separate parts interrelate in an original whole that he revealed to the reader only in stages.

Whether the trinity is a true synthesis or simply a conclusion, as some historians suggest, is thus debatable.[43] Either way, Clausewitz's choice of the word trinity (*Dreifahltigkeit*) seems quite deliberate, for it conveys the sense that the parts of war are distinct in their own right, yet at the same time each belongs to an indivisible whole. It obviously resembles the Christian trinity, which centers on the mystery of three-spirits-in-one, a metaphor Clausewitz's Protestant and Catholic contemporaries would have recognized instantly.

The wondrous trinity reflects the same objective–subjective construct Clausewitz used elsewhere in *On War*, which is one of the reasons many of his interpreters have misunderstood it.[44] As we have seen, by objective characteristics, Clausewitz meant universal elements, those common to all wars. Accordingly, in the objective sense, the trinity consists of the force of basic hostility, the play of chance and probability—which also includes the elements of danger, physical exertion, uncertainty, and friction in general— and the subordinating or guiding influence of purpose.[45] Let us examine each of these more closely.

## Purpose

The purpose we wish to achieve is the first consideration we must take into account when determining the military aim, the amount of violence, and the level of effort we should employ in any given war. Returning to Clausewitz's purpose-means hierarchy, the purpose of the war helps establish the tasks for strategy, for the engagements, for the military forces, and helps determine whether the war should be offensive or defensive in nature. It is also the standard by which we will measure the ultimate success or failure of the war, though the purpose of course may change, and likely will, as events unfold. If the engagements and campaigns have gone in our favor, our purpose might not change. If they have not, we might need to adjust it according to what is feasible under the resulting circumstances. Probability will again come into play, however, as our decisions will be based on likelihoods rather than certainties.

As the historian Hans Delbrück noted more than a century ago, Clausewitz's prefatory note of 1827 reveals that he came to regard war in a dualistic sense, that is, according to two different purposes: (*a*) where the goal is to defeat the enemy completely (conquest or regime change), or (*b*) where the intention is to arrive at a negotiated settlement.[46] Contrary to the claims of some of scholars, Clausewitz never abandoned this basic dualism.[47] At the end of Book VIII 'The Plan of War', for instance, he identified different planning considerations for wars where a negotiated settlement is sought (chapters 7 and 8) and wars in which the goal is the complete defeat of the enemy (chapter 9). Even in Book I, chapter 2 'Purpose and Means in War', he warned against mistaking a war of conquest for a war of limited aims, indicating the dualism persisted in his thinking. If the stakes are low and a commander is able to accomplish his aims through limited means, then he is justified in doing so; however, he would be well advised to keep in mind that he is following 'circuitous ways' and that if his enemy attacks him directly with a 'sharp blade', he needs more than a 'mock one' with which to defend himself.[48] In other words, we should not delude ourselves into believing that we face an enemy pursuing a limited purpose, when in fact he is after much more. While he acknowledged that each type of war might have endless variations and gradations, he nonetheless continued to see war itself in terms of two fundamentally different types, or natures. It is also clear that he continued to see all-out war as superior to its more restricted counterpart.

## Chance

'There is no human activity', Clausewitz urged, 'that is so constantly and so universally affected by chance as war'.[49] The absolute, the so-called mathematical, are never part of the reckoning that takes place in the art of war. Instead, from the outset war involves the play of possibilities, probabilities, and good and bad fortune. Laplace referred to probability in this way:

Probability is relative in part to our ignorance, in part to our knowledge. We know that of three or a greater number of events a single one ought to occur; but nothing induces us to believe that one of them will occur rather than the others. In this state of indecision it is impossible for us announce their occurrence with certainty.[50]

This definition, which became widespread in the early nineteenth century, helps bring into clearer focus Clausewitz's sense of the term probability. Laplace defined chance as the number of favorable cases divided by the number of possible ones.[51] This sense accords well with Clausewitz's belief that chance made war much like a game of cards (*Kartenspiel*).[52] Drawing a favorable card is a matter of chance, that is, the number of desired outcomes divided by the number of possible outcomes. How one plays the hand one is dealt is another matter. We can extend Clausewitz's metaphor to a game of poker, and thus include elements like trying to calculate whether our hand is better than our opponent's, reading his style, his body language, betting small or risking all, bluffing, deterring, concealing, and attempting to deceive. As history shows, these activities correspond to the ways statesmen and senior military leaders often behave toward their adversaries. This is also the realm in which one's creative spirit, or genius, is free to roam, that is, able to make the most of its opportunities.

Estimating an opponent's purpose is, therefore, a task for judgment. It is a matter of probability deduced from what an opponent is likely to do given his character, his available means, and his foreign and domestic political situations. Chance, or probability, not only has an effect on war at the highest levels, it also influences the activities of units and individual soldiers. A column might take the wrong road, and thus arrive too late to influence the outcome of a battle. The loss of a talented commander at a critical point in an engagement might cause a unit to break and run, just when it was on the verge of defeating its opponents.

## Hostility

Clausewitz maintained that war involves hostile feelings, such as hatred or enmity, as well as hostile intentions, such as the desire to reduce another's power or influence; hostile intentions can exist without hostile feelings, but the former can ignite the latter. He thus identified two basic types of hostility: hostile feelings or animosity; and hostile intentions. The former need not exist, and often do not, or are not very strong, for war to occur; the populations of two warring states need not have any basic animosity toward one another for the states to be at war.

On the other hand, hostile intentions—one state advancing its interests at the expense of another's—are almost always present. Anything one state does, however minor, that limits the power of another can be considered a hostile act. States can, of course, mobilize the hostile feelings of their citizens, as part of making war. Also, hostile feelings can be aroused by war, whether political leaders wish them to be. They can exist before the war, and persist long after it. Or, they can come into being because of the war, only to fade away when it ends.

Clausewitz thus counted hostility as one of war's fundamental forces, though it could exist independent of war, or could seem virtually absent. The level of hostility could fluctuate in intensity from one conflict to the next, or even multiple times within the same war. Conceivably, a change in the degree of hostility could be severe enough to make it tantamount to a change in kind. As mentioned previously, Clausewitz considered the wars of Napoleon—in which hostility reached new levels—substantially different from those of Frederick, where it was not as significant a factor.[53]

In summation, Clausewitz believed all wars have these basic forces or tendencies in common regardless of when or where they are fought, though naturally the intensity and significance of these forces fluctuates or varies from one war to another, and often many times in the same war. By war's subjective characteristics, on the other hand, he meant those institutions or representative bodies which, unlike war's objective elements, may be valid only for a particular time and place.[54] In the subjective sense, therefore, each tendency of the trinity corresponds to a separate institution, though not only to that institution. The populace (*das Volk*), for instance, which includes the populations of any society or culture, corresponds to basic hostility. Similarly, the military commander and his army (*der Feldherr und sein Heer*), which represents the warring bodies of any period, relates to chance and probability. Finally, the term government (*die Regierung*) includes not just heads of state, but any ruling body, any 'agglomeration of loosely associated forces', or any 'personified intelligence', that endeavors to use war to accomplish some purpose.[55]

Clausewitz uncovered the importance of these three institutions during his brief historical survey of warfare in Book VIII, a survey that parallels, perhaps not surprisingly, those found in Lloyd's and Bülow's works.[56] Of course, as Clausewitz indicated, making distinctions between government, military, and people can be somewhat artificial: governments can display hostility as much as peoples or militaries; chance can influence the development of policy as much as it can the course of military events; purpose can affect the level of hostility as much as it can the actions of the military. Thus, the relationship between the forces and the institutions is not exclusive.

The trinity conveys the sense that none of the tendencies of the nature of war is a priori more influential in determining the shape and course of actual conflict than any other. Thus, to single out policy or politics as *the* central element of war's nature is to distort the intrinsic balance implied by the mere concept of the trinity itself, and ultimately to compromise its dynamism. Put differently, while *Politik* exerts a subordinating influence over war for the purpose of realizing its goals, its influence runs up against, and is in turn reduced or elevated by, the play of chance and the force of basic hostility.

These latter forces affect the kinds of ends that war can achieve as well as the extent to which it can attain them. Consequently, policy's influence over war is never absolute; not only should it not act as a 'despotic lawgiver', it is actually impossible for it to do so, unless chance and hostility are somehow removed.[57]

As we shall see, Clausewitz also stressed that the influence of policy is limited, too, by the conditions and processes from which it emerged, in a word, by politics. The trinity thus reinforces the point that war is not an 'independent thing', and can be regarded as a whole only when it is considered within its social and political contexts.[58]

## CONCLUSIONS AND IMPLICATIONS

Although history shows wars vary widely in form, it also reveals that they have certain objective characteristics in common, namely, hostility, chance, and purpose, all of which contribute to a universe of war characterized by violence, danger, friction, uncertainty, and physical exertion. These characteristics vary constantly in relative importance and levels of intensity, and we find them present in the conflicts of antiquity as well as contemporary wars, to include the global war on terror. The purposes in conflict in the war on terror are, for instance, not unlike those of the Thirty Years War in which religious and secular aims were inextricably intertwined; they were as numerous as the many belligerents involved. While many identify with the jihadist vision of al-Qaeda, or at least are inspired by it, others pursue seemingly secular purposes, such as political self-determination.

For its part, al-Qaeda's leadership has portrayed the group as a vanguard of sorts in a worldwide jihadist movement, a global *intifahda*, reflective of a general Islamist awakening. The group's explicit purpose is to 'move, incite, and mobilize the [Islamic] nation' to rise up and end Western interference in Islamic affairs and to recast Islamic society according to Salafist interpretations of Islamic law.[59]

The stated purposes of the United States and its coalition partners, in contrast, are to reduce terrorism in general to an 'unorganized, localized, nonsponsored' phenomenon, and to persuade all responsible nations and international bodies to adopt a policy of 'zero tolerance' for terrorism, and to agree to delegitimize it, much like 'piracy, slave trading, and genocide' have been in the past.[60]

The purposes for each side cannot be achieved by violence alone, and in fact require much more in the way of political, social, and economic resources, but that would hardly disqualify it from being a war. Cultural norms and expectations surely influence how each side chooses to wage the conflict, and how it prefers to define the ends it seeks.[61] However, that important fact provides little basis for maintaining, as some scholars have done, that culture now supplants policy or politics, and that this somehow negates Clausewitz's theory. In short, both the United States and al-Qaeda are clearly using, or attempting to use, armed force to achieve ends that are as political as they are religious or secular in nature.

Hostility clearly runs high in this war, which is actually a war within wars. This hostility, the result of years of real and perceived injustices and repression, informs the policy choices, strategies, and tactics of all parties involved. As a consequence, the populace is both a weapon and a target, physically and psychologically, in this form of war. Al-Qaeda and those terrorist groups with regional rather than global visions, such as Hamas and Hizballah, have turned their constituencies into effective weapons by creating strong social, political, and religious ties with them. These groups have become an integral part of the social and political fabric of Muslim societies by addressing everyday problems: establishing day cares, kindergartens, schools, medical clinics, youth and women's centers, sports clubs, social welfare, programs for free meals and health care; in contrast, most government bodies in the Middle East, generally perceived as corrupt and ineffective by Muslim communities, have failed to provide such basics.[62] Hamas and Hizballah have also achieved substantial political representation in their respective state governments.

Put differently, many of these extremist groups, whether their purpose is local or global, have become communal and political activists for their constituencies. Those constituencies have, in turn, become an important weapon in the arsenal of such groups by providing the means to facilitate the construction and maintenance of considerable financial and logistical networks and safe houses, all of which aid in the regeneration of the groups, as well as providing other support.[63] The role of communal activist does not, of course, preclude using tactics of disinformation, fear, and intimidation to keep one's constituencies loyal; hence, not only is an adversary's populace a target, so is one's own, especially for purposes of recruiting and other kinds of assistance.

Paradoxically, the increase in information and the spread of information technology brought about by globalization have amplified rather than reduced chance and uncertainty. Recent polls indicate that few people are certain about which side is winning the war on terror, or how to wage it.[64] The vast array of information technology with which US and coalition forces are now equipped has done little to help locate improvised explosive devices before they kill, to locate and avoid ambushes, and—perhaps most important of all—to distinguish noncombatant friend from irregular foe. To be sure, the key to accomplishing one's objectives in counterinsurgency operations, as in any kind of military operation, is timely and reliable intelligence. However, the entire process of intelligence gathering and assessment is clearly more art than science.[65]

Moreover, experts do not agree on the root causes of extremism, or that any necessarily exist. Nor, therefore, do they agree on the nature of, or even the need for, enduring solutions to the problem. Poverty, demographic trends, globalization, religious extremism, failed or failing states, repressive regimes, unresolved conflicts, US and Western foreign policies, lack of education, and alienation and rage have all been offered, individually or in combination, as principal causes of terrorism.[66] All are eminently plausible, and an examination of local conditions might lead to identifying which particular combination of causes may be responsible for the rise of a specific terrorist group; yet consensus has not materialized. Instead, the theories of experts remain at odds, perhaps not so much in the broad strokes, but in the details, where it matters.[67] In short, the greater access to information and the larger number of expert opinions available to the public have amplified rather than reduced uncertainty, which in turn hampers development of a comprehensive, integrated strategy capable of going beyond military action.

Terrorism, guerrilla wars, and conventional wars—which are arguably false categories in any case—all share the same objective nature, though the level of violence might be lower in the first two than in the last.[68] Each act of violence in a terrorist or guerrilla war, however infrequent, could have great political significance, which only shows how a little violence can go a long way. The subjective natures of each kind of war differ in obvious respects, particularly as regards the tactics and types of forces employed. Of course, two wars of the same kind can in fact differ markedly from another in both objective and subjective natures, depending on the belligerents involved, the objectives at stake, and the weapons at hand. Hence, Clausewitz saw the nature of war, not just its character—its subjective characteristics—as dynamic.

Furthermore, the subjective means employed in the waging of war directly affect the war's objective characteristics, causing them to increase or diminish in both intensity and significance. The employment of nonlethal weapons or precision munitions or strict rules of engagement or other methods can reduce the amount of violence. Likewise, the use of advanced information technologies can decrease some forms of uncertainty. However, such objective characteristics can never be eliminated entirely, because they are as commonplace—and as omnipresent—as reality itself. To remove them completely would be tantamount to taking reality out of real war. The military historian van Creveld misses the point when he refers to these characteristics as unremarkable, for Clausewitz's aim was to produce a theory that reflected reality, and corrected the false theories of his day.[69]

Variations in war's objective characteristics can also cause direct changes in its subjective qualities. A modification in a war's political purpose, for instance, can make belligerents use, or refrain from using, certain types of weapons or methods. In the Cold War, both sides determined that the violence of a nuclear exchange was to be avoided, as the vast destruction likely to be wrought by such an escalation would be self-defeating. Thus, each side worked toward limiting the objective element of violence, which in turn gave the Cold War a unique subjective nature, since the emphasis shifted away from conventional conflict toward the use of proxy insurgencies and counterinsurgencies.

The shift in purpose is not always multilateral, however. The subjective nature of the war in Iraq shifted from a conventional conflict to that of a complex civil war, or insurgency.[70] In the larger global war on terror, al-Qaeda and its ilk seek to intensify the element of violence by acquiring weapons of mass destruction (and by other means), while the United States and its allies and strategic partners endeavor to prevent that escalation from happening. In other words, the objective and subjective natures of war are not separate phenomena but rather aspects of the same phenomenon.

Appreciating when a conflict's subjective nature has changed, or anticipating how it might change, is critical to accomplishing one's aims, or recognizing that they must change. Hence, we must refrain from using knowledge of war's nature as a template to dictate courses of action. In other words, coming to grips with the nature of *the* war at hand helps generate questions that can lead to a better grasp of the potential power and apparent limitations of a particular form of war.

The dynamic relationship that exists between war's objective and subjective natures underscores the need to understand not only the nature of war in general, but also the nature of the particular war at hand. While it is important to understand the nature of one's tool or weapon, a sword perhaps, it is also valuable to know whether it is a broadsword or a rapier. Depending on the situation, one could be more useful or more risky than the other. What is more, since war, as Clausewitz said, only exists where there is resistance, we would do well to know what type of weapon our foe will use, and whether we are sparing for ceremony's sake, or are going for the kill.

In a perfect world, understanding the nature of war would preclude attempts to use armed conflict to achieve something it cannot. It would alert us to the fallacy of developing rigid, one-sided theories or formulae that purport to guarantee victory. The nature of war, as Clausewitz presented it, and which history validates, is too dynamic for that. The interdependent relationship between the subjective and objective natures of war enables us to choose weapons and ways of fighting that might reduce violence, friction, and physical exertion.

However, because our actions take place in the physical world and not in a vacuum and because our opponent can take preemptive action or introduce effective countermeasures, the results of such measures can never be certain. An element of risk is, therefore, unavoidable. Knowledge of the nature of war is, thus, important because it informs the choices that political leaders make when deciding to resort to war to achieve certain aims, or when making decisions about force structure; it also informs the choices that commanders make when equipping and training their troops for war.

In sum, the Clausewitzian nature of war rests on the fundamental cause–effect relationships involving the forces of purpose, chance, and hostility. These forces both influence and are influenced by one another, reflecting the dynamism of actual war in a universal and a particular sense. The remaining chapters of this section will describe the other major elements that make up the Clausewitzian universe of war.

## NOTES

1. Compare: Colin S. Gray, 'How Has War Changed since the End of the Cold War?', *Parameters*, 35/1 (spring 2005), 14–27; and R. D. Hooker, Jr, 'Beyond *Vom Kriege*: The Character and Conduct of Modern War', *Parameters*, 35/2 (summer 2005), 4–17; the former is a scholar, the latter a practitioner, but both argue Clausewitz's views are correct.
2. For an introduction to these debates, see Jan Angstrom, 'Introduction: Debating the Nature of Modern War', in *Nature of Modern War*, 1–20, who identifies three major debates: (*a*) whether nonstate warfare is essentially new, (*b*) whether the revolution in military affairs (RMA) will change the nature of war, and (*c*) whether war is becoming more 'virtual' or 'postmodern'.
3. This makes the nature of war different from its essence or spirit, a term Heuser, *Reading Clausewitz*, 189, sought to substitute for nature; it would be more correct to say the essence of war is violence. Clausewitz's reference to war's trinity as three 'lawgivers' reveals he was after the fundamental laws that influence war. *Vom Kriege*, I/1, 213; *On War*, 89.
4. *Vom Kriege*, VIII/3B, 973; *On War*, 593.
5. Only the first half of the note is presented here; Carl von Clausewitz, in W. M. Schering (ed.), *Geist und Tat: Das Vermächtnis des Soldaten und Denkers*

(Stuttgart, Germany: Kröner, 1941), 309–11, reproduces it in its entirety; for a slightly different translation see Aron, *Clausewitz*, 59.
6. *Vom Kriege*, I/1, 191, emphasis original; *On War*, 75.
7. Alan D. Beyerchen, 'Clausewitz, Nonlinearity, and the Importance of Imagery', in David Alberts and Thomas Czerwinski (eds.), *Complexity, Global Politics, and National Security* (Washington, DC: National Defense University, 1997), 153–70, explains the importance of Clausewitz's use of metaphor.
8. *Vom Kriege*, VI/7, 644; *On War*, 377.
9. *Vom Kriege*, IV/9, 453; *On War*, 248.
10. For a similar interpretation, see John E. Tashjean, 'Pious Arms: Clausewitz and the Right of War', *Military Affairs*, 44/2 (April 1980), 82–3, which argues Clausewitz was challenging the legalistic or moral definitions of his day. One the other hand, one could also apply the term duel to the struggle between heads of state in time of war, John Lukacs, *The Duel: The Struggle between Churchill and Hitler, 10 May–31 July 1940* (New York: Ticknor & Fields, 1991).
11. Prussia's Law Code of 1794 made dueling illegal, and imposed strict penalties for those who practiced it: three to six years detention for a challenge, ten years to life as well as loss of noble title and honorable position for actually dueling, and capital punishment for killing someone in a duel. Enforcement of the law was not consistent, however, and the penalties were relaxed significantly after 1880. Kevin McAleer, *Dueling: The Cult of Honor in Fin-de-Siècle Germany* (Princeton, NJ: Princeton University Press, 1994), 21–2.
12. McAleer, *Dueling*, 21–2.
13. *Vom Kriege*, IV/8, 449; *On War*, 245.
14. *Vom Kriege*, I/1, 191, emphasis original; *On War*, 75. Compare the 1873 Graham translation: 'War therefore is an act of violence intended to compel our opponent to fulfill our will'. Carl von Clausewitz, *On War*, 3 vols., trans. J. J. Graham (London: Kegan Paul, Trench, Trübner, 1908), vol. I, 2.
15. This was an explicit rejection of Bülow's claim that the 'modern system' would resolve war with less bloodshed, as well as other views, such as those of the philosopher Immanuel Kant, which held out hope that enlightenment could achieve some sort of 'Perpetual Peace'. Bülow, *Modern System of War*, 222–43. Azar Gat, 'Clausewitz's Political and Ethical World View', *Political Studies*, 37 (1989), 97–106, shows the similarity of Clausewitz's outlook with those of his contemporaries. On the implications of Clausewitz's apparent denigration of the importance of the law of war, see Martin van Creveld, 'The Clausewitzian Universe and the Law of War', *Journal of Contemporary History*, 26 (1991), 403–29.
16. *Vom Kriege*, I/1, 192, emphasis added; *On War*, 75. The phrase *wehrlos machen* has been translated as 'to disarm' or 'to render powerless'. Yet its literal meaning is to render defenseless, which falls between these two. A combatant stripped of weapons, or 'disarmed', can still cause harm, or resist our will. A 'powerless' enemy, in contrast, has no *power* or ability to fulfill our will. The sense that

*wehrlos* conveys, therefore, is that of an opponent unable to defend himself, but not necessarily incapable of carrying out our will.
17. *Vom Kriege*, I/1, 192–4; *On War*, 75–6.
18. *Vom Kriege*, I/1, 194–5; *On War*, 77.
19. *Vom Kriege*, I/1, 195; *On War*, 77.
20. *Vom Kriege*, I/1, 199–200; *On War*, 80.
21. *Vom Kriege*, I/2, 222; *On War*, 94.
22. *Vom Kriege*, I/1, 195–9; *On War*, 78–80: '6. Modifications in Reality', '7. War Is Never an Isolated Act', and '8. War Does Not Consist of a Single Blow without Duration'.
23. Donald Gillies, *Philosophical Theories of Probability* (London: Routledge, 2000), 14–24, discusses the basics of classical probability theory; Colin Howson, 'Personalistic Bayesianism', in J. P. Dubucs (ed.), *Philosophy of Probability* (Boston, MA: Kluwer, 1993), 1–12, does the same; Lorraine Daston, *Classical Probability in the Enlightenment* (Princeton, NJ: Princeton University Press, 1988), 192 ff., argues that probability theorists through the nineteenth century did not distinguish between objective (in nature) probability and those based on philosophical or logical uncertainties; Hacking, *Emergence of Probability*, agrees.
24. Pierre Simon de Laplace (1749–1827) was perhaps the first to put the objectivist or classical view into the vernacular; previously, it had been largely in Latin and inaccessible. His *A Philosophical Essay on Probabilities*, which was based a series of lectures dating to 1795, was first published in 1814, and went through several editions, many of which would have been available to Clausewitz along with works by other objectivists. Marquis de Laplace, *A Philosophical Essay on Probabilities*, trans. Frederick Truscott and Frederick Emory (New York: Dover, 1995).
25. *Vom Kriege*, I/1, 207–8, I/2, 216–18; *On War*, 85–6, 91–2.
26. Game or decision theory became something of a rage in the 1960s. Mary Ann Dimand and Robert W. Dimand, *A History of Game Theory*, vol. 1 (New York: Routledge, 1996), show that attempts to apply some form of game theory to decision-making trace back to the nineteenth century; *The Foundations of Game Theory*, 3 vols. (Lyme, NH: Edward Elgar, 1997), xv, is a collection of 'primary sources' to 1960 concerning game theory, the 'analysis of conflict and cooperation as games of strategy'.
27. This was another direct refutation of Bülow who claimed that the science of war was gradually making the qualities of courage and skilled judgment, or genius, obsolete; Bülow, *Modern System of War*, 187–92.
28. P. M. Baldwin, 'Clausewitz in Nazi Germany', *Journal of Contemporary History*, 16 (1981), 5–26, here 8, makes this error; for another example, see Henk W. Houweling and Jan G. Siccama, 'The Risk of Compulsory Escalation', *Journal of Peace Research*, 25/1 (1988), 43–56, esp. 44–5.
29. '1. Ältere Fassung, Entwürfe', in *Schriften–Aufsätze–Studien–Briefe*, Part I, vol. 2, 632.

30. *Vom Kriege*, VIII/3B, 973–4; *On War*, 592–3.
31. *Vom Kriege*, I/1, 196; *On War*, 78.
32. *Vom Kriege*, I/1, 196–200; *On War*, 78–80.
33. Honig, 'Clausewitz's *On War*'.
34. *Vom Kriege*, I/1, 200–1; *On War*, 80–1.
35. *Vom Kriege*, I/1, section 17, pp. 205–6; *On War*, 84.
36. *Vom Kriege*, I/1, section 18, p. 206; *On War*, 84–5.
37. Cimbala, *Clausewitz and Escalation*, 180–1, argues wrongly that Clausewitz saw friction only as a decelerating influence.
38. *Vom Kriege*, VIII/6B, 990; *On War*, 605.
39. *Vom Kriege*, I/1, 210–12; *On War*, 87–8.
40. *Vom Kriege*, I/1, 213, emphasis original; *On War*, 89. Howard and Paret translate *wunderliche* as 'remarkable' in the first edition of *On War* (1976) and as 'paradoxical' in the second (1989). The literal sense is retained here.
41. *Vom Kriege*, I/1, 191, emphasis original; *On War*, 75.
42. Archie J. Bahm, *Polarity, Dialectic and Organicity* (Albuquerque, New Mexico: World Books, 1988), 228.
43. Michael Howard, *Clausewitz* (New York: Oxford University Press, 1983), 73, considers it the latter.
44. An example of the trinity misconstrued is van Creveld, *Transformation* of War, 35–40, 125–6; the error is corrected in Christopher Bassford and Edward J. Villacres, 'Reclaiming the Clausewitzian Trinity', http://www.clausewitz.com/CWZHOME/Keegan/KEEGWHOL.htm.
45. These factors appear in *Vom Kriege*, Book I, chapter 3, and are addressed in more detail in chapters 4–7.
46. Hans Delbrück, 'Carl von Clausewitz', *Historische und Politische Aufsätze* (Berlin: Walther & Apolant, 1887); see also E. Kessel, 'Zur Genesis der modernen Kriegslehren', *Wehrwissenschaftliche Rundschau*, 3/9 (July 1953), 405–23.
47. Heuser, *Reading Clausewitz*, 34, points out that Clausewitz almost falls into the 'trap' of seeing war in terms of this simple dichotomy, but in the end he develops a more nuanced view of war. In fact, the first two chapters of *On War* reveal that Clausewitz saw those gradations *within*, not in lieu of, his framework of two different types of war.
48. *Vom Kriege*, I/2, 230; *On War*, 99.
49. *Vom Kriege*, I/1, 207; *On War*, 85.
50. Laplace, *Essay on Probabilities*, 6.
51. Laplace, *Essay on Probabilities*, 7.
52. *Vom Kriege*, I/1, 208; *On War*, 86.
53. *Vom Kriege*, VIII/3B, 970–4; *On War*, 592–3.
54. *Vom Kriege*, I/1, 212–13; *On War*, 85–6.
55. *Vom Kriege*, VIII/3B, 962, 964–5; *On War*, 588.
56. *Vom Kriege*, VIII/3B, 962–73; *On War*, 586–93.
57. *Vom Kriege*, I/1, 210; *On War*, 87.

58. *Vom Kriege*, I/1, 212; *On War*, 89.
59. 'Usama Bin Laden's Message to Iraq', *Al-Jazirah Television*, February 11, 2003; 'Bin Laden Interviewed on Jihad against U.S.', *Al Quds Al Arabi* (London), November 27, 1996; cited from 'Al Qaeda: Statements and Evolving Ideology', Congressional Research Service, June 20, 2005, 13. Kenneth Katzman, 'Al Qaeda: Profile and Threat Assessment', Congressional Research Service, February 10, 2005. See also Fawaz A. Gerges, *The Far Enemy: Why Jihad Went Global* (Cambridge: Cambridge University Press, 2005), who writes that al-Qaeda had been marginalized within the larger jihadi movement before 9/11, and launched its attacks in a bid to put itself at the forefront of the movement; Marc Sageman, *Understanding Terror Networks* (PA: University of Pennsylvania Press, 2004), underscores the role of small group dynamics in terrorist acts; Rohan Gunaratna, *Inside Al Qaeda* (Cambridge: Cambridge University Press, 2002), analyzes networks and social and economic support systems.
60. US Government, *National Strategy for Combating Terrorism*, Washington, DC: February, 2003, 13, 22–3; this goal includes diminishing conditions terrorists typically exploit, such as poverty, social, and political disenfranchisement, and long-standing political, religious, and ethnic grievances; reducing these conditions requires, among other things, fostering political, social, and economic development, good governance, the rule of law, and consistent participation in the 'war of ideas'. The Honorable Paul Wolfowitz, 'The Greatest Deeds Are Yet to Be Done', *Naval War College Review*, 47/1 (winter 2004), 13–19, esp. 15. John Gearson, 'The Nature of Modern Terrorism', in Lawrence Freedman (ed.), *Superterrorism: Policy Responses* (Oxford: Blackwell, 2002), 7–24, points out the risks of waging war on a tactic.
61. Jeremy Black, *War and the New Disorder in the 21st Century* (New York: Continuum Press, 2004), underscores the importance culture plays in defining war and success in war.
62. Shaul Mishal and Avraham Sela, *The Palestinian Hamas: Vision, Violence, and Coexistence* (New York: Columbia University Press, 2000), 18–26; Sami G. Hajjar, *Hizballah: Terrorism, National Liberation or Menace?* (Carlisle, PA: Strategic Studies Institute, August 2002); Gunaratna, *Inside Al Qaeda*, 55, 227, 230.
63. Ed Blanche, 'Al-Qaeda Recruitment', *Janes Intelligence Review*, 14 (January 2002), 27–8; Paul J. Smith, 'Transnational Terrorism and the al Qaeda Model: Confronting New Realities', *Parameters*, 32/2 (summer 2002), 33–46.
64. E&P Staff, 'Gallup: Only 1 in 3 Think US is Winning War on Terror', *Editor & Publisher*, July 5, 2005.
65. Scott Shane, 'Eavesdropping Isn't Easy, The Master at It Says', *New York Times*, August 17, 2005.
66. Margaret Purdy, 'Countering Terrorism: The Missing Pillar', *International Journal* (winter 2004–2005), 3–24; Karin von Hippel, 'The Roots of Terrorism: Probing the Myths', in *Superterrorism*, 25–39.

67. Compare: Anonymous [Michael Scheuer], *Imperial Hubris: Why the West Is Losing the War on Terror* (Washington, DC: Brassey's, 2004); Jessica Stern, *Terror in the Name of God: Why Religious Militants Kill* (New York: HarperCollins, 2003); Bernard Lewis, *Crisis of Islam: Holy War and Unholy Terror* (New York: Modern Library, 2003); Bruce Hoffman, *Al Qaeda, Trends in Terrorism, and Future Potentialities: An Assessment* (Santa Monica, CA: RAND, 2003); Gunaratna, *Inside Al Qaeda*.
68. M. L. R. Smith, 'Guerillas in the Mist: Reassessing Strategy and Low Intensity Warfare', *Review of International Studies*, 29/1 (2003), 19–37, demonstrates the problems with such categories, and serves as a corrective to Walter Laqueur, *Guerrilla Warfare: A Historical & Critical Study* (New Brunswick, NJ: Transaction, 1998), 110–12, which overlooks Clausewitz's larger framework.
69. Creveld, '*Transformation of War* Revisited', 3–5.
70. Andrew Krepinevich, 'How to Win in Iraq', *Foreign Affairs*, 84/5 (September–October 2005), 87–104; and 'The War in Iraq: The Nature of Insurgency Warfare' (Center for Strategic and Budgetary Analysis, June 2, 2004), which present one view on the difference between the nature of a conventional conflict and that of an insurgency, and how to address the latter. Krepinevich's model has, however, come under criticism for relying too heavily on the example of Vietnam. See Stephen Biddle, 'Seeing Baghdad, Thinking Saigon', *Foreign Affairs*, 85/2 (March–April 2006), 2–14.

# 4

# Policy, Politics, and Political Determinism

This chapter explores the relationships between war and policy, war and politics, and policy and politics as they appear in *On War*. As Clausewitz examined the relationship between war and policy in Book VIII, his thinking tended at times toward political determinism. In other words, he saw the social, cultural, economic, legal, and ethical circumstances as caused by policy. Consequently, he did not distinguish between political purposes and other kinds in his analyses, but rather rolled the latter into the former. His reasoning was simply that social, cultural, and other conditions could not be other than they were unless policy, the collective interests of the state, shaped them or allowed them to be shaped that way.

To be sure, policy itself is the product of the give-and-take that occurs between internal and external factors. However, for Clausewitz this was essentially political activity, or politics, as usual. By the term state we should understand that he meant any politically sovereign body, to include individual Tartar tribes, a definition that would also encompass our contemporary notion of nonstates. He did, however, consider the modern state the superior form of political expression. We should keep in mind, therefore, that he defined policy and politics rather broadly, perhaps too much so.[1]

As Chapter 3 revealed, Clausewitz's observation that war was the 'mere continuation of political activity (*Politik*) by other means' placed war firmly within the larger concept of politics, or inter- and intrastate relations. It meant that war had 'its own grammar, but not its own logic'; it was 'only a part of political activity' and 'in no sense an independent thing in itself'.[2] Scholars have given considerable privilege to this expression, referring to it as the Prussian's 'great dictum', and as Clausewitz's unique contribution to military thinking.[3] It is probably the passage most often quoted of Clausewitz's work, and many strategists in fact interpret it and similar expressions in *On War* to mean that the primacy of policy is the book's core message.[4]

We find similar interpretations in evidence in much of the military literature written after the Vietnam conflict and during the Clausewitzian renaissance, to include the memoirs of prominent American commanders.[5] One particular manifestation of this understanding of Clausewitz is the well-known Weinberger/Powell doctrine, which explicitly cites him. Briefly stated, the doctrine said that the United States should only use combat troops to protect vital national interests, and those actions must have clear political objectives and popular support; in effect, it tacitly acknowledged the primacy of policy even as it established restrictive guidelines, which were also political in nature, for the use of force.[6]

However, as we shall see, these interpretations, influenced perhaps too much by the shadow of the Cold War and the values of liberal democracy, obscure the nature of Clausewitz's observation that war is part and parcel of political activity on at least three counts. First, they transform what Clausewitz saw as a statement of fact, a description of a historically verifiable relationship, into a normative doctrine as to the way that relationship ought to function. Second, they confuse policy with politics. Today, we tend to see the former as the decision to protect or promote our interests and usually to do so in certain ways; we see the latter as the relations and conventions that develop among states (and nonstates) as they pursue their interests. Policy is often at odds with politics, as Clausewitz pointed out, and policy's failure to appreciate the power of political circumstances when waging war has often led to failure. Finally, the above views overlook the political determinism that crept into Clausewitz's thinking as he worked out the relationship between war and policy in Book VIII, and its significance for his overall theory of war.

## THE PRIMACY OF POLICY

Readers will find a number of statements in *On War* which lend credence to the belief that the primacy of policy became the core of Clausewitz's thinking. 'Policy', as he warned, is 'the intelligence and war merely the instrument, and not the reverse'.[7] Military conflict, Clausewitz maintained, 'does not suspend the intercourse of governments and peoples or subject them to its own laws', but instead 'political intercourse, in its essence, continues to exist, whatever the means it chooses to use'.[8] The 'political element does not force itself deep into the details of war', but it does influence the 'plan of the war as a whole, and that of the campaign, and often even that of the battle'.[9] Accordingly, since 'the conduct of war in its major aspects is thus policy itself, which takes up the sword in place of the pen', the subordination of the 'military point of view to the political one' is the only relationship that makes sense.[10]

Aside from a few exceptions, such statements seem to have made little impression on theorists and practitioners through the first half of the twentieth century. However, that changed after the experience of two devastating world wars, and threat of runaway escalation during the Cold War. Clausewitz's ideas concerning primacy of politics, and the *rational* and *measured* use of force they apparently implied, seemed worthy of renewed emphasis. For instance, Robert Osgood, perhaps the leading American theorist of limited war between the 1950s and the 1970s, made extensive use of certain parts of *On War* to build a case for the primacy of politics as a basis for his theory of applying force incrementally; he defined the primacy of politics in this way:

> The primacy of politics in war means, simply, that military operations should be conducted so as to achieve concrete, limited, and attainable security objectives, in order that war's destruction and violence may be rationally directed toward legitimate ends of national policy.[11]

The 'purpose of war', Osgood went on to say, was 'to employ force skillfully in order to exert the desired effect on the adversary's will along a continuous spectrum from diplomacy, to crises short of war, to an overt clash of arms'.[12] This principle, he explained, 'promised to make American power more effective, yet safer', and to assuage the fears of those who believed that a 'local crisis or war might expand into a nuclear holocaust'.[13] Other American political theorists of the Cold War era, such as Thomas Schelling, adopted the idea of the primacy of politics without necessarily referring to Clausewitz.[14] As Brodie later explained, the idea that policy was supreme was itself likely to be misunderstood, if not rejected outright:

> It suffers this fate for a number of reasons, one being that war does arouse passions, usually very strong ones, and another being that generals like to win decisively whatever contests they are engaged in, and do not like to be trammeled by a political authority imposing considerations that might modify that aim.[15]

Brodie and other scholars of his generation, in short, overemphasized the significance of the primacy of policy in the Prussian's theories, though they did so with good intentions. For instance, in considering such expressions as, 'policy will permeate all military operations and, in so far as their violent nature will admit, it will have a continuous influence on them', these scholars stressed the first part of the statement, namely, that policy will pervade military operations, while downplaying the important qualification—'in so far as their violent nature will admit'.[16]

Good intentions notwithstanding, representing Clausewitz in this way is ultimately as misleading as depicting him as the 'Madhi of Mass' or the 'apostle of total war', as Liddell Hart and others did decades earlier.[17] Both interpretations, in effect, destroy the balanced theory, and body of knowledge, Clausewitz sought to construct. As we saw in the previous chapter, his theory settled on a tripartite explication of war.[18] At first blush, the distortion produced by Brodie and others seems merely to correct the erroneous view that Clausewitz was an advocate of absolute war. Yet a closer examination reveals that this correction, in effect, goes too far; it willfully overlooks the basic premise of Clausewitz's argument, as well as the limits he placed on policy.[19] This overcorrection was shaped in no small way by the presentist concerns of historians and political and social scientists writing after the ruinous world wars of the twentieth century, and under the threatening shadow of the Cold War.

Within the strategic environment that followed World War II, apprehensions regarding the threat of a devastating nuclear exchange or of a major military escalation in a conventional sense between two powerful alliances—perhaps the most powerful the world had seen to that point—induced scholars to stress the role of policy in limiting war. From that motive it was but a small step to Osgood's concept of limited war, that is, the idea of restricting the use of force 'to a scale that is no greater than necessary to achieve the objectives at stake'.[20]

Clausewitz's many statements regarding the relationship between war and policy provided welcome support for this view. Here was an accomplished soldier and an important, if somewhat obscure and complex, military writer who came from as militaristic a tradition as one is likely to find. Yet, his life's work could nonetheless serve as a counterweight to such dangerous claims as General Douglas MacArthur's oft repeated assertion that in war there is 'no substitute for victory'.[21] For many scholars, such claims not only seemed to pervade the military mind, if left unchecked under the strategic circumstances of the Cold War, they could well lead to catastrophic, even suicidal, escalation.[22] It must be said, however, that the military mind was also all too aware of the difficulties of adapting the theory of limited war to practice, particularly the assumption that the level of violence can be adjusted with the precision of a rheostat to achieve a desired effect.[23]

Of course, the military mind was not the only enemy. Distressingly optimistic theories were advanced by some accomplished Cold War thinkers, such as the physicist Herman Kahn, who reportedly could boast of the highest IQ in American history; Kahn believed that the United States could actually win a nuclear war against the Soviet Union.[24] It was not altogether clear, however, what rational end might be served by such an exchange, which was likely to destroy most, if not all, of that which was to be defended or acquired. References to the primacy of policy helped underscore the point that armed conflict of any type should serve a higher purpose, and the benefits should outweigh the costs. There were, thus, several urgent reasons for representing Clausewitz's theories in a particular way.

The liberal-democratic values of Clausewitz's many interpreters naturally had an effect as well. Among other things, such values hold civilian control over the military as a prerequisite to safeguarding individual liberties, and rightly so.[25] During the widespread examination of the excesses of German militarism that followed World War II, scholars came to see Clausewitz as one of the few 'good' Germans whose admonitions regarding political control over the use of force supported western democratic ideals, especially those concerning civilian control over the military. Gerhard Ritter's multivolume work on German militarism, *Staatskunst und Kriegshandwerk* (translated into English as *Sword and Scepter*), for example, implied, if not explicitly stated, that if Germany's military and political leaders had understood Clausewitz as well as they claimed, World Wars I and II and their numerous atrocities might not have occurred.[26] The American social scientist Samuel Huntington went so far as to declare that Clausewitz's *On War* was, in fact, the 'first theoretical justification for civilian control' over the military.[27] In a more recent example, German historian Hans-Ulrich Wehler used Clausewitz to argue that statesmen have always possessed an 'inalienable right' to assert their authority over military leadership, even in wartime.[28]

This interpretation of Clausewitz's thought remains dominant today, even though his ideas concerning the relationship between politics and war were drawn from his historical analyses, the bulk of which concerned nondemocratic political systems.[29] It remains so, in fact, even though other scholars have argued that such interpretations portray Clausewitz as more politically enlightened, more open to the idea of limited war, and less doctrinaire than he actually was.[30]

## GRAMMAR VERSUS LOGIC

Contrary to what many scholars have maintained, Clausewitz placed some significant limits on policy's control over military operations. Policy, for instance, can influence military operations only to the extent that war's violent nature will allow, and military commanders are entitled to require that 'policy shall not be inconsistent with [war's] means'.[31] Additionally, he stressed '*if* policy judges the course of military events correctly, it is fully entitled to determine which events and which courses of action correspond with the aim of the war'; thus, a 'certain insight into military affairs must go hand-in-hand with the direction of political activity'.[32] Moreover, the 'political aim', Clausewitz reminded us, cannot act as a 'despotic lawgiver', or tyrant.[33] Even his statement that 'war has its own grammar, but not its own logic', which is usually understood to reinforce the idea that war is merely a political instrument, also places as many restrictions on policy as grammar does on speech.[34]

Simply put, political control over the use of force was, for Clausewitz, less a question of the proper relationship between civilian policymakers and military commanders, than a matter of subordinating an operational point of view to a strategic or, better, a grand strategic perspective. Whether the individual holding this perspective was a civilian or a member of the military was immaterial. Clausewitz gave examples of soldiers making poor statesmen, and vice versa. His two principal models for heads of state—Frederick the Great and Napoleon—arguably transcended military and civilian societies. What truly mattered was that the perspective itself was a unifying one, capable of encompassing the entire interests of the state or community, and, second, that it was the basis for wartime decisions.

More precisely, Clausewitz's concern throughout Book VIII, where his initial observations regarding the primacy of policy appear, was explaining why war seemed to assume different forms and serve diverse purposes over time. He realized the answer to that question would have a direct bearing on what the nature of war was, or whether it had one at all. That determination, in turn, would directly affect whether he could develop a universally valid theory of war.

## POLICY VERSUS POLITICS

As other scholars have remarked, the German word *Politik* means both *policy* and *politics*, and, unfortunately, this dual meaning has led to a great deal of confusion.[35] However, this difference does not always appear in English translations, which typically render *Politik* simply as policy. As Sir Michael Howard explained, the Howard–Paret translation inclines toward policy more than politics because 'policy is what states do', and because the term 'politics' carries a negative connotation in English.[36]

Clausewitz defined policy as the 'trustee' or 'representative of the separate interests of the whole community'.[37] The formulation of policy was an art rather than a science, a product of human 'judgment' and other qualities of 'mind and character'.[38] He also believed that states as well as nonstates arrived at policy decisions in similar ways, even if those ways might vary significantly in terms of their sophistication; his example of the Tartar tribes illustrates the case for nonstates, and puts paid to the mistaken notion that Clausewitz thought only in terms of the nationstate model, though, to be sure, that model was as important to him as it was to his contemporaries.[39] In fact, as we have said, he found it superior. The Tartar way of war, which to most observers seemed to consist mainly of wanton plunder and pillage, nonetheless served the various political interests of the tribes and their leaders; it was shaped by the types of resources that were available, the character of the tribes as a composite of Turkish and Mongol peoples, their nomadic culture and traditions, and the influence of Islam.[40]

As we have seen, Clausewitz's ideas concerning the centrality of *Politik* do not differ greatly from those of his competitors or his colleagues, though again he certainly pursued the issue farther than they did.[41] For instance, August Rühle von Lilienstern, who was a colleague of Clausewitz's at the War College in Berlin, revised the Prussian *Officer's Handbook* in which he wrote, 'war as a whole always has an ultimate political purpose', it is, in fact, undertaken 'to realize the political purpose upon which the State decided in view of the nation's internal and external conditions'.[42] As Clausewitz explained in a letter dated December 22, 1827: 'the entire plan of war proceeds directly from the political life (*Dasein*) of the two warring states, as well as their relations to each other', for 'war is nothing but the continuation of political struggles (*Bestrebungen*) with altered means'.[43] Like Machiavelli, Clausewitz and his contemporaries saw *Politik* as the struggle among states for the protection or advancement of their interests, and this struggle was considered natural, if not inevitable.[44]

However, in Clausewitz's usage, the term *Politik* assumes still other meanings, not all of which are recognized today. One such use lends credence to the argument that he had been influenced in important ways by Hegel, whose theories concerning the primacy of the state had gained considerable currency by the 1820s, albeit in diluted and diffused form.[45] In Book VIII, chapter 3B, 'On the Magnitude of the Military Purpose and its Corresponding Efforts', Clausewitz presented a brief survey that shows how the conduct of war over the ages had been determined by the historical 'period and its circumstances'.[46]

The half-civilized Tartars, the republics of antiquity, the feudal lords and commercial cities of the Middle Ages, kings of the eighteenth century, and finally, princes and peoples of the nineteenth century all waged war in their own way, conducted it differently, with different means, and for different aims.[47]

It is in this survey that the importance of three institutions—government, military, and populace—mentioned in the previous chapter begins to emerge. In the Middle Ages, for example, the political, military, and socioeconomic institutions of feudalism restricted military operations in both scope and duration, and thus made mediaeval wars quite distinctive in nature. Conflicts mainly involved the military in the form of vassals and servants and the people in terms of feudal levies, since no central government existed. The purposes of such wars, Clausewitz stated, were more to punish, than to subdue, and they tended to last no longer than was necessary to burn the enemy's castles and make off with his cattle. From the end of the seventeenth to the end of the eighteenth century, wars became a more forceful form of negotiation. Governments raised standing armies and, unlike the Tartars for whom the people and the military were the same thing, military and civilian societies became essentially separate spheres. The French Revolution at the end of the eighteenth century broke down many existing social, political, and military barriers, and enabled war to evolve into a more devastating form. The populace played a larger role in war, and under Napoleon military operations went beyond set-piece battles and sieges to striving for knock-out blows.[48] By the introductory chapter of *On War*, this triad of populace, government, and military had become the trinity of hostility, purpose, and chance.

## POLITICAL DETERMINISM

However, throughout this historical survey and in the ensuing discussion, the meaning of *Politik* expands to encompass not only the political conditions of the era, but also its dominant ideas and conventions, its military institutions and their capacities, as well as the general 'spirit of the age' (*Zeitgeist*).[49] Again, in Book VIII, chapter 6B, 'War is an Instrument of *Politik*', Clausewitz characterized the three principal institutions—government, military, and populace—that 'make up war and determine its main tendencies' as essentially political in nature, and in fact he considered them inseparable from 'political activity' itself.[50] *Politik* thus becomes a deterministic force that shapes history, establishes the character of peace as well as of war, while also using the latter as an instrument to achieve those ends that diplomacy alone cannot. This concept vaguely resembles Hegel's notion that international politics and war function as instruments advancing the dialectic of history.[51] Clausewitz, however, rejected the teleology inherent in Hegel's philosophy, except in one respect—that political entities are struggling to become states, and if states already, to become stronger ones.[52]

Such political determinism severely restricts policy choices, however. By way of illustration, Clausewitz referred to the 'three new Alexanders'— Gustavus Adolphus, Charles XII, and Frederick the Great—who aimed to use their 'small but highly disciplined armies to raise little states to the rank of great monarchies'. However, they had to content themselves with 'moderate results' due to the countervailing influence of a 'very refined system of political interests, attractions, and repulsions'.[53] This system, in turn, reflected the collective interests of the states of Europe, which desired to prevent any one state from gaining 'sudden supremacy' over the others. Furthermore, it is only when political conditions themselves change, as they did as a result of the French Revolution, that 'real changes in the art of war' can take place.[54] Political conditions, as Clausewitz pointed out in his study of the campaign of 1815, prevented Napoleon from assuming a defensive posture, which would have been more militarily advantageous.[55] More recently, General Clark complained about the extent to which political forces undercut not only military execution, but also the development of a unified political goal.[56] Thus, the wars of history owe their forms more to politics, the constellation of political conditions and interests, than to policy itself as the pursuit of particular interests. In other words, Clausewitz's argument often has less to with the primacy of policy than with the deterministic influence of politics, broadly defined.

At first glance, Clausewitz appears justified in arguing the primacy of policy, after having established the prevalence of politics. Yet, on closer examination, we see that this is not the case. If wars are essentially politically determined, then it is impossible for them not to have political purposes, in every case. For Clausewitz to argue, therefore, that the military point of view should be subordinate to the political one is redundant. In a politically determined world, it is simply not possible to have any other relationship. The social-political position and values of military society are the result of politics, at the root of which is a series of policies. Hence, a purely military perspective cannot exist at all, a point Clausewitz touched on later, but did not pursue.

In short, his argument amounts to saying that politics determines how we think and act; therefore, we should think and act politically. His logic thus breaks down when he shifts from describing how things are to how they ought to be, from the objective to the subjective or the normative; it is not necessary to argue that we must select military aims that serve political purposes, for under the conditions he described it is not possible for us to do otherwise. Policy, writ large, shaped our social structures, our mental outlooks, and assigned wealth and other resources; in short, it distributed power in a particular way. No individual policy can change these structures and ways of thinking *unless* the political conditions established, again, by Policy are ripe for it.

This circular reasoning is, of course, the result of *On War*'s author pushing an idea to its limits. Still, readers would do well to appreciate the contradiction between Clausewitz's drift toward political determinism and his basic assumption that we can make genuine nonpolitical, or apolitical choices.

## POLICY AND WAR

Clausewitz consciously, and understandably, oversimplified policy by defining it as the trustee of the various interests of the state or community. The head of state is essentially where those interests come together. Although he did so to avoid becoming bogged down in niggling details, the immediate consequence of dealing in such generalities is to strip friction from the strategic or policy level of war. Friction, as he maintained at great length elsewhere in *On War*, is an inevitable characteristic of real war, indeed, of physical reality in general. To omit it, as Clausewitz did in Book VIII, 'The Plan of War', is to obscure how difficult it is to arrive at a political purpose in the first place, and it assumes that there will be one purpose, rather than many competing ones. Indeed, the history of war shows that deciding on the purpose or purposes for which a war is to be fought, even if it occurs only in the mind of a head of state, is rich in friction.

This friction is something the late American historian Russell Weigley alluded to in his argument that politics tend to become an instrument of war rather than the other way around.[57] In part, Clausewitz addressed this point in Book I, chapter 1, 'What War Is', explaining that war may indeed modify political purposes, sometimes dramatically, but those new purposes still remain political in nature, through and through.[58] However, none of this is clear in Book VIII, nor does Clausewitz's development of it in Book I allow us to refute Weigley's argument entirely. Political activities carried out with violent tools may well be qualitatively different, that is, different in nature, from those conducted without such tools.

Furthermore, Clausewitz's argument regarding the primacy of policy holds true only from the standpoint of trying to ascertain war's true nature and to reconcile its apparent contradictions. Policy was the 'one single clear idea' that enabled the mind to grasp the 'true and the right' from the veritable mass of war's individual elements and their relationships.[59] He assumed, therefore, that war has a nature that can be fathomed. He could just as well have concluded, on the contrary, that war had no nature. Put differently, if we remove Clausewitz's desire to reconcile the contradictory nature of war from his discussions in Book VIII, we find no justification for the primacy of policy, and his argument begins to unravel.

Also, in Book VIII Clausewitz tended to refer to war as if it were an inanimate instrument, a single saber, rather than the dynamic conflict between opposing wills, the crossed sabers, he depicted in Book I. Instruments are usually, though not always, inanimate objects used against other inanimate objects: they do not fight back. Yet, as the previous chapter showed, Clausewitz argued that war itself did not exist until it met resistance. Instead of an inanimate tool, war is a dynamic activity involving opposing wills, each reacting to or attempting to preempt the other.[60] To be sure, war is a continuation of political activity with violent means. Yet, a fundamental question, which he did not pursue beyond a fusillade of assertions, is whether resistance by violent means does indeed create a unique *logic* for war.

Leaving aside these minor flaws, all of which affirm that *On War* is an unfinished work, Clausewitz also provided a number of significant caveats regarding political control over the use of force. In most cases, these statements refer both directly and indirectly to the nature of war. Curiously, this critical aspect of his thought has received too little attention over the years.[61] As we have seen, the nature of war can vary in degree so much so that, for all practical purposes, the sum of those variations would amount to changes in kind: we may be involved in a war of minimal violence in one moment, and a war of rapidly escalating violence in the next in which the original political motives are suddenly no longer worth the cost.

*Politik* must, therefore, understand that its instrument—a poor choice of terms in any case—is a dynamic one. War involves living forces rather than static elements; thus, it can change quickly and significantly in ways the logic of policy may not expect. Accordingly, when Clausewitz wrote that policy should not ask war to accomplish something against its nature, he spoke volumes.

## POLICY VERSUS THE TRINITY

In addition, the wondrous trinity tells us that no tendency is a priori more influential in determining the shape and course of war than any other. Thus, to single out policy or politics as *the* central element of war's nature is to distort the intrinsic balance of the trinity, and ultimately to compromise its dynamism. Put differently, while *Politik* exerts a subordinating influence over war to realize its purpose, its influence runs up against, and is in turn influenced by, the forces of violence and chance that are inherent in military operations as well as the force of basic hostility. These forces affect the kinds of ends war can accomplish, as well as the extent to which it can do so. In

## Policy, Politics, and Political Determinism 95

short, the forces of violence, chance, and hostility can influence *Politik* to such a degree that policy may have to increase or reduce its aims. Consequently, policy's influence over war is not absolute. It reacts, consciously or otherwise, to the vicissitudes of chance and to fluctuating levels of hostility (on both sides).

Moreover, since military operations take place in an atmosphere of chance and uncertainty, political leaders can increase the risks of policy failure by requiring commanders to ignore such factors in their planning, by eliminating reserve forces—which serve as a hedge against uncertainty—for example. Of course, it is the military's job to do whatever it can to reduce chance and, along with it, the risk of failure. This effort relates back to what Clausewitz called the grammar of war. The analogy is an appropriate one; for, as every author knows, errors in grammar can distort or corrupt the logic of the message one wishes to send.[62] Put differently, political considerations that override the grammar of war may run counter to the accomplishment of policy aims.

Policy failure in war can, of course, have significant consequences, such as revolution, economic collapse, or widespread civil unrest, even among nondemocratic regimes. It is in policy's interest, therefore, to avoid violating the grammar as well as the nature of war. And therein lays the rub, so to speak. Policy requires impartial input from the military in order to understand what the subjective nature and grammar of war are at any given time. Yet, impartial input, from any source, is difficult, if not impossible, to obtain. Each of the services in the US military, for example, has its own perspective and agenda. Each would find it difficult to provide objective military advice, even if it should wish to do so. It is at this point that we cross from the comparatively straightforward realm of policy to the more complex world of politics, as Clausewitz frequently did. The influence of policy is, therefore, limited by the existing political conditions, in a word, by politics.

Clausewitz's wondrous trinity, thus, negates the notion of the primacy of policy; it renders policy as purpose, and holds it a priori just as important as chance and hostility. Only when viewed historically, that is in an a posteriori sense, can we determine the extent to which each of those forces actually influenced the course of events.

## CONCLUSIONS AND IMPLICATIONS

In summation, Clausewitz's views regarding the relationship between war and policy and war and politics appear different in Book VIII, where his exploration of the topic began in earnest, than in the introductory chapter of Book I, where he appears to have arrived at a final resolution. As Clausewitz explained in his prefatory note of 1827, Book VIII was intended to serve as a sounding board of sorts for the revision of the rest of *On War*.[63] He intended to use Book VIII to work out his ideas concerning the relationship between war and policy, and the existence of two types of wars: those intended to achieve the complete defeat of an opponent, and those aimed at accomplishing lesser purposes.

Indeed, compared to the tightly argued first chapter of Book I, many of his discussions in Book VIII appear rather raw, marked by tendentious or even circular logic, and drift toward political determinism. Many of these chapters, in other words, have all the characteristics of a draft or a sketch, of an author thinking aloud on paper. The crystallization of his ideas appears in *On War*'s first chapter, in the form of the wondrous trinity, and the resolution he settles on is one of intrinsic tension, rather than equilibrium. Thus, to take Clausewitz's statements in Book VIII regarding the relationship between war and policy at face value, as many have done, is akin to finishing Schubert's eighth symphony.

Writing under the shadow of the Cold War, Clausewitz's interpreters tended to overemphasize one particular aspect of his trinity. While he did indeed maintain that policy provided the guiding intelligence for the conduct of war, he also insisted policy must not violate the grammar of war. Otherwise, it undermines the accomplishment of the very ends it has decided to use war to achieve in the first place. Book VIII which many scholars have construed as Clausewitz's argument for the primacy of policy is actually his effort to understand the apparently diverse nature of war. His concern in the rough draft that is Book VIII was primarily to reconcile the contradictions he perceived in the nature of war. He found that reconciliation in the perspective afforded by politics, but in so doing succumbed to political determinism, which like technological determinism, or any other sort, is a logical fallacy. Beyond that, he did not address the most important counterargument—that destroying the enemy's military capabilities as quickly as possible opens the door to achieving any political objective. There are, of course, many ways to demolish that counterargument. However, the point is that Clausewitz did not entertain any of them in Book VIII.[64]

Moreover, as we saw with his wondrous trinity, a theory of war would have to remain suspended above the dynamic forces of purpose, chance, and hostility. In other words, a theory that insisted on the primacy of policy was ultimately one-dimensional, and thus unrealistic in Clausewitz's eyes. That does not mean, however, that democracies are wrong to insist on the primacy of policy whenever they wage war, or that they should refrain from requiring strict civilian control over the military.

As some scholars have maintained, in democracies, civilians authorities have the right to be wrong: they should get the wars they ask for, even if they are not the ones they really want; in other words, military practitioners should not take creative liberties with the guidance they receive from their civilian heads.[65] The principles and values that underpin democracies were long in coming, and too important to risk losing in anything less than a war for national survival. Rather, it is only to say that Clausewitz finally settled on a different approach. In citing him as an authority to support our own arguments, therefore, we must first understand his basic premises and then ensure we fully appreciate the various twists and turns his thinking underwent as it evolved.

## NOTES

1. This chapter is based in part on Antulio J. Echevarria II, 'Clausewitz of the Cold War', *Armed Forces & Society*, 33/3 (2007); on Clausewitz's views regarding policy and the state, see Hugh Smith, 'The Womb of War: Clausewitz and International Politics', *Review of International Studies*, 16 (1990), 39–58; this article is a necessary counterpoint to Charles Reynolds, 'Carl von Clausewitz and Strategic Theory', *British Journal of International Studies*, 4 (1978), 178–90, which holds that despite Clausewitz's claims about the role of policy, much of his discussion of war lacks grounding in political context, thereby rendering it too theoretical or abstract.
2. *Vom Kriege*, VIII/6B, 990–1; *On War*, 605.
3. Michael Howard, 'British Grand Strategy in World War I', in Paul Kennedy (ed.), *Grand Strategies in War and Peace* (New Haven, CT: Yale University Press, 1991), referred to it as Clausewitz's 'famous dictum', 31; Brodie, 'A Guide', in *On War*, called it the Prussian's 'great dictum', 645; see also his *War and Politics* (New York: Macmillan, 1973), 8–11, and *Strategy in the Missile Age* (Princeton, NJ: Princeton University Press, 1965), 67–8, 97; similarly, Raymond Aron, *Peace and War: A Theory of International Relations* (New Brunswick, NJ: Transaction, [1966]2003), labeled it Clausewitz's 'famous formula', 23.
4. Eliot A. Cohen, *Supreme Command: Soldiers, Statesmen, and Leadership in Wartime* (New York: Anchor, 2003) and 'Strategy: Causes, Conduct, and Termination of War', in Richard H. Shultz, Jr, Roy Godson, George H. Quester (eds.), *Security Studies for the 21st Century* (Washington, DC: Brassey's, 1997), 364–6; Paul Kennedy, 'Grand Strategy in War and Peace: Toward a Broader Definition', in *Grand Strategies*, 1–10; John Baylis et al., *Contemporary Strategy I: Theories and Concepts*, 2nd edn. (New York: Holmes & Meier, 1987), calls Clausewitz the 'leading exponent of the political philosophy of war', 32.

5. Colin Powell with Joseph E. Persico, *My American Journey: An Autobiography* (New York: Random House, 1995); and Wesley K. Clark, *Waging Modern War: Bosnia, Kosovo, and the Future of Combat* (New York: Public Affairs, 2001). Norman H. Gibbs, 'Clausewitz on the Moral Forces in War', *Naval War College Review* (January–February 1975), 15–21, expresses concern that the value of Clausewitz's other theories has been overshadowed by the discussions regarding policy.

6. Bassford, *Clausewitz in English*, 204. The Powell doctrine emerged in 1991–2, as a modification of the doctrine Defense Secretary Casper Weinberger developed in 1984. The Weinberger doctrine consisted of six conditions for the commitment of US forces to combat: (*a*) it should only be done to protect vital interests, (*b*) and with the clear intention of winning, (*c*) commitment overseas demanded clearly defined military and political objectives, (*d*) and it must be continually reassessed and adjusted based on the changing conditions of the conflict, (*e*) commitment is contingent on the support of the American public, and (*f*) it should only occur as a last resort. Casper Weinberger, 'Speech delivered at the National Press Club', on November 28, 1984, reprinted in *Defense* (January 1985): 1–11. Powell discusses his doctrine in *My American Journey*.

7. *Vom Kriege*, VIII/6B, 993; *On War*, 607.

8. *Vom Kriege*, VIII/6B, 991; *On War*, 605.

9. *Vom Kriege*, VIII/6B, 992; *On War*, 607.

10. *Vom Kriege*, VIII/6B, 998; *On War*, 608.

11. Robert E. Osgood, *Limited War: The Challenge to American Strategy* (Chicago, IL: University of Chicago Press, 1957), 20; and *Limited War Revisited* (Boulder, CO: Westview, 1979), 10, which admitted that limited-war strategy was stimulated by the 'perceived imperative of military containment in the nuclear age', and its the underlying rationale was the 'Clausewitzian principle that armed force must serve national policy'.

12. Robert E. Osgood, 'The Post-War Strategy of Limited War: Before, During, and After Vietnam', in Anthony W. Gray, Jr and Eston T. White (eds.), *National Security Management: Military Strategy* (Washington, DC: National Defense University, 1983), 179–218, here 185.

13. Osgood, 'Post-War Strategy', 185.

14. Thomas C. Schelling, *Arms and Influence* (New Haven, CT: Yale University Press, 1966).

15. Brodie, 'Guide', 645.

16. Osgood, *Limited War*, 23–4; Brodie, 'Guide', 645, 706.

17. Cf. Bassford, *Clausewitz in English*, 129–131.

18. Robert Carlyle, *Clausewitz's Contemporary Relevance*, Strategic & Combat Studies Institute, no. 16, Ft. Leavenworth, 1995, provides a brief summary of Clausewitz's progression toward the trinitarian concept of war; whether Clausewitz ever had a monist conception of war is, however, debatable.

19. A point also made by Howard, 'The Influence of Clausewitz', in *On War*, 43, in a brilliant but all too brief essay.

# Policy, Politics, and Political Determinism 99

20. Osgood, *Limited War*, 26.
21. MacArthur's Address to Joint Meeting of Congress, April 19, 1951; cf. D. Clayton James, *Refighting the Last War: Command and Crisis in Korea, 1950–3* (New York: Free Press, 1993), 51; see also Brodie, 'Guide', 644.
22. Compare: Freudenberg, 'A Conversation with General Clausewitz', 68–71, and Greene, 'Foreword', in *On War* (Jolles), xiii.
23. For all its faults, Harry Summers's *On Strategy: A Critical Analysis of the Vietnam War* (Novato, CA: Presidio [1982] 1995) uses Clausewitz to expose some of the difficulties in the theory of limited war.
24. Herman Kahn, *On Thermonuclear War* (Princeton, NJ: Princeton University Press, 1960); and *Thinking about the Unthinkable* (New York: Horizon, 1962), which was introduced by Raymond Aron, who praised *On Thermonuclear War*, 9.
25. Osgood, *Limited War*, 26–7, states as much on both counts.
26. Gerhard Ritter, *Staatskunst und Kriegshandwerk: Das Problem des Militarismus in Deutschland*, 4 vols. (Munich, Germany: R. Oldenbourg, 1954). See also the work by the German expatriate Alfred Vagts, *A History of Militarism: Civilian and Military* (New York: Meridian, 1959). While the first edition was published in 1937, and thus predated Ritter's work and the influences of the Cold War, it was not well known until the revised edition appeared in 1959; this edition included chapters on the growth of militarism during World War II and its aftermath.
27. Samuel P. Huntington, *The Soldier and the State: The Theory and Politics of Civil–Military Relations* (Cambridge, MA: Harvard University Press, 1985), 58; Eliot A. Cohen, *Citizens and Soldiers: The Dilemmas of Military Service* (Ithaca, NY: Cornell University Press, 1985), 22–24, takes a similar view.
28. Hans-Ulrich Wehler, *The German Empire, 1871–1918*, trans. Kim Traynor (New York: Berg, 1989), 154.
29. See textbooks such as John Spanier and Steven Hook, *American Foreign Policy since World War II*, 14th edn. (Washington, DC: Congressional Quarterly, 1998); and works addressing civil–military relations in the United States, such as Peter D. Feaver and Richard H. Kohn (eds.), *Soldiers and Civilians: The Civil–Military Gap and American National Security* (Cambridge, MA: Massachusetts Institute of Technology, 2001); and Suzanne C. Nielsen, *Political Control over the Use of Force: A Clausewitzian Perspective* (Carlisle, PA: Strategic Studies Institute, 2001).
30. Honig, 'Clausewitz's *On War*', argues that *Vom Kriege* displays more tension on the issues of political control and the imperative of destruction than is evident in *On War*; Gat, *Origins of Military Thought*, maintains that Clausewitz's views derived more from Prussian theories regarding the nature and primacy of the state (*etatisme*) than those of Western-style democracy; C. B. A. Behrens, 'Which Side Was Clausewitz on?', *New York Review of Books* (October 14, 1976), 41–4, raises the issue of Clausewitz's political inclinations.
31. *Vom Kriege*, I/1, 210, VIII/6B, 995; *On War*, 87, 607.

32. *Vom Kriege*, VIII/6B, 994, emphasis added; *On War*, 607.
33. *Vom Kriege*, I/1, 210; *On War*, 87.
34. *Vom Kriege*, VIII/6B, 991; *On War*, 605.
35. The same point is made in Wallach, 'Misperceptions of Clausewitz' *On War*', 213–39.
36. Sir Michael Howard, conference on 'Clausewitz in the 21st Century', Oxford University, March 18, 2005, question and answer session; Honig, 'Clausewitz's *On War*', points out that the Howard–Paret translation is 'remarkably consistent' in translating *Politik* as 'policy' rather than politics: *Politik* appears nine times in chapter 1, Book I, but is translated as 'politics' only once; in chapter 6B, Book VIII, *Politik* is translated as 'policy' in twenty-seven of forty-two cases, and as 'politics' only twice; in addition, the adjective *politisch* is often translated as the noun 'policy'. Honig distinguishes policy as 'a specific course of action pursued by an authority' from politics or 'the medium, the *milieu*, or the system or body (as in 'body politic'), which gives meaning to political activity'.
37. *Vom Kriege*, VIII/6B, 993; *On War*, 606.
38. *Vom Kriege*, VIII/3B, 961–2; *On War*, 586.
39. *Vom Kriege*, VIII/3B, 962 ff.; *On War*, 586 ff. Carl Schmitt, 'Clausewitz als politischer Denker, Bemerkungen und Hinweise', in *Clausewitz in Perspektive*, 442, makes the point that Clausewitz thought in terms of the state, but what is often overlooked is his concept of the state was broader, than the one commonly used today.
40. Douglas S. Benson, *The Tartar War* (Chicago, IL: Maverick, 1981). Again, the Tartar example is also found in the works of Lloyd and Bülow.
41. Peter Paret, 'Die politischen Ansichten von Clausewitz', in *Freiheit ohne Krieg?*, 333–48.
42. R[ühle] von L[ilienstern], *Handbüch für den Offizier zur Belehrung im Frieden und zum Gebrauch im Felde*, 2 vols. (Berlin: G. Reimer, 1817–18), II, 8; cf. Paret, *Clausewitz*, 314–15, and Heuser, *Reading Clausewitz*, 30.
43. The letter was to Major von Roeder, in 'Zwei Briefe des Generals von Clausewitz. Gedanken zur Abwehr', *Militärwissenschaftliche Rundschau*, 2 (1937), Sonderheft, 6. Partial English translations are offered in Peter Paret, *Understanding War: Essays on Clausewitz and the History of Military Power* (Princeton, NJ: Princeton University Press, 1992), 123–9; Wallace P. Franz, 'Two Letters on Strategy: Clausewitz' Contribution to the Operational Level of War', in *Clausewitz and Modern Strategy*, 171–94, provides some analysis. Honig, 'Interpreting Clausewitz', challenges the translations.
44. Felix Gilbert, 'Machiavelli: The Renaissance of the Art of War', in Paret (ed.), *Makers of Modern Strategy*, 11–31, and Paret, *Clausewitz*, 169–208.
45. As noted previously, Herberg-Rothe, 'Clausewitz und Hegel', argues that Hegel's influence on Clausewitz was greater than acknowledged hitherto; Gat's treatment in *Origins of Military Thought* is fair; W. M. Schering, *Die Kriegsphilosophie von Clausewitz* (Hamburg, Germany: Hanseatische, 1935) is considered to

have taken the issue of Hegel's influence too far; see Paret, *Clausewitz*, 84, 370, 443; and Baldwin, 'Clausewitz in Nazi Germany', 20–1.
46. *Vom Kriege*, VIII/3B, 962; *On War*, 586.
47. *Vom Kriege*, VIII/3B, 962; *On War*, 586.
48. *Vom Kriege*, VIII/3B, 962–74; *On War*, 586–94.
49. *Vom Kriege*, VIII/3B, 974; *On War*, 594. The last three books (*Defense*, *Attack*, and *The Plan of War*) reflect this historicist perspective.
50. *Vom Kriege*, VIII/6B, 991; *On War*, 605.
51. G. W. F. Hegel, *Philosophy of History*, trans. J. Sibree (New York: Dover, 1952). A similar teleology with regard to the role of war is evident in Kant's works; see Yirmiyahu Yovel, *Kant and the Philosophy of History* (Princeton, NJ: Princeton University Press, 1989), 8, 151–3.
52. Paret, *Clausewitz*, 438.
53. *Vom Kriege*, VIII/3B, 966–8; *On War*, 593–4.
54. *Vom Kriege*, VIII/6B, 997; *On War*, 610.
55. 'Feldzug von 1815', in *Schriften–Aufsätze–Studien–Briefe*, II, 956–8.
56. Clark, *Waging Modern War*, 417–61.
57. Weigley, 'Military Effectiveness', 341.
58. *Vom Kriege*, I/1, 211–12; *On War*, 87–8.
59. *Vom Kriege*, VIII/1, 951; *On War*, 577.
60. See e.g. *Vom Kriege*, II/3, 303–4; *On War*, 149.
61. The exception is Gallie, 'Clausewitz on the Nature of War', in *Philosophers of Peace and War*, 37–65, which identifies the flaws in the logical structure Clausewitz uses in Book I/chapter 1 of *On War*, but does not explore the Prussian's nature of war in depth.
62. A point Clausewitz also makes, *Vom Kriege*, VIII/6B, 995; *On War*, 605.
63. *Vom Kriege*, 'Nachtricht', 179; *On War*, 69–70.
64. However, as we have seen, he explored them in Book I, chapter 2 'Purpose and Means' from the standpoint of weighing cost vs. benefit.
65. Peter D. Feaver, 'The Civil–Military Problematique: Huntington, Janowitz, and the Question of Civilian Control', *Armed Forces & Society*, 23 (1996), 154.

# 5

## Genius, Giving the Rule to Art

This chapter examines Clausewitz's understanding of military genius, but to do so it must first lay out his concept of general friction, which included incidental friction, danger, physical exertion, uncertainty, and chance. Military genius, the harmonious balance of intellectual and character traits, helped offset these disruptive influences.[1] However, Clausewitz, who derived his concept of genius from Kant's definition—an innate gift that gives the rule to art—saw it as more than the counterpoise to friction. For Kant, genius set new rules in the field of art; similarly, for Clausewitz, military genius established new rules for the art of war, or strategy.[2] These new rules led to new forms or models, which other artists or practitioners would emulate.

As we know, Clausewitz criticized the military theorists of his day for overlooking individual talent or aptitude, among other psychological factors. They proffered rules that were not fit for general practice, let alone genius; in fact, Enlightenment writers tended to place genius outside the realm of what could be understood scientifically. They regarded genius as a rare, inexplicable, and therefore inconvenient, phenomenon. As Clausewitz noted, genius was seen as existing 'above the rules' because it was considered beyond comprehension.[3]

In his chapter on military genius, Clausewitz sought to rectify this error, first, by affirming the existence of genius, and then by subjecting it to scientific analysis in order to ascertain its principal characteristics.[4] This analysis of the human qualities which contribute to superior judgment was seminal, though it may appear vague and fragmented to modern readers. True to the Enlightenment's spirit of inquiry, Clausewitz examined a phenomenon the Enlightenment itself had essentially marginalized. Today, genius is hardly treated scientifically; instead, we find it supplanted by 'expert theory' or similar thinking, or relegated to the realm of popular literature.[5] Scholarly military history, for instance, now looks more closely at military institutional or organizational effectiveness, what it is, and how to achieve it.[6] Both history and theory have, in some respects, gone beyond assessing the influence of major personalities to understanding processes and organizations.[7] Thus, an examination of Clausewitz's concept of genius breaks both old and new ground.

## FRICTION

The concept of friction developed as part of Clausewitz's lifelong effort, inherited in part from Scharnhorst, to explain why war in theory differed so markedly from 'war as it actually is—*der eigentliche Krieg*'.[8] We find two types of friction mentioned in *On War*: general friction, and incidental friction or chance. General friction was Clausewitz's collective term for those elements that make up the atmosphere of war, and turn it into a resistant medium. *On War* offers two different lists of the elements of friction. The first appears in book I, chapter 3, 'On Military Genius', and includes: danger, physical exertion, uncertainty (*Ungewißheit*), and chance.[9] The second is found in book I, chapter 8, 'Closing Observations of Book I', and mentions: danger, physical exertion, military reports or intelligence (*Nachrichten*), and incidental friction.[10] Thus, in the first list uncertainty replaces intelligence, and chance supplants incidental friction. Yet these discrepancies should not overly concern us. Uncertainty and intelligence both pertain to elements that affect the mind of the military commander. Chance and incidental friction influence the functioning of the military instrument as part of the machinery of war. Although the terms are clearly different, they nonetheless have a great deal in common.[11]

Clausewitz's letter to Marie, dated September 29, 1806, appears to be his earliest use of the term friction; in the letter he complained to Marie of the resistance or 'friction' Scharnhorst encountered as he repeatedly, but fruitlessly, attempted to propose a coherent plan for Prussia's impending clash with France. 'How much must the effectiveness of a gifted man be reduced', he wrote, 'when he is constantly confronted by the obstacles of convenience and tradition, when he is paralyzed by constant friction with the opinions of others.'[12]

Of all the elements of general friction, Clausewitz believed danger and physical exertion were the most influential, and therefore the most significant. These two are also the elements that most distinguish war from other political or social activities: the other elements of friction are more or less present in everyday life. For that reason, critics such as van Creveld maintain that Clausewitz's theory is unremarkable.[13] This criticism, however, misses the point, since Clausewitz was attempting to ground his theory in reality or, more precisely, in the everyday life of war.

## DANGER

'Combat', Clausewitz said, 'gives birth to the element of danger, in which all military activities must live and move, like the bird in the air and the fish in water.'[14] It affects the emotions as well as the intellect; with regards the former it generates a desire to flee, while with respect to the latter it allows fear and anxiety to creep into one's thinking. Danger, as Clausewitz explained, is often thought of in a romantic light, but appears quite different in reality. The excitement of a cavalry or bayonet charge might sweep away one's fear for a few moments, but those moments were fleeting. Exposure to the 'air' of danger is a more general affair that outlasts the rush of adrenaline and gradually wears down one's courage. As novices who do not know war, we might find danger attractive at first, but this view changes the closer we move to the fighting. At the front lines, we see officers protect themselves from shot and shell by using man-made structures or features of terrain for cover; the instinct for self-preservation thus competes with, and at times overcomes, self-discipline and sense of duty:

Suddenly someone we know is hit—a shell strikes home among the crowd and causes involuntary reactions—we begin to feel that we are no longer quite so calm and collected; even the bravest soul loses his composure somewhat.[15]

The sight of the maimed and fallen begins to tell on the novice, whose initial feeling of attraction to danger is replaced by a keen desire to avoid it. Only an extraordinary individual can withstand such impressions when exposed to them for the first time and still exercise judgment effectively. Over time, we become more accustomed to danger, but it never fails to have at least some adverse effect on our perception and judgment.

Clausewitz, thus, saw danger as a factor that adversely affects the perceptions and decisions of officers and enlisted troops; as he said, it refracts the light of reason in unique and inevitable ways.[16] While everything seems clear when considered from a position of comfort and safety, the presence of danger makes it much more difficult to determine the right course of action. Danger is still a factor for a commander who may be far from the actual fighting: it bears down on him, like the weight of responsibility, whenever he must make a decision regarding battle, knowing its outcome may mean tremendous loss of life and may put his country in jeopardy. Courage, both physical and emotional, is the natural counterpoise to danger, but courage is also more than that because, like genius, it has a power of its own.

## PHYSICAL EXERTION

Likewise, physical exertion, in Clausewitz's view, impaired perception and judgment at least as much as danger.[17] Judgments made under conditions of numbing frost, debilitating heat and thirst, and enervating hunger and fatigue would not necessarily hold up under objective analysis; however, he thought that more often than not they would prove reasonable in light of the subjective circumstances in which they were made. In other words, decision-making in a sterile, classroom environment where the right course of action is plain to see, was very different from deciding what to do under strenuous conditions, where human endurance and the instinct for self-preservation tend to warp one's view. A realistic appreciation for how far one's officers and troops can go under difficult circumstances to include danger is, therefore, of immense importance. In this case, subjective knowledge—valid for the individual and the specific circumstances—trumps objective knowledge. In a larger sense, therefore, one of most important qualities of genius is the ability to appreciate when objective knowledge must yield to subjective knowledge.

Physical exertion, like danger, Clausewitz maintained, is an indefinite quantity, which fluctuates in terms of its intensity and influence.[18] It is difficult, therefore, to estimate how it will affect a commander's decisions, and the performance of his troops.

## UNCERTAINTY

Clausewitz had nothing but cautionary remarks regarding the reliability of military reporting or intelligence (*Nachrichten*)—or simply information—which many today see as the key to success in war.[19] Indeed, some authors see information as the basis of an unfolding revolution in military affairs.[20] This view is, of course, hotly contested.[21]

Although the term *Nachrichten*, by which Clausewitz meant the 'collective knowledge of the enemy and his country, and thus the foundation of one's notions and actions', can be translated as intelligence, it seems best to render it in the broader sense of military reports.[22] The latter sense underscores the raw nature of many of the reports commanders had to deal with in the Napoleonic era, and provides a better impression of Clausewitz's perspective. The military reports of Clausewitz's day stand in direct contrast to the deliberate processes of analysis that information is subjected to today before it becomes intelligence. Both the military reporting of two centuries ago and the intelligence of today, of course, involve subjective interpretation, and the latter, as recent conflicts have shown, is not necessarily more reliable than the former.

However, the onus of interpreting information is not just the commander's or that of his principal staff, but is becoming ever more widely distributed, both laterally and vertically. A brigade or regimental commander today might well have responsibility for an area the size of the battlefield at Waterloo. Commanders must still, as ever, use their experienced judgment to assess the overall value of intelligence. However, most of the information-gathering and verification is done for them by their staffs.

The common thread that links uncertainty and military reports in Clausewitz's view is the imperfect nature of information. He did not deny the importance of information, but he warned of its fluid nature and advised against taking reports at face value:

> A great many of the reports one receives in war are contradictory, an even greater number of them are false, and by far the greatest number are overshadowed by apparent uncertainty. What we must require of officers, therefore, is a certain ability to discern [fact from fiction], which only subject-matter expertise, an understanding of human nature, and good judgment can provide. The law of probabilities must guide them.[23]

The imperfect nature of information affects decision-making even before the conflict begins, when one is far removed from danger. 'The great uncertainty of all data (*Datis*) in war', Clausewitz wrote, 'means that all actions must be carried out to a certain extent as if in a twilight, which as within a fog or under the glow of the moon distorts things and makes them appear more threatening.'[24] In the thick of the fight, reports tend to arrive in rapid succession, which in turn helps magnify the degree to which the reality of the situation is distorted. The natural tendency, particularly in the heat of battle, is to exaggerate the negative. Even prewar planning is subject to being influenced by worst-case scenarios. So, the uncertainty of the information itself is only half of the problem; the other is the natural psychological tendency to accentuate the negative. Together, both increase the challenges facing the commander. Knowledge, talent, and especially judgment, Clausewitz believed, were the commander's best defenses against the assaults of uncertainty.

## CHANCE

As noted earlier, Clausewitz included chance as part of the wondrous trinity. A closer look reveals that he viewed chance as the arbitrary influence of an infinite number of events or circumstances:

An example of chance is the weather. Here, fog prevents the enemy from being discovered in time, a cannon from firing at the right moment, a report from reaching the commanding officer; there, rain keeps a battalion from arriving, or another from arriving on time because instead of three hours it had to march for perhaps eight, and the cavalry from effectively charging because it is weighed down in sodden soil, etc.[25]

We can think of such incidents or circumstances, as *On War* suggests, as a sort of incidental friction, not concentrated on a few points as in mechanics itself, but as occurrences distributed randomly across the entire military instrument.[26] Chance, or incidental friction, is exceedingly difficult or impossible to account for in any war plan, since its possible occurrences are endless. Incidental friction makes even the simplest thing difficult, and creates a gap between war in the physical world and war on paper:

Consider, for instance, a traveler who, late in the day, is but two stops from the end of his day's journey—four or five hours more, with fresh horses posted along the way; it should be easy. However, at the next stop he finds no horses, or only worn out ones; the terrain becomes hilly, the roads poor, and night falls, and after much strenuous effort he is only too happy to arrive at the next stop and accept whatever meager accommodations he finds.[27]

Moreover, when combined with the other elements of general friction—danger, physical exertion, and uncertainty—the effects of incidental friction are often magnified. Indeed, we might say the elements of friction tend to compound one another, which is another point Clausewitz's passages on friction attempted to make.

Interestingly, the paragraph cited above never mentions war. Incidental friction is not peculiar to war, but a part of everyday life. We may encounter a great deal of incidental friction—as well as the other elements of general friction—by simply commuting to work in a crowded metropolis, for instance. Since the number of deaths and injuries on major highways exceeds those due to military action, we could say the element of danger is certainly present; nor are the effects of physical exertion and uncertainty absent.

So, in one respect, Clausewitz's identification and analysis of general friction is indeed unremarkable: it is a recognized and accepted condition of physical reality. It is unlikely he would have used the term friction in his letter to Marie unless he was reasonably sure she would have understood what he meant by it. Explaining the difference between war on paper and war in the physical world was a topic that intrigued not only Scharnhorst and Clausewitz, but others in the Berlin Military Society.

What does make the concept remarkable, however, is that so many of the theories of Clausewitz's day tended to exclude, or at best minimize, the influence of friction. Jomini's theories, for instance, do not necessarily assume a world without friction. Instead, his underlying assumption is that if a commander were to hold fast to the proposed principles, and use them as guidelines, he would succeed in the face of the confusion and chaos of battle. Thus, adherence to simple principles was, for Jomini, the way to beat danger, physical exertion, uncertainty, and chance.

Clausewitz's concept of friction may well state the obvious, as van Creveld claims. However, it was patently obvious to the Prussian theorist that such a statement was necessary. Omitting such an acknowledgment from a theory that purported to reflect objective knowledge would have rendered the work dubious from the outset.

## GENIUS, A BALANCE OF INTELLECT AND CHARACTER

Military genius, according to Clausewitz, consisted of a harmonious balance of several qualities belonging to reason (*Verstand*) and passion (*Gemüt*), or what we might refer to, while admittedly taking some liberties, as sense and sensibility.[28] The latter category included energy (*Energie*), steadfastness (*Festigkeit*), resolve (*Standhaftigkeit*), strength of temperament (*Gemütsstärke*), and strength of character (*Charakterstärke*).[29]

As mentioned earlier, these served as a counterweight to the elements of danger, physical exertion, uncertainty, and chance, which made up the atmosphere of war; they also represent counterstatement to Bülow's theory. Energy was necessary to overcome the resistance of one's enemy as well as the inertia of one's own military machine; it might take the form of a commander's personal quest for glory, or his desire to satisfy his own honor.

Although these motives were often regarded as negative, Clausewitz believed they could prove more powerful, and thus more valuable, than other passions, such as patriotism, fanaticism, and revenge. Steadfastness and resolve go hand-in-hand: the former refers to the ability to stay focused when confronted by sudden adversities; the latter means the capacity to remain committed over the long haul. Strength of temperament best equates to self-discipline, the ability to listen to the voice of reason in the midst of even the strongest of emotional appeals—to maintain one's perspective. Strength of character, a common term throughout the nineteenth and most of the twentieth century, means strength of conviction, which might stem from many factors, but—ideally—came from an unshakeable belief in correct principles; in contrast, obstinacy was blind adherence to unfounded or incorrect ideas, and thus was a perversion of strength of character, and so was to be avoided. Once again, therefore, we see the importance of objective knowledge in the formulation of judgment.

In a sense, all of these qualities fall under the heading of physical and psychological courage. Physical courage means the ability to function in spite of the debilitating influence of danger and the physical privations of war; psychological courage refers to the capacity to accept responsibility, to make decisions in times of crisis.

Yet, the central point of this chapter of *On War* is that all of these qualities would come to naught without the use of the intellect. The ability to penetrate the fog of uncertainty that surrounds events in war, and to exercise sound judgment, was essential. This higher use of the intellect required a certain *coup d'œil*—an innate ability to see in an instant the true significance of manifold things or events, to grasp the situation completely and precisely even as it unfolded.[30] Put simply, *coup d'œil* describes the ability to see simultaneously with the physical as well as the mind's eye. As mentioned previously, this talent could be nurtured by acquiring correct knowledge of war.

Together, these were the qualities essential for successful command at high levels, and Clausewitz believed one could find them in evidence in each of history's great military commanders: Alexander, Hannibal, Gustavus Adolphus, and Frederick the Great. However, he did not limit genius only to such lofty heights. In his view, true genius was the harmonious union of the traits of temperament and intellect in such a way that each cooperated with, rather than opposed, the others. While some scholars believe Clausewitz's model for genius was Napoleon, it was probably Scharnhorst, whose traits were balanced.[31] Napoleon's character was weighted toward arrogant recklessness, and thus not balanced enough for true genius.[32] In Clausewitz's studies of the 1814 and 1815 campaigns, moreover, he more than once sought to deflate the Corsican's growing legend, though he clearly admired aspects of his way of waging war.[33] The officer he most admired was his friend and mentor Scharnhorst, to whom he owed a great deal.

Possessing all the qualities mentioned above was not enough to qualify as a genius, however; they also had to work together. The message was, simply, that favoring one type of quality, such as energy, led to an imbalance, a character flaw that adversity would overwhelm, or an adversary would exploit.

## GENIUS AND THE RULES

However, there was more to genius than balance. True genius rose above talent, according to Kant. Clausewitz's description of genius closely resembles that advanced in Kant's *Critique of Judgment* (1788–90), which defined genius as:[34]

...the talent (natural gift), which gives the rule to art. Since that talent itself, as an innate productive ability of the artist, belongs to nature, we may put it this way: *Genius* is the innate psychological aptitude (*ingenium*), *by which* nature gives the rule to art.

...The psychological powers whose union, in certain individuals, comprise *genius* are imagination and understanding....

[Genius] is the exemplary originality of the natural gifts of an individual in the *free* employment of his cognitive faculties.[35]

Kiesewetter's *Outline of Logic* amplifies the Kantian concept of genius in this way:

We distinguish between a brilliant mind (*Kopf*) and a genius; a brilliant mind is one who makes discoveries in science, a person who, with respect to knowledge, is original. A genius is that person who, in works of fine art, delivers exemplary products; the one who, with respect to the production of works of taste, achieves originality.... Works of genius are, however, inexplicable, and the genius himself cannot say how he brought them forth. Both—brilliance and genius—are gifts of nature, talents; Newton was a brilliant mind, and Horace, a genius. The products of genius can, of course, arouse the creative forces in a similarly gifted individual, and inspire that person to accomplish similar works; however, the master cannot teach others how he created his original works.[36]

A key element in Kant's definition of genius is, thus, the quality of originality.[37] Works of genius are by necessity original works. A genius cannot just follow existing rules or models; otherwise his works would not be original. Rather, by virtue of his innate talent, nature provides him special rules or concepts by which to operate, and his finished works in turn provide the models, or rules, for others to emulate. In this way, different schools in art, and thought, develop.

Kant, in fact, went to some length to explain that genius was an aptitude for art, itself a 'human skill', and not for science, a 'practical form of theoretical faculty'.[38] In science, rules determine how one must proceed; in art, skill is its own rule. Furthermore, a genius has a concept in mind of that which he wishes to create, even though that concept is unknown to the public; hence, genius presupposes a certain understanding of the materials and their proper use in realizing the concept. Clausewitz echoed similar ideas when he stressed that:

The rules of strategy are grounded in the means that we possess, and to be sure not merely in *cannon, troops, fortresses*, but also in any advantages that are available which are of a *psychological* nature, and therein also belongs the genius of the commander. Whoever possesses genius should make use of it; *that is entirely within the rules!*[39]

As previously noted, Clausewitz saw means as subjective in nature. They change from war to war, perhaps even from battle to battle. The means used in one may not be available in the next. As the means change, so must the rules. It is the particular quality of genius that it can create new rules from new means. Importantly, the final product is subjective in nature; it is thus valid for that individual only, and may not be suitable for replication:

> However superbly a great military commander does things, there is always something subjective in the way in which he does them; if he has a certain style, a good portion of it is a product of his individuality, which does not always accord with the individuality of the person who imitates his style.[40]

We also find evidence of Clausewitz's acceptance of Kant's definition of genius in *On War*'s discussion of theory. According to Kant, creating something required first having a concept (*Begriff*) of that thing. Every concept, in turn, needed rules, or cause-and-effect relationships, that served to define it, and distinguish it from other things. Making war, in other words, first required a concept of war, which in turn needed rules or laws that helped define it, and thereby distinguish it from other social activities. All of this underscores the importance of his frequent use of the term concept (*Begriff*) of war, as discussed earlier.

When Clausewitz wrote: 'What genius does must at once be the perfect rule, and theory can do nothing better than to show how and why this is so', he was completely in agreement with Kant's concept of genius.[41] Genius, as Kant explained, makes its own rules, insofar as its innate talent will allow. These rules then become the guidelines, or models, which those of lesser talent emulate, even ape. The risk inherent in that emulation, of course, is that the model established by genius might be too subjective for widespread replication.

Applying the methods of Napoleon (if indeed we are to consider him a genius) to other times and places without taking into account the differences in circumstances could prove dangerous. 'That danger', Clausewitz continued, 'is what theory should prevent through clear and intelligible critical analysis'.[42] A universally valid theory, moreover, should capture, not the specific rules used by genius, for that would require analyzing countless historical cases individually, but rather the underlying causal linkages that make those rules, and others, possible. This, as we know, was Clausewitz's intent.

## GENIUS AND ROMANTICISM

Kant's emphasis on originality became part of a growing intellectual movement associated with the German *Aufklärung*, or Enlightenment, and its

Romanticist reaction. The movement and its countermovement involved men of education and letters such as Johann Gottlieb Fichte (1762–1814), Johann Gottfried von Herder (1744–1803), and Johann Wolfgang von Goethe (1749–1832), all of whom sought to establish, among other things, a uniquely German cultural identity.[43] Nor was Kant's treatment of genius wholly original in the way it attempted to account for the sublime in art without subverting Enlightenment ideals of reason and rationality. Similar attempts had already appeared in British philosophy some years before.[44] We also saw that tendency expressed in Lloyd's work, though Bülow merely attempted to dismiss it from the 'modern system of war' altogether. The invention and reinvention of genius as a concept has a long history that need not concern us here. The point is merely that by the time Clausewitz embraced the notion of genius itself, the concept was already in full bloom, and had been widely discussed in scholarly and popular literature.

Although it might be tempting to see Clausewitz's exposition of military genius as an attempt to balance the Enlightenment's preference for rational explanation with the Romanticist inclination toward intuitive understanding, this was not likely the case.[45] Unlike Goethe's concept of genius, as revealed in his masterful work *The Sorrows of Young Werther*, Clausewitz's version did not derive from the excessive irrationalism of the German Counter-Enlightenment and Romanticist movements, which rejected the systematic thinking of the eighteenth century and its 'deification of the intellect'.[46] Goethe, the renowned man of letters, believed that genius, which acted spontaneously rather than through meditation, followed its own inner laws which had to be 'felt' rather than 'grasped'.[47] In this respect, Goethe's concept of genius resembled Clausewitz's.

However, unlike the man of letters, the military theorist believed that correct knowledge, or understanding, also played an important role. Whereas Goethe's genius acted spontaneously (and sometimes self-destructively), as in the case of young Werther, Clausewitz's genius took action only after correctly assessing the overall situation. This assessment might occur so rapidly as to seem spontaneous, but the actions taken by genius always followed the insight gained by means of knowledge, experience, and the commander's special *coup d'œil*, his use of the physical as well as the mind's eye to see the situation clearly. Eventually, the mature Goethe would come to resolve the apparent contradiction between the need for a work of genius to be original and the reality that an artistic tradition, however weak or strong, inevitability influenced a work of genius, even if only negatively through the rejection of that tradition. Goethe came to see the true mark of genius as consisting not in originality, but in the lasting impression the work left on the present and subsequent generations, that is, how it enriched daily life through the power to astonish.[48] Under this criterion, *On War* might qualify as a work of genius, even though Clausewitz himself might not.

## GENIUS AND KNOWLEDGE

As we have seen, Kant believed that genius was the combination of imagination and understanding; the former referred to one's conceptual skills, and the latter to knowledge of one's craft. In adapting Kant's concept of genius to military command, Clausewitz acknowledged the importance of both components. He valued conceptual skills highly, as noted earlier, and thought the education and training of an officer should develop them. We also know, based on the time he spent writing *On War*, he greatly valued understanding. Strategy, as he said, was part science and part art, though neither wholly the one nor the other. Genius clearly applied to that part of strategy that was art, and thus required skill in execution; however, a commander needed both skill and knowledge to be successful. He need not know everything there was to know about war, of course, but he had to know what was appropriate for his level of command, and he needed the ability to translate that knowledge into skill. Clausewitz's concept of genius, like Kant's, thus presupposed a certain knowledge of one's craft.

Knowledge of the craft of war can, of course, take many forms. As Clausewitz wrote:

A true quality of genius belongs to every level of command, from lowest to highest, though history and posterity reserve the title of genius only for those who have served at the highest position—that of commander-in-chief—for here the demands on understanding and psychological makeup are much greater....

Bringing an entire war or its great acts, its campaigns, to a brilliant end requires exceptional insight into the higher relations of the state. The conduct of war and political intercourse here become one, and the military commander is simultaneously the statesman....

We say: the military commander becomes the statesman, but he must not stop being the commander; from his perspective he grasps the entire political situation on the one hand, while on the other he is precisely aware of what he can accomplish with the means at his disposal.[49]

Accordingly, the knowledge a commander requires may range from a grasp of the larger political situation to an understanding of what particular military forces can accomplish. In most cases, that knowledge will be subjective, by its very nature. It will thus tend to decay over time, so it must be updated frequently. Genius must therefore not only master war's objective knowledge, it must also continuously seek to upgrade its own subjective knowledge.

As a case in point, upgrading subjective knowledge was a critical function of the Prussian–German general staff as it evolved under Count Helmuth von Moltke (1800–91).[50] Not only was the planning function of the general staff responsible for revising the original war plan as the conflict unfolded, it was also charged with war-gaming potential scenarios even before hostilities commenced. War-gaming for the campaign against Denmark, for instance, began some eighteen months before the actual conflict broke out; the same kinds of activities took place during the several months that preceded the wars against Austria and France.[51]

In each case, the general staff considered numerous factors, such as the nature of the terrain, the location and capacity of transportation networks, and the advantages of different march routes and troop deployments. The results, in turn, generated reasonable estimates of an opponent's best courses of action, and served as the basis for revising mobilization timetables and march orders, as well as for providing sound military advice to the political architect of each of these wars, Bismarck. In other words, the general staff updated significant portions of Moltke's subjective knowledge both prior to, and during, a conflict. What such testing could not capture, of course, was the ebb and flow of psychological factors, such as the morale of the adversary's troops and the will of the indigenous population to resist. And there was, of course, no guarantee that the enemy would adopt any of the courses of action the general staff considered. Everything, as Clausewitz said, was matter of probability; thus, judgment—more than any process—would prove the deciding factor.

Nonetheless, upgrading subjective knowledge, as the general staff accomplished it resembled the way in which a chess grand master (genius?) before a match tests numerous combinations and variations beginning with the opening moves through the end game. Contrary to popular opinion, chess masters do not rely solely on being able to think ahead twenty or thirty moves during a game. Instead, they study in advance which combinations would not succeed in certain situations. During the game, pattern recognition—and memory recall—take control. The master's skill comes into play with his innate ability to recognize a familiar pattern from an otherwise complex assortment of pieces of different ranges and capabilities, and to recall the best move for that situation.[52]

Without such an ability to recognize patterns in an opponent's deployments, Moltke might have remained a mediocre and obscure chief of staff. As one of his biographers notes, however, he appears to have had an aptitude for conceptual thinking, or imagination, which goes hand-in-hand with pattern recognition.[53] The risk of this approach, of course, is that new situations can emerge that do not fit recognizable patterns. Thus, the rapid recognition of a truth is distinct from intuitive insight, where an answer is divined correctly despite an inadequate knowledge base.

## A LEGACY OF GENIUS?

The same emphasis on war-gaming as an aspect of planning, of updating subjective knowledge even though that term was never used, remained important to Moltke's successors. Schlieffen and the younger Moltke valued diligent staff work, the heart and soul of planning, perhaps to a fault. However, the elder Moltke's legacy of genius, its astonishment value, had everything to do with the dramatic results he achieved on the battlefield. Together, the exemplary victories at Königgrätz (1866) and Sedan (1870) left the impression that it was possible to execute quick, decisive campaigns, and near-perfect battles.

Clausewitz's emphasis on the harmonic balance of sense and sensibility was lost in the many debates over the nature of Moltke's genius versus that of Napoleon. Instead of an emphasis on balance, military genius drifted toward the pursuit of excellence, or virtuosity, on the battlefield. As a consequence, it had less to do with originality and more to do with achieving perfection.[54] All too often, this interest was used to justify excluding political influence from the development of military strategy and from the actual conduct of war. Political leaders were believed to have little or no understanding of the nature of war, or the use of military force. That belief proved correct with respect to Germany's political leadership during the four decades or so between the time Bismarck stepped down as chancellor and Hitler seized dictatorial powers. Still, it was not just the political leadership that had trouble grasping the nature of war, which continued to change during that time frame; many generals failed to understand it as well. In any case, the inability to use grammar properly does not necessarily mean one's logic is flawed.

Consider the example of Germany, in World War II. Several of its military commanders rose to prominence and achieved fame: the names of Erich von Manstein, Heinz Guderian, Erwin Rommel, Herman Balck, and Friedrich von Mellenthin come to mind. Some of them even explicitly valued intuition, expressed as a *Fingerspitzengefühl* or 'fingertip feeling' for the terrain and the dispositions of the enemy aspect of military genius, that had much in common with *coup d'œil*.[55] Certainly, some of the battle plans they conceived, such as Manstein's concept for the invasion of France in 1940, were innovative, if not wholly original, in their use of available means to accomplish rapid military victories. Liddell Hart, in fact, wrote that Manstein, whom he believed to be

Germany's ablest commander of the war, clearly possessed 'military genius'.[56] Yet, Liddell Hart, who was not without his own agendas, also concluded that Germany's general staff system produced officers who shunned novel ideas, and were decidedly 'lacking in genius'.[57]

In any case, none of these commanders astonished posterity to the extent that Napoleon or the elder Moltke did (unless of course one considers the German army's documented complicity in acts of barbarity).[58] Nor did any of them demonstrate what might qualify as a convincing grasp of the larger political situation, as it evolved over the course of the war. Their focus throughout remained, as Manstein revealed, solely on destroying the enemy's military forces:

> While strategy must unquestionably be an instrument in the hands of the political leadership, the latter must not disregard—as did Hitler to a great extent when fixing operational objectives—the fact that the strategic aim of any war is to smash the military defensive power of the enemy. Only when victory has been secured is the way open to the realization of political and economic aims.[59]

What Manstein meant by strategic aim was closer to the Clausewitzian *Ziel*, than to *Zweck*. On the other hand, as Clausewitz made clear, subordinate commanders, such as Manstein, have a much more limited sphere within which to apply their intellectual talents.[60] So, in a sense, Manstein's limited perspective, as well as those of his contemporaries, is to be expected. One's perspective is necessarily limited by one's education and training. It might be unwise, in other words, to ask military commanders for advice in applying political or economic power, for which they have little expertise.

Still, the biographies of these commanders, few of which can be considered critical, do not reveal whether their personalities ever truly achieved the Clausewitzian balance of sense and sensibility. They might have had Clausewitz's key attributes, but we cannot determine their proportion. Recent scholarship suggests that systemic problems and cultural conceits proved more important in Germany's defeat in World War II than did individual deficiencies in talent.[61] If so, then what some authors have argued with respect to the apparent attempt to institutionalize genius, military excellence, in the general staff must be judged a failure.[62]

## CONCLUSIONS AND IMPLICATIONS

Contrary to the opinion of some scholars, Clausewitz's concept of friction is not an explanation for why some wars do not reach the absolute. According to this view, 'friction and chance were, for Clausewitz, problems which were likely to distort the plans of political leaders and commanders by *slowing them down*', whereas with modern nuclear weapons those forces might act 'in the opposite direction', that is, by speeding up military activity, thereby causing 'inadvertent escalation'.[63] Any number of actions might occur in a conventional conflict between India and Pakistan, for instance, which could cause one side to escalate to nuclear weapons because it believes, albeit incorrectly, that the other is doing the same.

However, this view is wrong on several counts. First, friction—particularly in the form of uncertainty—is, as Clausewitz said, just as likely to slow down military activity as it is to accelerate it.[64] The more frequent tendency is to exaggerate the capabilities of one's opponent, which in turn generally, but certainly not always, leads to inaction rather than action. Friction is merely the cause of the misjudgment; the misjudgment itself, influenced by the political and social conditions of the day, is what causes the subsequent deceleration or acceleration of military activity. At times the forces that drive war are strong enough to overcome inertia or friction; at other times they are not.[65] Second, this view assumes a direct link between the forms of escalation that culminate in absolute war and war as it appears in reality.[66]

Nonetheless, as we have seen, nuclear war, or any real approximation of total war, does not equate to absolute war. Rather, absolute war and real war are actually products of two parallel lines of inquiry: the first concerns the concept of war examined in a strictly logical sense, the second investigates war's appearances in the physical world. The first line of inquiry shows that war, as a pure concept, can do nothing but escalate, ad infinitum, for there are no forces intrinsic to it that would ever act in a limiting way. This limitless escalation Clausewitz termed absolute war, but he clearly indicated that it is a logical absurdity, not unlike the idea of a circle with four corners. In the physical world, in contrast, whether war escalates at all is essentially a guessing game, an estimate of probabilities. Clausewitz determined from historical study that most wars, in fact, do not escalate for several reasons: the influence exerted by the political purpose, which includes the human tendency to misjudge an adversary's intentions and capabilities; the natural superiority of the defense over the attack, which often brings about a standstill in the fighting; and the general political and social (to include technological) conditions under which the war itself began.

In sum, friction itself does not prevent war from escalating; rather, it keeps war from being executed *perfectly*, or as it was originally conceived in prewar planning. So long as friction is a part of the physical world, it seems safe to assume it will be a part of war. The remedies sought through better technology, more realistic training, and the cultivation of experience may help reduce friction. However, it is better to take such measures and still anticipate encountering friction than to expect it to disappear.

As noted earlier, Clausewitz's concept of military genius was founded on a harmonious balance of qualities of temperament and intellect. While some of these may be more prominent than others, none should be at odds. The concept invariably reveals his prejudices regarding what qualities commanders needed, not only to succeed in war, but to be exceptional. While he endeavored to offer a systematic analysis of genius, what we have instead are one individual's views developed in an era well before psychology became a field of scientific inquiry.

We could apply Clausewitz's concept of genius equally well to military professionals and guerrilla and terrorist leaders. According to some accounts, Osama bin Laden demonstrated the conceptual skills of a genius with the uniqueness of the bombings of 9/11; however, by other accounts, he meddled in the planning of that attack to the point of nearly sabotaging it, and seriously miscalculated how the attack itself would benefit al-Qaeda and its desire to become the dominant force in the larger jihadist movement.[67] Nor is it entirely clear that bin Laden's traits of temperament and intellect were balanced, due, at least in part, to his religious extremism. It is difficult to analyze one's strategy and tactics critically if they are considered divinely inspired. His attacks on 9/11 undoubtedly broke conventional rules, even astonished, if not appalled, the global public. He once enjoyed considerable popularity, even tangible support, among Muslims worldwide, though some polls taken in 2005 show that confidence in bin Laden and his tactics have declined among at least some Muslim populations; Muslim intellectuals have also spoken out against 'bin Ladenism'.[68] Whether any of that will amount to anything significant, however, remains to be seen. None of this is meant to suggest that we should exalt bin Laden as a military genius, but to show that the concept itself, as a framework of analysis, is not limited to conventional military figures.

Clausewitz's views were not only informed by historical study and personal experience, they were shaped by the popular literature and the philosophical debates of his day. He owed an obvious intellectual debt to the Enlightenment in general and to Kant in particular. Romanticism may have opened a few intellectual doors for him, but the path he took was that of systematic analysis, pursuing it as far as possible, capped, ultimately, by judgment. Yet one point is imminently clear in *On War*, namely, that the only factors capable of reducing the influence of intangibles such as chance, uncertainty, danger, and physical exertion in war are other intangibles: the combat experience of a military force and the skill—even genius—of its commander. That this contribution to military theory should make *On War* a work of genius says much about the treatise itself and its competition, both then and now.

## NOTES

1. Daniel Moran, 'Strategic Theory and the History of War', in *Strategy in Contemporary World*, 29–31, eloquently describes Clausewitz's concept of genius as 'the intelligence and willpower of the commander that moves the machinery of war forward, despite the friction that impedes it'.
2. Clifford J. Rogers, 'Clausewitz, Genius, and the Rules', *Journal of Military History*, 66/4 (October 2002), 1167–76, with a response by Jon T. Sumida; this is a brief but interesting debate, in which Rodgers challenged Sumida for stating that Clausewitz believed 'genius rises above the rules'. Such a belief would have undermined the value of rules, which any sound theory requires, and would not have been Clausewitz's intent, especially in a book designed to advance theory. However, both sides of the debate have overlooked Clausewitz's interest in genius's ability to create new rules. Genius can rise above the old rules, as the genius of Gustavus Adolphus and Napoleon did, and use ways and means in different combinations to create new rules: 'for the rules are grounded in the means we possess', and include psychological factors such as genius itself. 'Über die Strategie des Herrn von Bülow', in *Verstruete kleine Schriften*, 81.
3. *Vom Kriege*, II/2, 283; *On War*, 136.
4. *Vom Kriege*, I/3, 'Der kriegerische Genius', 231–52. Despite a growing body of military history, comparatively little concerns military genius: Edward H. Bonekemper III, *A Victor, Not a Butcher: Ulysses S. Grant's Overlooked Military Genius* (Washington, DC: Regnery, 2004); Alt Kaltman, *The Genius of Robert E. Lee: Leadership Lessons for the Outgunned, Outnumbered, and Underfinanced* (Paramus, NJ: Prentice-Hall, 2001); N. G. L. Hammond, *The Genius of Alexander the Great* (Chapel Hill, NC: University of North Carolina Press, 1997); Cecil B. Currey, *Victory at Any Cost: The Genius of Viet Nam's General Vo Nguyen Giap* (Washington, DC: Brassey's, 1997); and Carlo D'Este, *Patton: A Genius for War* (New York: HarperCollins, 1995). One of the first efforts, Col. (Ret.) T. N. Dupuy, *A Genius for War: The German Army and the General Staff, 1807–1945* (Englewood Cliffs, NJ: Prentice-Hall, 1977), is not scholarly.
5. Thomas H. Killion, 'Clausewitz and Military Genius', *Military Review*, 75/4 (1995), 97–100, is an attempt to connect Clausewitz's concept to such contemporary theories.
6. For examples of popular literature, see Harold Bloom, *Genius: A Mosaic of One Hundred Exemplary Creative Minds* (New York: Warner, 2002), 11, which actually defines genius similar to Kant, as 'a transcendental awareness capable of broadening the consciousness of others through exemplary works'. One reason for the decline in scholarly interest was the emergence of so-called scientific measures, such as the Intelligence Quotient (IQ), to restrict entry into elite academic institutions; Catherine Morris Cox, *Genetic Studies of Genius*, vol. II, *The Early Mental Traits of Three Hundred Geniuses* (Standford, CA: Stanford University Press, [1926] 1969), was perhaps the first example of such abuse.

Stephen Jay Gould, *The Mismeasure of Man* (New York: W.W. Norton, 1981), challenges the traditional criteria for identifying genius.
7. For instance, Williamson Murray, Macgregor Knox, and Alvin Bernstein, eds., *The Making of Strategy: Rulers, States, and War* (Cambridge: Cambridge University Press, 1994), examines processes and other factors instead of key individuals, which was the focus of the classic *Makers of Modern Strategy*.
8. Paret, *Clausewitz*, 71.
9. *Vom Kriege*, I/3, 237; *On War*, 104.
10. *Vom Kriege*, I/8, 265; *On War*, 122.
11. The discrepancies could well be evidence of the progress, or lack thereof, of Clausewitz's revisions, as uncertainty and chance relate more closely to the topics discussed in the first chapter of *On War*, where the Prussian theorist introduced the idea of probability.
12. Paret, *Clausewitz*, 124; Paret credits Rothfels, *Clausewitz*, 90, for identifying this as Clausewitz's first use of the term friction; see also Barry D. Watts, *Clausewitzian* Friction and Future War, McNair Paper no. 52; and the Revised Edition, McNair Paper no. 68 (Washington, DC: Institute for National Strategic Studies, 1996 and 2004), 7, 1, respectively.
13. Creveld, 'Transformation of War Revisited', 13–15.
14. *Vom Kriege*, II/2, 286; I/1, 207–8; *On War*, 138, 85–6.
15. *Vom Kriege*, I/4, 253–4; *On War*, 113.
16. *Vom Kriege*, I/4, 254; *On War*, 113.
17. *Vom Kriege*, I/5, 256; *On War*, 115.
18. *Vom Kriege*, I/5, 257; *On War*, 115.
19. David Kahn, 'Clausewitz and Intelligence', in *Clausewitz and Modern Strategy*, 117–25, maintains that technology has partially invalidated Clausewitz's view, but contemporary events show Kahn may have given too much credit to technology. Not surprisingly, some intelligence officers argue that Clausewitz undervalued intelligence; see Victor M. Rosello, 'Clausewitz's Contempt for Intelligence', *Parameters*, 21/1 (spring 1991), 103–14; William M. Nolte, 'Rethinking War and Intelligence', in Anthony D. McIvor (ed.), *Rethinking the Principles of War* (Annapolis, MD: Naval Institute, 2005), 419–39, brings the argument up to date, while acknowledging the verity of Clausewitz's views.
20. Admiral Bill Owens, *Lifting the Fog of War* (New York: Farrar, Straus, Giroux, 2000) is perhaps the best example of such thinking in recent works.
21. Lawrence Freedman, *The Transformation of Strategic Affairs*, Adelphi Paper no. 379 (London: International Institute for Strategic Studies, 2006), 16–26, outlines the opposing views; Colin S. Gray, *Strategy for Chaos: Revolutions in Military Affairs and the Evidence of History* (London: Frank Cass, 2002) is more detailed, and critical.
22. *Vom Kriege*, I/6, 258; *On War*, 117.
23. *Vom Kriege*, I/6, 258; *On War*, 117.

## Genius, Giving the Rule to Art 121

24. *Vom Kriege*, II/2, 289; *On War*, 140.
25. *Vom Kriege*, I/7, 262; *On War*, 120. Katherine L. Herbig, 'Chance and Uncertainty in *On War*', in *Clausewitz and Modern Strategy*, 95–116, attempts to trace the various linkages Clausewitz made between chance and uncertainty, but he essentially saw them as two separate concepts.
26. *Vom Kriege*, I/7, 261; *On War*, 119.
27. *Vom Kriege*, I/7, 261; *On War*, 119.
28. *Vom Kriege*, I/3, 246; *On War*, 110.
29. *Vom Kriege*, I/3, 238; *On War*, 104.
30. *Vom Kriege*, I/3, 234–5; *On War*, 102. Duggan, *Napoleon's Glance*, 3–5, sees this quality as the core of Clausewitz's concept of genius. However, as we have seen, Clausewitz's concept is also a fairly complex balance of sense and sensibility, as well as a talent for innovation.
31. 'On the Life and Character of Scharnhorst', *Historical and Political Writings*, 85–109.
32. 'Campaign of 1812 in Russia', *Historical and Political Writings*, 201–2; see also Moran, 'Strategic Theory', 29–30.
33. In his study of the 1815 campaign, Clausewitz set the record straight about Napoleon's 1814 campaign, where the Corsican claimed to have defeated vastly superior numbers. 'Feldzug von 1815', in *Schriften–Aufsätze–Studien–Briefe*, II, 960–1.
34. *Vom Kriege*, I/3, II/2.
35. Compare: Immanuel Kant, in Wilhelm Weischedel (ed.), *Kritik der Urteilskraft* (Frankfurt, Germany: Suhrkamp, 1974), section 46, pp. 241–2, section 49, pp. 253, 255; Immanuel Kant, in Ernst Behler (ed.), *Philosophical Writings* (New York: Continuum Press, 1986), 224, 233, 235; and Paret, *Clausewitz*, 161.
36. Kiesewetter, *Grundriss*, Part II, 113.
37. For the value of originality, see Brig. Gen. J. P. Kiszely, 'The Contribution of Originality to Military Success', in Brian Holden Reid (ed.), *The Science of War: Back to First Principles* (London: Routledge, 1993), 24–48.
38. Eva Schaper, 'Taste, Sublimity, and Genius: The Aesthetics of Nature and Art', in Paul Guyer (ed.), *The Cambridge Companion to Kant* (Cambridge: Cambridge University Press, 1999), 388–91.
39. 'Über die Strategie Herrn von Bülows', in *Verstreute kleine Schriften*, 81; emphasis original.
40. *Vom Kriege*, II/4, 310–11; *On War*, 154.
41. *Vom Kriege*, II/2, 284; *On War*, 136.
42. *Vom Kriege*, II/4, 311; *On War*, 154.
43. Beiser, *Romanticism*, 57–83, 189–221.
44. Cassirer, *Philosophy of the Enlightenment*, 312–33.
45. Gat, *Origins of Military Thought*, 139–55.
46. On German Romanticism, see Beiser, *Enlightenment*, 189–260; Gordon A. Craig, *The Germans* (New York: Meridian, 1983), 190–212; Sheehan, *German History*, 326–41.

47. Michael Beddow, 'Goethe on Genius', in Penelope Murray (ed.), *Genius: The History of an Idea* (Oxford: Blackwell, 1989), 98–112.
48. Beddow, 'Goethe', 106–11.
49. *Vom Kriege*, I/3, 250–1; *On War*, 111–12.
50. Although Moltke attended the Berlin War College in 1823 while Clausewitz was serving as its director, the two had little, if any, contact. Yet, in an interview in 1890, Moltke named *On War* as one of the books that most influenced him, even though it is obvious from his writings that he disagreed with some of Clausewitz's theories. Kessel, *Moltke*, 108; Reinhard Stumpf (ed.), *Kriegstheorie und Kriegsgeschichte. Carl von Clausewitz, Helmuth von Moltke* (Frankfurt, Germany: Deutscher Klassiker, 1993) places their theories side-by-side.
51. Bucholz, *Moltke and German Wars*, 77–81, 112–13, 154–9. Some of the functions that Moltke's general staff performed resemble those of the US military's regional combatant commands, which do scenario and contingency planning.
52. F. Gobet and H. A. Simon, 'Pattern Recognition Makes Search Possible', *Psychological Research*, 61 (1998), 204–8, and 'The Roles of Recognition Processes and Look-ahead Search in Time-constrained Expert Problem Solving: Evidence from the Grandmaster-level Chess', *Psychological Science*, 7 (1996), 52–5; F. Gobet and A. D. de Groot, *Perception and Memory in Chess: Studies in the Heuristics of the Professional Eye* (Assen, the Netherlands: van Gorcum, 1996); D. H. Holding and R. I. Reynolds, 'Recall or Evaluation of Chess Positions as Determinants of Chess Skill', *Memory & Cognition*, 10 (1982), 237–42.
53. Bucholz, *Moltke and German Wars*, 32–3, 103–4.
54. Compare Schlieffen, 'Der Feldherr', in *Gesammelte Schriften*, 2 vols. (Berlin: E. S. Mittler, 1913), 3–10; and Freytag-Loringhoven, 'Eine Zeit der Rückganges in der Kriegskunst', *Vierteljahreshefte für Truppenführung und Heereskunde*, II, 4 (1905), 597–608.
55. William DePuy, *Generals Balck and von Mellenthin on Tactics: Implications for NATO Doctrine* (Alexandria, Egypt: Defense Technical Information Center, 1980).
56. Erich von Manstein, *Lost Victories*, trans. Anthony Powell, fwd. Capt. B. H. Liddell Hart (Novato, CA: Presidio, 1982), 13.
57. B. H. Liddell Hart, *The German Generals Talk* (New York: Morrow Quill, 1979), 299; on Liddell Hart, see Brian Bond, *Liddell Hart: A Study of His Military Thought* (New Brunswick, NJ: Rutgers University Press, 1977).
58. Omar Bartov, *Hitler's Army: Soldiers, Nazis, and War in the Third Reich* (Oxford: Oxford University Press, 1991).
59. Manstein, *Lost Victories*, 276; Erich v. Manstein, *Verlorene Siege* (Bonn, Germany: Athenäum, 1957), 307.
60. *Vom Kriege*, I/3, 249; *On War*, 111.
61. Geoffrey Megargee, *Inside Hitler's High Command* (Lawrence, KS: University Press of Kansas, 2000).
62. Dupuy, *Genius for War*, fails to appreciate this point.

63. Stephen J. Cimbala, *Clausewitz and Escalation: Classical Perspective on Nuclear Strategy* (London: Frank Cass, 1991), 180, and *Clausewitz and Chaos: Friction in War and Military Policy* (Westport, CT: Praeger, 2001); Richard Ned Lebow, 'Clausewitz and Crisis Stability', *Political Science Quarterly*, 103/1 (spring 1988), 81–110.
64. *Vom Kriege*, I/1, 206; *On War*, 84.
65. *Vom Kriege*, I/1, 209–10; *On War*, 87.
66. See especially, Cimbala, *Clausewitz and Escalation*, 181–3.
67. Gerges, *Far Enemy*, 187–92, and 232–4.
68. 'Support for Terror Wanes among Muslim Publics', The Pew Global Attitudes Project, Washington, DC, July 14, 2005, 2, 6.

# Part III

# Strategy, Balancing Purpose and Means

The first of the following three chapters discusses Clausewitz's concept of strategy, which centered on the use of violence, or the threat of it, as its sole means. The second covers his treatment of a number of strategic principles, some of which were in vogue in his day, and others he discovered in the course of his own observations. The last chapter examines his most misunderstood principle, the center of gravity, in an effort to shed light on the concept's advantages and limitations.

Many of Clausewitz's critics maintain that his definition of strategy—the 'use of engagements to accomplish the purpose of the war'—is too narrow for contemporary warfare.[1] One critic, in fact, goes so far as to say that Western strategic thinking is in a crisis due to the 'domination of a Clausewitzian strategic doctrine that is inappropriate to combating or solving likely conflicts facing the West'.[2] Others look to build on the foundation the Prussian theorist laid, arguing that while he did not have the lexicon of today's strategist available to him and could only grasp at concepts we take for granted, his realization that 'war is a contest of wills' can serve as a useful basis for any contemporary concept of strategy.[3] Still others see little need to modify his definition, maintaining that the Clausewitzian concept of strategy still serves as the basic 'bridge that relates military power to political purpose'.[4] Indeed, this view predominates in many defense universities and staff colleges today. We would do well, therefore, to take a close look at his concept of strategy.

We should remember, first of all, that Clausewitz's definition was in part a reaction to contemporary views, such as von Bülow's, which dismissed, or sought to marginalize, the importance of fighting. Application of the correct geometric angles, or other formulae could obviate the need for battle. 'The history of our times', Clausewitz declared, 'has destroyed this illusion', and, he added, 'if theory can warn of such errors, it would provide those who heed its warning a valuable service'.[5] In short, the emphasis Clausewitz placed on the principle of destruction (*Vernichtungsprinzip*) was not due to a preoccupation with decisive battles, but to a desire to bring military theory back to the reality of war; it had less to do with annihilation, and more to do with using destruction over artificial or 'mechanical' measures.

As the first chapter will show, Clausewitz's definition of strategy, which is founded on a dynamic relationship between purpose and means, is both more limited and broader than many interpretations allow. It is more limited in the sense that it acknowledges only one means, combat or violence, and it was clearly not intended to be anything other than a wartime strategy; by design, it concerns only the employment of the military instrument of power, and only in wartime. The definition is broader in the sense that its means also involve the *threat* of violence, which is more significant than it might appear at first blush, since it includes virtually all military operations and forms of war, to include those in which fighting rarely occurs.

Under Clausewitz's view of strategy, there was also 'no such thing as victory'.[6] Victory belonged to the realm of tactics. Strategy's portion was success, and it succeeded whenever it set the conditions for tactical victories properly, and fully exploited those victories. Thus, strategy made tactical victories possible, and linked them together in a purposeful way. The concerns of the strategist and those of the tactician, though different, were, therefore, intertwined.

The second chapter shows that many of the strategic principles Clausewitz examined in Book III 'On Strategy' correspond to the principles of war (or operations) military practitioners recognize today. His tone throughout Book III, however, is cautionary—pointing out the limitations of those principles, and warning his readers not to view them as keys to victory. As his undated prefatory note indicates, he later found several more principles in the course of writing Books VI and VII. The existence of these principles, he believed, suggested that it might be possible to formulate a theory for the art of war, or strategy, which he had previously discounted due to the complex nature of strategy. Hence, Clausewitz not only believed strategic principles existed for the conduct of war, but also that they were crucial to theory. Nonetheless, those principles he expounded on have hitherto received only scant attention, with the notable exception of the center of gravity, for which the opposite is true. It is the subject of the last chapter.

## LAWS, PRINCIPLES, AND RULES

Before proceeding with our discussion of Clausewitz's strategic principles, we must first understand how he distinguished between laws, principles, and rules, and how they fit into his larger explanatory scheme of cause and effect.

Borrowing again from Kant—or more precisely Kiesewetter—Clausewitz saw physical events as governed by a logical hierarchy of laws (*Gesetze*), principles (*Grundsätze*), rules (*Regeln*), regulations and directives (*Vorschriften und Ausweisungen*), and procedures (*Methoden*).[7] Each category is less authoritative and less comprehensive than its predecessor. The last two, regulations and procedures, do not appear to have been derived from Kant, but rather from Clausewitz's own military experience.

## Laws

Laws form the first and most fundamental part of the hierarchy:

Law, the most universal concept that is equally applicable to both understanding and action, in its literal sense clearly has something subjective and arbitrary about it; yet it also expresses that very thing upon which we and our environment depend. From the standpoint of understanding, law is the relationship of things and their effects to one another. From the standpoint of wanting to take action, law is the determinant of action, and in this sense it is equivalent to the terms legal or illegal.[8]

Accordingly, in Clausewitz's view, laws were derived from the major cause-and-effect relationships that explain why things happen the way they do in the physical world. Examples outside the domain of war include the law of gravity, the laws of motion, and the laws of attraction and repulsion that govern magnetic objects. Without such laws, neither principles nor rules are possible.

Kiesewetter's *Outline of Logic* sheds further light on the definition of a law, which Clausewitz's use of the term elsewhere in *On War* also follows. Kiesewetter explained that laws must be both 'universal and necessary'.[9] They must apply everywhere, and they must be ineluctable in terms of logic. The law of gravity, for example, applies everywhere, and it is a force for which physics must account. If it were removed, another identical law would have to take its place. Otherwise, it would be impossible to perform simple physics calculations, and a great many occurrences in the physical world would thus go unexplained. As Kiesewetter further clarified, 'laws are universal rules whereby multifarious elements are brought together in unity'.[10] In short, laws bring unity and order to what otherwise would be nothing more than random, unrelated events.

Consequently, Clausewitz could claim that 'fighting (*das Gefecht*) is the highest *law* of war'.[11] While he believed that the purposes war served were many, he held that only one means, fighting or combat, existed for accomplishing them. Even in cases where fighting did not actually occur, the threat of it was present and invariably influenced events, especially if one side or the other decided to avoid combat because it perceived that the probability of achieving a favorable outcome was low. Avoiding something because we fear its effects only reinforces its significance.

Moreover, as Clausewitz pointed out, armed forces were raised, trained, organized, equipped, and otherwise prepared for a single reason only, to fight. All the time, money, and other resources that went into creating a military force were intended to make it more effective at one activity, fighting. Fighting—the use of violence, or the threat of violence, to achieve the purpose of the war—thus 'winds its way through the whole fabric of military activity and holds it together'.[12] Violence was thus the key ingredient that distinguished war from other social and political phenomena, as well as the unifying law that held his theoretical system together.

Yet, while maintaining that combat was the supreme law of war, Clausewitz could also argue—without contradiction—that *laws of action* were not necessary for constructing a valid theory of strategy. He distinguished between laws as explanations of cause-and-effect relationships, and laws that prescribed action; the nature of war was too variable and diverse for laws of action to work consistently.[13] In other words, even though battle is the supreme law of war, we cannot conclude on that basis that we must act in a certain way—that is, use a particular strategy, or deploy our forces in a specific manner—every time war breaks out. Rather than searching for such laws, Clausewitz proposed to search for that which was universally true about war. If laws, principles, and rules emerged in the process, he would acknowledge them and incorporate them into his theory. Thus, understanding the cause-and-effect relationships that underpinned war did not mean we could predict the outcome of a war, which was still a function of probabilities. It could, however, provide food for the nourishment of judgment.

## Principles

The next element of the logical hierarchy, principles, Clausewitz defined as deductions that reflected the 'spirit and sense' of a law. Principles were thus more elastic than laws, though their scope was actually more limited. If the law of combat governs war, the principle of mass governs certain operations within war; it is thus more flexible than a law, but applies to a more limited part of the subject. Any number of principles might fall under a single law; however, laws cannot be subordinated to principles.

Clausewitz divided principles into two types: objective, those valid for all; and subjective, those valid only for an individual. In the latter case, a principle was essentially the same as a maxim.[14] By way of illustration, the principles he outlined for the Prussian crown prince in the essay entitled, *The Most Important Principles for the Conduct of War*, equate to maxims more than guidelines.[15] He declared, for instance, that the maxim of pursuing 'one great decisive aim with force and determination' should take 'first place among all causes of victory in the modern art of war'.[16] Some of Clausewitz's interpreters have mistaken this particular maxim as the essence of his theory, but we should see this essay on *The Most Important Principles* as subjective in nature, valid for the crown prince and the wars of his day. Clausewitz clearly regarded them as such.

As Clausewitz explained in Book II, chapter 2, 'On the Theory of War', he initially thought developing strategic principles was too difficult because change and uncertainty were greater in strategy than tactics. He, therefore, offered the following examples of tactical principles: cavalry must not be used against unbroken infantry, except in emergencies; firearms should not be discharged until the enemy is within effective range; one should hold back as many troops as possible for the final phase of the fight.[17]

Throughout *On War*, Clausewitz stressed the importance of grasping the meaning behind principles, rather than treating them as rigid rules. Applying principles was, in his mind, a matter of experienced judgment, and also required a certain intuition or sensibility. The tendency in stressful situations such as war is to reach for checklists that prescribe action, rather than to exercise one's judgment. The modern military theorist, J. F. C. Fuller, purportedly abandoned his quest to develop principles of war because the British army had begun to treat them as prescriptive rules.[18] Fuller's principles had essentially become laws, rather than reflecting the spirit and sense of laws.

## Rules

The next element in the hierarchy, rules, Clausewitz defined, in a manner most confusing to the reader, as general 'laws of action'.[19] Rules were less authoritative and less comprehensive than principles. Nonetheless, they were, like laws, derived from war's underlying cause-and-effect relationships. The primary difference between rules and laws, as he attempted to explain, was that the former admitted of exceptions, while the latter did not. Clausewitz offered the following example to illustrate his point: as a rule, when our adversary begins to withdraw his artillery, it means he is giving up the fight. The decision to concede the field of battle is the cause; the withdrawal of the artillery is the effect. The effect, in turn, becomes a cause if, for instance, it prompts us to attack to exploit the apparent vulnerability of our foe. The exception that proves the rule is, of course, that the withdrawal could be a trick to lure us into attacking prematurely. Hence, the need for judgment.

As Clausewitz noted, the chain of causality that underpins rules resembles the way in which we apply shortcuts in mathematics. For instance, it is not necessary for us to prove Pythagoras' theorem—that the square of the hypotenuse of a right triangle equals the sum of the squares of the other two sides ($a^2 + b^2 = c^2$)—every time we apply it. We merely identify it, take the shortcut it affords, and move on to solve the remainder of the problem. In a sense, however, Clausewitz's example of mathematical shortcuts failed him: for Pythagoras' theorem, which is universally valid for all right triangles, can never have an exception in quite the same way as the withdrawal of an opponent's artillery can.

## Regulations and Procedures

*On War* defines regulations as drill instructions, and procedures as methods, such as those outlined in most field manuals.[20] While regulations and methods might seem too trivial to bother with in an objective theory of armed conflict, Clausewitz considered them critical to the conduct of war, since the sum of individual actions has a significant bearing on the larger outcome. A military force that does not encourage individual initiative, for instance, must fight differently than one that does, and may well be at a disadvantage because of it. Also, regulations and procedures tend to build and reinforce certain habits of thought and perception; these in turn lay some solutions bare, while masking others. Regulations and procedures are, as he pointed out, designed to work in *most* situations, and on average point to the correct solution. They are especially valuable at the lower ranks, or when a military's skill and experience levels are slight. Regulations and procedures thus provide an obvious and crucial link between preparation for war and how it is conducted.

Clausewitz also acknowledged the value of drill and repetition: 'through the constant repetition of a formal exercise, a sense of *readiness, precision,* and *security* is attained in the movement of troops which diminishes the natural friction, and makes the machine operate more easily'.[21] However, he also underscored the harm mechanical repetition could cause if it worked its way to the higher ranks, with commanders imitating the methods of great generals without first analyzing and reflecting on them. Only a 'tolerable theory, a sensible analysis of the conduct of war', can provide commanders an opportunity to educate themselves, and avoid 'mindless imitation'.[22]

## NOTES

1. *Vom Kriege*, III/1, 345; *On War*, 177.
2. Jan Willem Honig, 'Strategy in a Post-Clausewitzian Setting', in *Clausewitzian Dictum*, 109; see also Jeff Huber, 'Clausewitz is Dead', *Proceedings*, 127/3 (March 2001), 119–21, who asserts that for 'Clausewitz "the aim of all action in war is to disarm the enemy"' and that 'this has not been true in any U.S. war since World War II'.
3. Beatrice Heuser, 'Clausewitz's Concept of Strategy and its Relevance for Today', conference paper, 'Clausewitz in the 21st Century', Oxford University, March 21, 2005; see also Uwe Hartmann, *Carl von Clausewitz and the Making of Modern Strategy* (Potsdam: Miles, 2002), 42–6.
4. Colin S. Gray, *Modern Strategy* (Oxford: Oxford University Press, 1999), 17; see also Richard K. Betts, 'Is Strategy an Illusion?', *International Security*, 25/2 (fall 2002), 5–50, who describes it as the 'link between military means and political ends', 5.
5. *Vom Kriege*, IV/11, 470; *On War*, 259–60.
6. *Vom Kriege*, VI/3, 622; *On War*, 363.
7. *Vom Kriege*, II/4, 305–6; *On War*, 151–2.
8. *Vom Kriege*, II/4, 305; *On War*, 151.
9. Kiesewetter, *Grundriss*, I, 7.
10. Kiesewetter, *Darstellung*, Part II, 9.
11. *Vom Kriege*, I/2, 229; *On War*, 99; emphasis added.
12. *Vom Kriege*, I/2, 225; *On War*, 97.
13. *Vom Kriege*, II/4, 305–06; *On War*, 151–2.
14. *Vom Kriege*, II/4, 305; *On War*, 151.
15. Grundsätze des Kriegführens'. Although Clausewitz admitted his principles for the crown prince were 'hastily drawn up', he nonetheless believed they were sound in content. 'Grundsätze', 1047.
16. 'Grundsätze', 1047.
17. *Vom Kriege*, II/4, 307; *On War*, 152.
18. John I. Alger, *The Quest for Victory: The History of the Principles of War* (Westport, CT: Greenwood, 1982), 122–3.
19. *Vom Kriege*, II/4, 306; *On War*, 152.
20. *Vom Kriege*, II/4, 305–7; *On War*, 152.
21. *Vom Kriege*, II/4, 309; *On War*, 153; emphasis original.
22. *Vom Kriege*, II/4, 310; *On War*, 154.

# 6

# Combat, War's only Means

As noted earlier, Clausewitz's definition of strategy, 'the use of engagements to accomplish the purpose of the war', recognizes only one means, combat or fighting. Yet it is actually broader than his critics admit, and demonstrably valid even in today's postmodern setting. In judging his definition unfit, his detractors typically commit at least one of two classic errors: first, they mistake conclusions he drew from the pure concept of war, that is, war considered from a strictly logical standpoint, as reflective of his approach to strategy; second, they overlook the critical point that his definition of war's means includes not only violence, but the *threat* of violence.[1]

In contrast to contemporary definitions of strategy, Clausewitz's concept places the onus on strategy itself to establish conditions that would increase the likelihood of tactical victory, and then to take an active role in exploiting that victory once it is achieved. Contemporary views tend to require tactics to find a way to succeed within the parameters set by strategy. The essential difference, then, is that under Clausewitz's concept, strategy facilitates tactical success, while contemporary definitions, influenced in part by the doctrine of limited war, tend to circumscribe it. This chapter examines each of these important aspects of Clausewitz's concept of strategy.

## THE CENTRALITY OF COMBAT

Clausewitz spent the entire Book IV 'The Engagement' examining what he referred to as war's only genuine means, fighting, which ranged in magnitude from a simple encounter or engagement (*Gefecht*) to a major battle (*Schlacht*): fighting, or combat, regardless of its magnitude or extent, he said, 'is the only real means in war; everything else merely supports it'.[2] He defined an engagement as the 'bloody and destructive clash of physical and psychological forces', in other words, naked combat or fighting.[3] The purpose of fighting, he went on to say, was to destroy the combat capacity of one's adversary; hence, the principle of destruction was the dominant characteristic of war. In fact, this 'simple idea' (*einfache Vorstellung*) formed the underlying purpose of all engagements:

> Every engagement has its own particular purpose which is subordinate to the general one...but we can regard the complete or partial destruction of the adversary the exclusive purpose of all engagements.[4]

Although Clausewitz's definition pertains to the engagement in its 'absolute form' (*absoluten Gestalt*), that is, as a microcosm of war itself, it is still broader than his critics allow. He did not equate destruction to complete annihilation, as many of his later interpreters did, and in some cases still do.[5] Rather, he defined it simply as diminishing an opponent's forces at a rate proportionally greater than that suffered by friendly forces.[6] Destruction could range from 'total' to 'a degree only sufficient to prevent the foe from carrying on the fight', and one could achieve the foe's destruction 'by killing or wounding, or by other means'.[7] Moreover, he later expanded his definition of engagements, adding that they might serve other purposes besides destruction, such as conquest or defense of an area or an object, and deceiving an enemy; the purpose of an engagement, thus, depends on circumstances.[8] Yet these qualifications are missed by most of his interpreters.

Clausewitz's discussions in Book IV lack the conciseness and crisp organization we find in *On War*'s introductory chapter. The transition between the pure concept and its modifications in reality in ways that are not always apparent to the reader. Consequently, many of his critics (as well as some of his advocates) have taken his pure concept of the engagement for his overall view. His pure concept of the engagement parallels his pure concept of war, which centers on the following ideas: (*a*) destruction of the enemy's armed forces is the main principle (*Prinzip*) of war and the primary way of achieving the military aim (*Ziel*), (*b*) destruction is accomplished mainly by means of the engagement, (*c*) only major engagements produce major results, (*d*) results are greatest when all engagements are combined into a single battle, and (*e*) the commander can direct events with his own hands only in a major battle.[9] These ideas, in turn, are consistent with his pure concept of victory: (*a*) complete or partial destruction of the enemy's armed forces, (*b*) occupation of his country, and (*c*) breaking his will to fight.[10] Specifically, tactical victory occurred when an opponent suffered (*a*) greater loss of physical forces, (*b*) greater loss of psychological forces (morale), or (*c*) when he visibly abandoned his intentions.[11] The pure concepts thus have a logical consistency, but they do not reflect war in reality.

As readers recall, Chapter 2 of this study revealed that Clausewitz's pure concept of war obeys the strict laws of logical necessity. In contrast, material or real war, the crux of his general understanding of war, falls under the laws of probability. Hence, Clausewitz's observations regarding the engagement or victory—as derived from the pure concept of war—do not necessarily apply to material war. Readers might do well, therefore, to consider his use of the pure concept of war as something of a foil, or a straw man, which he establishes only to refute later.

Clausewitz noted that in real war fighting served many purposes, ranging from such petty motives as celebrating the birthday of a monarch, satisfying military honor, or nourishing the vanity of the commander, to larger goals, such as capturing territories for use in negotiations, or outright conquest.[12] Regardless of the purpose, all wars involve only one means, violence, whether or not that means is widespread or of high intensity. We must consider Clausewitz's emphasis on *Vernichtungsprinzip* within the context of his desire to expose and replace the 'completely false views, tendencies, and fragments of systems, whereby theory thought it had elevated itself above common practice'.[13] As he explained, he was seeking to 'counter that most ingenious idea', which considered it possible to 'shorten the road' to victory by applying small amounts of violence with precision to achieve a 'paralysis' of the enemy's physical forces and his will to fight.[14] Unfortunately, many of Clausewitz's detractors simply overlooked such statements, arguing, as did Liddell Hart, famous architect of the so-called 'indirect approach', that the Prussian theorist had merely 'reduced the art of war to the mechanics of mass slaughter'.[15]

To be sure, Clausewitz's views originated with his observations that the conduct of war had changed with the French Revolution and the rise of Napoleon, both of which contributed to bringing the principle of destruction to the fore.[16] Indeed, he clearly believed Napoleon, more than history's other great commanders, had brought war nearest to its 'absolute' form, taking war to a heretofore unsurpassed level of escalation by mobilizing the hostility of the French populace to an unparalleled extent, by pursuing the extreme military aim of rendering an opponent defenseless, and by exerting the utmost violence or force. Consequently, the battles of the day were essentially fights to the finish: 'the warlike element, aroused by national interests, has broken out and is following its natural course'.[17] As he went on to say:

We consider a major battle to be a decisive element, though admittedly not the only one, that would be necessary in a war or a campaign... [even] an intended battle is, to the extent allowed by circumstances, to be considered the temporary means—and thus the center of gravity (*Schwerpunkt*) of the entire war plan.[18]

However, the reason for Napoleon's success, as Clausewitz discussed in Book VIII, was not so much that the Corsican followed the true spirit of war, but rather that new political and social conditions permitted commanders who wanted to seek decisive battles to do so.[19] How long this would remain the case no one could say: 'Barriers, which to a certain extent exist only due to lack of knowledge of what is possible, are not so easily erected again once they are torn down'.[20] Still, future conditions, Clausewitz realized, could differ substantially from those of his day.

## THE THREAT OF COMBAT

Although combat might occur infrequently in some forms of conflict, in Clausewitz's view that did not invalidate fighting itself as an underlying law of war. As long as the threat of combat was present, which it invariably is, it remained valid as a cause-and-effect relationship. The 'decision by arms', Clausewitz explained, 'is for all major and minor operations in war what the simple settling of accounts is in commerce; however remote this transaction is, however seldom such settlements occur, they could never be absent entirely'.[21]

Historically, anticipation of an unfavorable outcome has often induced one party, or both, to avoid combat. The Italian *Condottieri*, for instance, while making great displays of martial virtue, typically shunned the actual task of fighting—bloody outcomes being bad for business.[22] Similarly, warrior monarchs of the eighteenth century frequently found victories on the battlefield almost Pyrrhic in nature, which explains the greater emphasis on maneuver: as Frederick the Great said of his victory at the battle of Torgau (1760), where he lost more than a third of his troops, it was 'an event that preserves us from great misfortunes, rather than a triumph', and he refused to let his adjutants post the numbers.[23]

The avoidance of open confrontation was the case as well in the Cold War, since NATO and the Warsaw Pact both determined that victory would cost nearly as much as defeat, with little actually gained in the end. The same logic applies to guerrilla warfare and terrorism, where one side chooses to avoid a stand-up fight, since its chances of winning by that route are slight.[24] In other words, if battles and engagements did not occur, it was because the anticipation of their likely outcomes influenced the decisions and actions of the belligerent parties. A show of force, for instance, can accomplish its purpose without firing a shot—this validates rather than undermines the value of force as a strategic tool. 'Every strategic act', concluded Clausewitz, eventually 'comes back to the idea of an engagement, because strategy is the use of military forces, and the idea of the engagement lies at the root of that use'.[25] Therefore, whether fighting actually occurred or its outcomes were merely imagined, the cause-and-effect relationship, the law, of combat remained in his eyes universally valid.

Some of Clausewitz's critics argue that because his definition of strategy, like his concept of war in general, holds destruction, or the threat of it, at its center, it does not apply to those forms of war, like insurgency or guerrilla warfare, in which fighting is peripheral. The British officer and military writer T.E. Lawrence, who guided Arab tribes in partisan activities against the Turks in World War I, said of guerrilla wars, that 'more than half the battle' takes place behind the front lines, in the minds of the belligerent and neutral populations, and that guerrillas have 'many humiliating material limits, but no moral impossibilities'.[26] In such wars, violence is generally dispersed, with the guerrillas seeking to avoid major battles, at least initially; military activity is usually limited and decentralized at the outset, with the front seemingly 'nowhere and everywhere'.[27]

The essential ingredient for waging guerrilla or Peoples' wars, according to Mao Zedong, is not overwhelming force, but patience. Such wars, in other words, are often 'nasty, brutish, and long'.[28] A Maoist Peoples' war, which became the model followed in China (1946–58), Vietnam (1946–54, 1958–75), and Cuba (1956–59), typically consist of three phases: (*a*) creating and consolidating a political base of support among the population, (*b*) expanding that base by bold attacks to force one's opponent on the defensive, and (*c*) launching a full-scale counteroffensive.[29] Conventional wisdom says the main target of attacks launched in phases 1 and 2, even if they strike military and other security forces, is actually popular opinion. The goal of such attacks is to create a 'general climate of insecurity', which causes the public to lose confidence in the government's ability to protect it, and to build support for the insurgency.[30] This selective use of violence for political purposes only confirms Clausewitz's views regarding the law of combat.

Clausewitz was certainly aware of the significance of insurgencies, guerrilla wars, and partisan activities. He addressed such wars directly, if all too briefly, in chapter 26 'Arming the Populace' of Book VI, referring to such conflicts collectively as an 'observable fact (*Erscheinung*) of the nineteenth century', and he provided some valuable insights into their nature.[31] In 1810 and 1811, he even delivered a series of lectures at the War College on the subject of small wars (*Kleinkrieg*), which were based on his analyses of French operations in the Vendee and the Spanish insurrection against Napoleon.[32] For the most part, the lectures aimed at instructing junior officers in tactics and techniques appropriate for countering guerrillas and partisans.[33] He did, however, strongly urge the Prussian monarchy to pursue a strategy of insurrection against Napoleon after the defeat at Jena-Auerstädt; he was, thus, clearly aware of the advantages of that form of war. Clausewitz, like Jomini, also acknowledged that such small wars were an effective means of resisting an invading force by disrupting its lines of communication, harassing and attacking its small detachments, and destroying its supply depots.[34]

What T.E. Lawrence said of guerrilla wars, of course, holds true of all wars. If we learn only one thing from Clausewitz's *On War*, it ought to be that all wars, regardless of form or type, are much more political than they seem. As Samuel Huntington reminded us, forms of war differ completely from types of war. The former is a 'variety of military activity involving particular military forces, weapons, and tactics', such as naval blockades, conventional ground campaigns, and air bombardments.[35] The latter is a kind of interaction based on the nature of the participants, their goals, and the resources they use; types of war include: total war, general war, limited war, and revolutionary war.[36] Others have underscored the point that Clausewitz's conception of the nature of war, and its relationship with the political environment of any given time, makes his theories compatible with conflicts of lesser intensity.[37]

Moreover, *On War* clearly acknowledges the utility of other, seemingly less bloody, strategic measures—such as dividing or rendering ineffective an opponent's alliance, or gaining new allies, or initiating favorable political events—which could directly influence the political balance of power, and thereby increase one's probability of success; such measures would 'offer a much shorter way to the aim than the destruction of the hostile armed forces'.[38] In other words, Clausewitz saw 'many ways to the aim and not every case is tied to the overthrow of the opponent'.[39] However, here again, the threat of force underpins the effectiveness of all such efforts: 'Every strategic combination rests only on tactical successes, and these overall—in bloody as well as bloodless solutions—are the actual fundamental causes of the decision'.[40]

## STRATEGY'S 'QUIET LABOR'

Under Clausewitz's view, strategy aligns the military aim (*Ziel*) with the war's overall purpose (*Zweck*), thus fulfilling a critical interpretive function. The military aim, in turn, provides the focal point for the war plan, and sets the aim and parameters for each campaign plan.[41] In this way, strategy's interpretive function also helps to integrate separate military actions into a larger scheme. However, neither strategy's task nor Clausewitz's contribution to strategic theory ends there: strategy also performed critical preparatory and finishing functions. In other words, in contrast to contemporary practice, as exemplified in the Gulf war of 1990–1 and in Kosovo, where strategy delimited tactical objectives, Clausewitz expected strategy to maximize the probability as well as the rewards of victory.[42] 'Strategy', in short, 'determines when, where, and with what forces, the fighting will occur; by means of this threefold determination it exerts a very important influence on the outcome of the engagement'.[43]

This activity was the 'quiet labor' of strategy, for which the strategist rarely received recognition.[44] Strategy performed its labor by providing every possible advantage to the commander whose task it was to win the engagements. Such advantages included, but were not limited to: having the greatest possible numerical superiority over one's opponent, making the best use of the geographic circumstances of the theater of war, and implementing measures to protect one's lines of communication and supply. *On War* actually identifies five elements of strategy which influence the outcome of engagements: (*a*) intellectual and psychological factors, such as the genius of the commander and the experience and spirit of the military force; (*b*) physical elements, which included the size, composition, and the nature of the arms of the military force; (*c*) mathematical or geometrical factors, such as lines of operation and converging attacks; (*d*) geographical elements, such as the influence of rivers, mountains, and other types of terrain; and (*e*) statistical factors, such as logistical support and maintenance.[45]

At first glance, these elements seem more operational or tactical than strategic in nature. However, Clausewitz rightly believed that decisions made by political and military leaders either prior to or during a conflict would influence tactical situations either directly or indirectly. As J.C. Wylie, an erstwhile strategic theorist and naval officer, remarked: 'The Congressman voting on a military appropriation is, in a very real sense indeed, making a fundamental strategic decision'.[46] Similarly, a political decision to enter a conflict without waiting to secure a few more allies or coalition partners could adversely affect physical elements, such as size of friendly forces, when it came time to fighting battles. Likewise, political considerations could well preclude using certain geographical elements in the defense of one's territory.

Although the elements of strategy were not difficult to comprehend, they were not necessarily easy to apply. 'Everything in war is very simple', as Clausewitz famously remarked, 'but the simplest thing is difficult'.[47] That intangible quality, judgment, was once again the key. As we have seen, Clausewitz's concept of genius—or the balanced mix of judgment and courage—is in many respects the counterpoise to the inherent unpredictability and friction of war.[48] *On War* does make it clear, in any case, that one of strategy's critical, if unheralded, tasks is to create the best possible conditions for winning battles or engagements.

We find little evidence in Clausewitz's works that he considered the possibility that a military success, if too great, might prove counterproductive to accomplishing the war's political purpose. In the 1973 Arab–Israeli war, the United States gave material support to Israel early on, but only enough for it to achieve a limited military victory, thereby requiring it to come to the negotiating table in good faith.[49] In contrast, Clausewitz, not unlike other military thinkers of the nineteenth century, seems to have believed that the greater the military victory, the more completely it served the political purpose. He did not dismiss moral or ethical issues with regard to the conduct of war, as the advocate of just-war theory, Michael Walzer, has claimed, but instead rolled them into politics, or rather political conditions, which help shape how war is fought in different eras.[50]

Notably, Clausewitz recognized only two levels of war: strategic, which, again, he defined as the use of battles to achieve the political purpose of the war; and tactical, meaning the art of winning battles or engagements. Nonetheless, he made frequent use of modern operational terms—such as the campaign plan (*Feldzugsplan*), a theater of war (*Kriegstheater*), and zones of operation (*Heergebiete*).[51] Much of what he had to say on those subjects, therefore, pertains to the operational level of war, even though that level did not formally exist in the military theory or doctrine of his day.[52] Clausewitz considered the close linking of purpose and means created by strategy important even on campaign. War plans were inevitably based on assumptions which might prove incorrect as events unfolded. Hence, Clausewitz advocated making strategic decisions as close to the front as possible so strategy could appreciate changes in the situation as they occurred, and then could quickly modify the campaign plans or the overall war plan accordingly. 'Strategy', he insisted, 'can not, even for a moment, withdraw its hand from the task'.[53] The conduct of operations was not a separate level of war, as it is regarded today, but an integral part of strategy.

In any case, the invention of the operational level of war—which ostensibly ties strategy and tactics more closely together—has not necessarily improved the conduct of war from the standpoint of linking purpose and means. Some analysts argue that the operational level of war does not apply in all cases, and that we ought not to let it become a rigid framework.[54] Others maintain that modern information technologies and speed of movement have combined to force the levels of war to merge or blend together.[55] Indeed, the operational level of war may have inadvertently created an excuse for tacticians to avoid thinking strategically, and for strategists to avoid considering military problems from a tactical perspective. In any case, Clausewitz saw strategy and tactics as inextricably linked: the former presupposes the success of the latter, and 'must never be considered as something independent'.[56] Whenever a change occurs in the nature of tactics, therefore, that change must also influence strategy.[57]

Clausewitz also insisted that strategy must exploit any tactical victory thoroughly; in other words, it had to perform a critical finishing function: 'If tactics has conducted the battle, if the result is at hand, be it victory or defeat, strategy makes such use of it as is possible in accordance with the overall purpose of the war'.[58] Those purposes may vary, he noted, and may seem far removed from the fighting. For Clausewitz, the exploitive function of strategy primarily took the form of physical pursuit, relentlessly chasing a defeated enemy to make his destruction as complete as possible. 'Without pursuit', he explained, 'no victory can have a significant effect'.[59] Again, he regarded pursuit as a strategic rather than a tactical matter: tactical results happen within the scope of battle, and especially within the period of exhaustion and disorder—the moment of crisis—that occurs just before the decision; in contrast, strategic results come about outside the scope of battle, after its conclusion, and after the total effect of the individual engagements is felt.[60] As he further explained, in the case of pursuit, 'strategy approximates tactics' in order to complete its task, and thus strategy's foremost concern is always to demand the 'fullest completion of the victory'.[61]

The energy with which we choose to pursue our foe, Clausewitz believed, largely determines the extent of our success. In his view, the ability to envision and prosecute pursuit beyond the battlefield required a strategic perspective. Tacticians typically busy themselves with consolidating gains, accounting for casualties, policing up stragglers, collecting prisoners, and otherwise reorganizing and rearming their forces. Strategists, on the other hand, look to prevent the enemy from fleeing and living to fight another day; strategists should think not only about sending troops after the foe, but ahead of him, anticipating where the opponent's line of retreat might take him and dispatching forces in those directions. Thus, even prior to the battle, strategy must consider ways of maximizing an adversary's losses through the exploitation of tactical victory. Even if the outcome of a battle or an engagement is never wholly predictable, giving thought to exploitation beforehand prepares commanders and their staffs to recognize opportunities when they occur. Every victory, however great, eventually reaches its culminating point—where its temporal and spatial influence begins to diminish—and strategists must always bear that in mind.[62] In other words, winning the battle itself was only part of the task; the second, more critical part was to exploit it, and exploitation, for Clausewitz, was essentially a race against time and across space.

## A THEORY OF DECISIVE BATTLE?

Clausewitz's *On War* is a combat-centric theory of war, with war revolving around the activity of fighting just as Copernicus' planetary system revolved around the sun, rather than a theory advocating pursuit of victory through decisive battles. The gist of Book IV is simply that fighting is the purpose that underpins all military activity, and if we want to inflict major results on an opponent's forces, we must seek a major engagement, a battle. Clausewitz's efforts to construct a combat-centric theory of war, which he equated to a revolution in military theory, had a greater physical impact on the conduct of war than he could have foreseen, though most of it was due to the influence of Napoleon's way of fighting than the arguments in *On War*. This was particularly true in the case of Clausewitz's German heirs, especially his most famous beneficiary, the elder Moltke. Like Clausewitz, Moltke saw strategy as the application of established principles for the purpose of bringing about conditions favorable for tactical success: strategy was a 'free, practical, artistic activity' that took advantage of unexpected opportunities and reacted to unpredictable factors, such as 'weather, illnesses, railway accidents, misunderstandings, and disappointments'.[63] Yet, for Moltke, tactics were pre-eminent: once strategy established the conditions for victory it was to fall 'silent' until tactical success was achieved. Tactics, for its part, was in all cases to accomplish the most complete destruction of the foe possible under the circumstances.

Interestingly, Clausewitz saw the completion of the victory as a function of strategy, while Moltke considered it the responsibility of tactics. For Moltke, strategic principles thus yielded to tactical ones once the battle began. Afterward, strategy became active again and made use of the results of tactical success for the purposes of the war.[64] Moltke often equated grand strategy to policy—the province of statesmen—and insisted that while policy had the right to establish the goals for the conflict, and could change them when it saw fit to do so, it had no right to interfere with the conduct of operations. Also, contrary to Clausewitz's belief that asking military commanders to provide purely military advice was nonsensical, Bismarck asked Moltke for precisely that kind of advice before each of the campaigns in the wars of unification—Denmark (1864), Austria (1866), and France (1870–1)—and Moltke, of course, obliged him.[65] In short, Moltke acknowledged the importance of the logic of war, but insisted that the grammar took precedence during the actual fighting.

Moltke is credited with saying that strategy is nothing more than an 'ad hoc system of expedients'.[66] However, rather than developing campaign strategies on the fly as this statement might imply, Moltke and his staff actually ran and reran numerous scenarios until he had a clear sense of the opportunities and pitfalls that awaited him, and his foe, if certain situations occurred in the campaign. In this way, he was able to contemplate in advance how best to respond to crisis situations; even though the actual situations that occurred never completely matched the scenarios that were war gamed, this process gave Moltke a considerable edge over his adversaries.[67] In other words, his campaigns in the wars of unification were much more than an ad hoc—or wait-and-react—approach in action.

Schlieffen's approach to strategy, in direct contrast to Moltke's, was closer to Clausewitz's in one respect, but well removed in another. As regards military strategy, Schlieffen placed strategic requirements—at least with regard to land forces—before tactical considerations. Not only should strategy determine where, when, and with what forces the fight should take place, it should also dictate the tactical methods to be used to ensure the most complete victory. This perspective, which many in his day, and since, have criticized for being too restrictive, marks a decisive break from the Moltkean tradition, and tends toward the approach in vogue today. Rather than tactical success *pulling* strategy, as per Moltke's view, Schlieffen felt strategy should *push* tactics to achieve a certain kind of success, one that best served the purposes of military strategy. It might be decisive victory in one sector, but a holding action in another. The battles along the front were to be considered as a totality, as a *Gesamtschlacht*.[68] However, Schlieffen also believed, in contradistinction to Clausewitz, that military strategy should take precedence over the war's political purposes. If military victory could not be achieved, any discussion of political purposes was superfluous.

The emphasis on decisive battles continued to characterize not only the German way of war, but also that of the West overall, well into the twentieth century.[69] The tendency, particularly in the US military has been to separate the grammar from the logic of war, and to forget that each is meaningless without the other.[70] In some ways this partitioning is inevitable. We separate purpose and means in order to study them more closely. Yet, in practice, we should think of them as complementary components of a dual-law, similar in nature to the law of supply and demand, where changes in the one invariably affect the other. Unfortunately, when pushed, strategists tend to prefer purpose, while tacticians incline toward means. The imminent historian of strategic thinking, Bernard Brodie, for instance, stressed that 'the influence of the purposes on the means must be continuing and pervasive'.[71] In contrast, the accomplished theorist of naval tactics, Wayne Hughes, opined that:

Strategy and tactics are best thought of as handmaidens, but if one must choose, it is probably more correct to say that tactics come first, because they dictate the limits of strategy.... Strategy is paramount in determining the aims of the tactician. But strategy is limited by means. An assessment of means—the combat power available and its utility to achieve strategic objectives—starts with an adequate understanding of the tactical employment of forces in battle.[72]

Again, neither logic nor grammar is meaningful without the other. Yet the history of war shows that the two are at odds more often than not.

The manner in which Clausewitz's definition of strategy links purpose and means closely resembles that of the ends-ways-means concept that characterizes contemporary strategic theory. Under his definition, the term means includes the activity of fighting as well as the forces which do the fighting; contemporary theory would refer to fighting as a 'way', or a method, as distinct from the means, the military forces themselves.[73] A prerequisite for good strategy, as for good war-making, however, is an understanding of the nature of the various purposes we might wish to pursue as well as of the means—the activity or method as well as the tool—we use, and how each influences the other. Advancing that understanding is basically the point of On War.

## CONCLUSIONS AND IMPLICATIONS

Although Clausewitz was well aware that, at the highest levels, little difference existed between policy, strategy, and the actions of statesmen, his definition of strategy as 'the use of engagements for the purpose of the war' only pertained to the application of force in wartime. It is, thus, purely a military strategy, though it can be seen as providing the conceptual foundation for contemporary strategic theory such as that advanced by Colin Gray, who defines strategy as 'the use that is made of force and the threat of force for the ends of policy'.[74] Similarly, Richard Betts calls strategy 'the link between military means and political ends'.[75] Even Liddell Hart, one of Clausewitz's earliest and most resolute critics, defined strategy in a like manner, as 'the art of distributing and applying military means to fulfill the ends of policy'.[76] Yet, unlike contemporary theorists, Clausewitz did not address the full gamut of military means, or how we should integrate them with other means, such as economic or diplomatic. He did not discuss sea power, for instance, or its potential role, though he certainly knew that British naval power had a hand in the defeat of Napoleonic France.[77] Naval theorists Alfred Thayer Mahan and Julian Corbett would later adopt some of Clausewitz's principles to their theories of war at sea.[78] Nonetheless, On War seems written principally for army rather than naval commanders. Today, we also look to integrate not only naval, air, space, and land power, but also diplomatic, economic, and informational means to achieve our strategic purposes, even if that integration tends to elude us in practice. Still, the rather narrow focus of On War does not compromise its explication of war's fundamental relationships.

At root, Clausewitz's approach to the purpose–means dynamic, though certainly influenced by the ideas of Machiavelli, is closer to the 'structural realism' school of thought in the sense that the sum of political conditions—alliances, coalitions, treaties, norms, and customs—created by states and nonstates tend to constrain what the policies of any one of them can achieve through the use of violence.[79] Revolutions in the use of violence occur when one state correctly perceives that conditions have changed enough to allow a different, perhaps an expanded, use of force to accomplish its aims, and acts accordingly. This is a remarkably nontechnological view which challenges those theorists who claim new technology is causing a general revolution in war.[80] For Clausewitz, the relative advantages and disadvantages of particular technologies emerged as a matter of historical chance, and would become part of the general balance of political power, the political conditions, that characterized the particular age, and even if they altered the destructive power of the means of war, they did not undermine the fundamental cause–effect relationship that existed between purpose and means, and on which his theory rested. It is not necessary, therefore, to add a technological dimension to his strategic concept, as some scholars have proposed, since this dimension is already accounted for in Clausewitz's broad concept of politics.[81]

The use of military forces in peacetime is clearly not the subject of *On War*. However, contemporary military strategy also covers the peacetime use of military forces. These forces routinely accomplish important tasks such as the training of allies and coalition partners, and practicing deployments and redeployments, which advance national interests by keeping strategic relationships renewed. Peace may be the ultimate object of war, as Clausewitz acknowledged, but war, as he defined it, occurs whenever one party resists the violent actions of another. That definition actually captures the state of affairs in many of the so-called peace operations taking place across the globe today. Nor would it be wrong to extend the definition to include counterterrorism and counterdrug, and similar operations, where the bulk of the forces involved are paramilitary or law-enforcement in nature.

Moreover, as we have seen, the principle of destruction that underpinned Clausewitz's theory did not equate to a doctrine of decisive battles, though many of his successors obviously took it that way. Even in the unrevised *On War*, which is characterized by ambiguities and contradictions, it is clear that he saw not annihilation, but combat and the threat of combat as war's fundamental, indeed only, means. In fact, the threat of combat also provides the foundation for the types of missions military forces are already performing in the new post-Cold War strategic environment, and will likely continue to perform for some time to come:

- *Show of Force*—activities to reassure allies, deter threats, and gain influence.
- *Arms Control*—locating, seizing, and destroying weapons; support to arms control regimes.
- *Peace Operations*—supporting diplomatic efforts to establish peace settlements and treaties.
- *Noncombatant Evacuations*—relocating threatened civilian noncombatants.
- *Humanitarian and Civic Assistance*—assistance conducted in conjunction with military training.
- *Security Assistance*—providing defense articles, military training, and related services.
- *Support to Counterdrug Operations*—interdiction of illicit drug traffic.
- *Combating Terrorism*—offensive and defensive measures to counterterrorism.
- *Foreign Internal Defense*—assisting governments in combating lawlessness and insurgency.
- *Support to Insurgencies*—logistical and training support to insurgencies opposing hostile regimes.
- *Domestic Support Operations*—supporting state and local governments in emergencies.
- *Foreign Humanitarian Assistance*—supporting other governments in emergencies.[82]

If current trends in peace operations are any indication, such missions will continue to increase in number. For instance, in 1990, as the Cold War ended, the United Nations had five peacekeeping operations underway, excluding those on the Korean peninsula, involving about 10,000 troops; whereas in 2006, it had 18 such operations taking place with nearly 73,000 troops involved, and peacekeeping costs had risen from $800 million in 1990 to $41 billion in 2006.[83] Trends-based analysis is always risky, but general trends are often all strategists have to go on.[84]

Accordingly, contemporary strategists and theorists who claim Clausewitz's definition of strategy is obsolete have overlooked the many ways in which force and the threat of force are already being used in this postmodern era. Such uses will not necessarily secure every political purpose, but they are prerequisites. Force cannot solve economic, demographic, health, and other problems, particularly those aggravated by globalization, but it can provide security mechanisms for protecting key personnel, installations, and other essential resources.

To be sure, Clausewitz could not always keep his own subjective views from interfering in his search for objective knowledge. Nonetheless, stating a preference for one method is not the same as claiming all other methods are invalid.

## NOTES

1. For example of these errors, see Huber, 'Clausewitz is Dead', 119–21; John E. Shephard, '*On War*: Is Clausewitz Still Relevant', *Parameters* (September 1990), 85–99; Thomas H. Etzold, 'Clausewitzian Lessons for Modern Strategists', *Air University Review*, 4 (May–June 1980), 24–8; Peter Moody, 'Clausewitz and the Fading Dialectic of War', *World Politics*, 31/3 (April 1979), 417–33.
2. *Vom Kriege*, IV/1, 419, IV/3, 422; *On War*, 225, 227.
3. *Vom Kriege*, IV/4, 429; *On War*, 231.
4. *Vom Kriege*, IV/3, 423; *On War*, 227.
5. Jehuda L. Wallach, *The Dogma of the Battle of Annihilation: The Theories of Clausewitz and Schlieffen and Their Impact on the German Conduct of Two World Wars* (Westport, CT: Greenwood, 1988); and 'Misperceptions of Clausewitz' *On War* by the German Military', in *Clausewitz and Modern Strategy*, 213–39. Jan Philipp Reemtsma, 'The Concept of the War of Annihilation: Clausewitz, Ludendorff, Hitler', in Hannes Heer and Klaus Naumann (eds.), *War of Extermination: The German Military in World War II, 1941–1944* (New York: Berghahn, 2000), 12–35, expands Wallach's argument by contending that wars of annihilation could not occur without the cultural space that allows them to be thought; however, Reemtsma misinterprets Clausewitz's pure concept of war, and likewise his concept of absolute war.
6. *Vom Kriege*, IV/4, 427; *On War*, 230.
7. *Vom Kriege*, IV/3, 423; *On War*, 228–9.
8. *Vom Kriege*, IV/5, 437; *On War*, 236–37.
9. *Vom Kriege*, IV/11, 467; *On War*, 258.
10. *Vom Kriege*, I/2, 214–15; *On War*, 90–1.
11. *Vom Kriege*, IV/4, 433; *On War*, 233–4; the last condition, Clausewitz stated, provided the only real proof of victory, though it might not mean a great deal if the opponent's intention was to conduct a deliberate withdrawal throughout his theater of operations. He also clearly valued destroying an adversary's psychological forces, breaking his will to fight, over demolishing his physical forces, or occupying his territory. Loss of morale was the 'predominant cause of a decisive outcome'. *Vom Kriege*, IV/4, 429; *On War*, 231. It was, in fact, the means by which one achieved a significant margin of victory, since major physical losses tended to occur as the result of a considerable drop in morale: 'The psychological effects resulting from the outcome of a major engagement are greater on the side of the victor than on that of the vanquished: they lead

to greater losses in physical forces, which then react on the psychological forces, and thus continue to reinforce and intensify each other. On this psychological effect, therefore, we must place special weight. It goes in an opposite direction on one side than on the other; just as it undermines the energies of the vanquished so it elevates the forces and energies of the victor. Yet, its principal effect is on the vanquished, since it becomes the direct cause of further losses....' *Vom Kriege*, IV/10, 460–1; *On War*, 253. Physical and psychological forces thus went hand in hand. Their effects essentially were mutually reinforcing; at times the mere threat of incurring physical losses could carry sufficient psychological power to induce an adversary to surrender, thereby making an actual battle unnecessary.

12. *Vom Kriege*, III/18, 416; *On War*, 222.
13. *Vom Kriege*, IV/3, 424; *On War*, 228.
14. *Vom Kriege*, IV/3, 424; *On War*, 228; this appears to be a reference to Jomini's decisive points.
15. *Vom Kriege*, IV/11, 470; *On War*, 230; Liddell Hart, *Strategy*, 342 his strategy of the indirect approach has been criticized as little more than an expansion of the principle of surprise. Bassford, *Clausewitz in English*, 128–35, shows that Liddell Hart's private papers reveal that he actually understood Clausewitz's views, but misrepresented them; see also Jay Luvaas, 'Clausewitz, Fuller and Liddell Hart', in *Clausewitz and Modern Strategy*, 197–212.
16. Jay Luvaas, 'Student as Teacher: Clausewitz on Frederick the Great and Napoleon', in *Clausewitz and Modern Strategy*, 150–70.
17. *Vom Kriege*, IV/2, 421; *On War*, 226.
18. *Vom Kriege*, IV/11, 471; *On War*, 260.
19. Clausewitz was certainly well aware of the advantages of a Fabian strategy. Notably, the actual reference he used closely resembles that found in Machiavelli's *Art of War*, which includes a discussion of Fabius Cuncator's strategy of avoiding battle with Hannibal; Niccolò Machiavelli, *The Art of War*, trans. Ellis Farnesworth, intro. Neal Wood (New York: Da Capo, 1990), 125.
20. *Vom Kriege*, VIII/3B, 973; *On War*, 593.
21. *Vom Kriege*, I/2, 226; *On War*, 97.
22. Neither Clausewitz nor Machiavelli thought highly of the *Condottieri*, which means contractors; Howard, *War in European History*, 25–7, reveals that the *Condottieri* did more fighting than is commonly supposed. Chris van Aller, 'Machiavelli and Clausewitz on the Political Determinants of National Security', *Defense Analysis*, 13/1 (1997), 5–18, highlights important similarities in Machiavelli's and Clausewitz's thinking.
23. cf. Robert B. Asprey, *Frederick the Great: The Magnificent Enigma* (New York: Ticknor & Fields, 1986), 543; on Torgau, see Dennis E. Showalter, *The Wars of Frederick the Great* (Harlow, UK: Longman, 1996), 281–96; in Frederick's case, of course, he often had to rely on battle where other monarchs did not.
24. William O. Staudenmaier, 'Vietnam, Mao, Clausewitz', *Parameters*, 7/1 (1977), 1–11, is an incisive reminder that Clausewitz's theory of war applies equally

well to conventional as well as unconventional forms of warfare; certainly Mao thought so.
25. *Vom Kriege*, IV/3, 423; *On War*, 227.
26. T. E. [Thomas Edward] Lawrence, *Seven Pillars of Wisdom: A Triumph* (New York: Anchor, [1926]1991), 195. See also Frank G. Hoffman, 'Small Wars Revisited: The United States and Nontraditional Wars', *Journal of Strategic Studies*, 28/6 (December 2005), 913–40.
27. Mao Tse-Tung, *On Guerrilla Warfare*, 2nd edn., trans. Samuel B. Griffith II (Baltimore, MD: Nautical & Aviation, 1992); and *Basic Tactics*, trans. Stuart R. Schram (New York: Praeger, 1966).
28. Kalevi J. Holsti, *The State, War, and the State of War* (Cambridge: Cambridge University Press, 1997), 40.
29. For adaptations of Mao's theory, see General Vo-Nguyen-Giap, *People's War, People's Army: The Viet Cong Insurrection Manual for Underdeveloped Countries* (New York: Praeger, 1962). Che Guevara, *Guerrilla Warfare*, 3rd edn., Brian Loveman and Thomas M. Davies Jr (eds.) (Wilmington, DE: Scholarly Resources, 1997), which contains updated case studies for the 1990s. See also Robert A. Doughty and Ira D. Gruber et al. (eds.), *Limited Warfare in the Nuclear Age* (Lexington, KY: D.C. Heath, 1996).
30. Walter Laqueur, *Guerrilla: A Historical and Critical Study* (London: Weidenfeld & Nicholson, 1977), 403–4.
31. *Vom Kriege*, VI/26, 799; *On War*, 479.
32. For the lectures, see 'Meine Vorlesungen über den kleinem Krieg, gehalten auf der Kriegs-Schule 1810 und 1811', in *Schriften–Aufsätze–Studien–Briefe*, vol. I, 208–599.
33. Werner Hahlweg, 'Clausewitz and Guerrilla Warfare', in *Clausewitz and Modern Strategy*, 127–33, which is an English translation of 'Clausewitz und der Guerilla-Krieg', in *Freiheit ohne Krieg*, 349–58.
34. Robert B. Asprey, *War in the Shadows: The Guerrilla in History* (London: Macdonald, 1975), 164.
35. Samuel P. Huntington, 'Guerrilla Warfare in Theory and Practice', in Franklin M. Osaka (ed.), *Modern Guerrilla Warfare: Fighting Communist Guerrilla Movements, 1941–61* (New York: Macmillan, 1964), xv–xvi.
36. M. L. R. Smith, 'War and Only War: Analysing the False Categories of Low Intensity Conflict', in *Nature of Modern War*, 21–44, makes a similar point, maintaining with some force that 'guerrilla warfare' and 'low intensity war' are 'flawed abstractions;' and 'Guerrillas in the Mist: Reassessing Strategy and Low Intensity Warfare', *Review of International Studies*, 29 (2003), 19–37, which argues that such wars can only be understood within Clausewitzian parameters.
37. Stuart Kinross, 'Clausewitz and Low Intensity Conflict', *Journal of Strategic Studies*, 27/1 (March 2004), 35–58.
38. *Vom Kriege*, I/2, 218–19; *On War*, 92–3.
39. *Vom Kriege*, I/2, 221; *On War*, 94.
40. *Vom Kriege*, VI/8, 659; *On War*, 386.

41. *Vom Kriege*, III/1, 345; II/1, 277; *On War*, 176–7.
42. Lawrence Freedman and Efraim Karsh, *The Gulf Conflict, 1990–1991: Diplomacy and War in the New World Order* (Princeton, NJ: Princeton University Press, 1993), 403–5; James Kurth, 'First War of the Global Era: Kosovo and Grand Strategy', in *War over Kosovo*, esp. 87–9; Clark, *Waging Modern War*, 420–40.
43. *Vom Kriege*, III/8, 373; *On War*, 194.
44. *Vom Kriege*, IV/12, 475; *On War*, 263.
45. *Vom Kriege*, III/2, 354; *On War*, 183. He discussed psychological elements further in Book III, chapters 3–7, 10; physical elements in Book III, chapters 8, 9, 11–14; geometric elements in Book III, chapter 15, and Book VI, chapters 4, 14, 24; statistical elements in Book III, chapters 16, 18, and in Book V, chapters 14–16; and geographic elements are discussed in several chapters in Books V, VI, and VII.
46. J. C. Wylie, *Military Strategy: A General Theory of Power Control* (Annapolis, MD: Naval Institute, 1989), 13.
47. *Vom Kriege*, I/7, 261; *On War*, 119.
48. Daniel Moran, 'Strategic Theory and the History of War', in John Baylis, James Wirtz, Eliot Cohen, and Colin S. Gray (eds.), *Strategy in the Contemporary World* (Oxford: Oxford University Press, 2002), 17–44.
49. Yaacov Bar-Simon-Tov, *Israel, the Superpowers, and the War in the Middle East* (New York: Praeger, 1987), 296–306.
50. Michael Walzer, *Just and Unjust Wars: A Moral Argument with Historical Illustrations* (New York: Basic Books, 1977), 22–5; and *Arguing about War* (New Haven, CT: Yale Nota Bene, 2005); Brian Orend, *Michael Walzer on War and Justice* (Montreal, Canada: McGill Queen's, 2000); Paul Christopher, *The Ethics of War and Peace: A Introduction to Legal and Moral Issues* (Upper Saddle River, NJ: Prentice-Hall, 2004) challenges Walzer.
51. Antulio J. Echevarria II, 'Clausewitz: Toward a Theory of Applied Strategy', *Defense Analysis*, 11/3 (October 1995), 229–40; Franz, 'Two Letters on Strategy', *Clausewitz and Modern Strategy*, 171–94.
52. The operational level of war did not appear in US military doctrine until the 1982 edition of FM 100–5, *Operations*. Milan Vego, 'Operational Art and Doctrine', in Anthony D. McIvor (ed.), *Rethinking the Principles of War* (Annapolis, MD: Naval Institute, 2005), 167–87, provides a solid introduction to operational art. On the emergence of the operational level of war, see Michael D. Krause and R. Cody Phillips (eds.), *Historical Perspectives of the Operational Art* (Washington, DC: Center of Military History, 2005); Robert M. Citino, *Blitzkrieg to Desert Storm: The Evolution of Operational Warfare* (Lawrence, KS: University Press of Kansas, 2004); Shimon Naveh, *In Pursuit of Military Excellence: The Evolution of Operational Theory* (London: Frank Cass, 1997); B. J. C. McKercher and Michael A. Hennessy (eds.), *The Operational Art: Developments in the Theories of War* (Westport, CT: Praeger, 1996).
53. *Vom Kriege*, III/1, 345; *On War*, 177.

54. Martin Dunn, 'Levels of War: Just a Set of Labels?', *Research and Analysis*, Newsletter of the Land Warfare Studies Center, no. 10, 1996. For the opposing view, see Lt. Gen. John Kiszely, 'Thinking about the Operational Level', *RUSI Journal*, 150/6 (December 2005), 38–43, which maintains that without the operational level, strategic success would be little more than 'the sum of tactical victories'.
55. Douglas A. MacGregor, 'Future Battle: The Merging Levels of War', *Parameters*, 22/4 (winter 1992–93), 33–47.
56. *Vom Kriege*, VI/8, 658; *On War*, 386.
57. *Vom Kriege*, IV/2, 420; *On War*, 226.
58. *Vom Kriege*, III/8, 373; *On War*, 194.
59. *Vom Kriege*, IV/12, 475; *On War*, 263.
60. *Vom Kriege*, III/12, 391; *On War*, 208.
61. *Vom Kriege*, IV/12, 480–1; *On War*, 267.
62. *Vom Kriege*, VII (chapter 22): this chapter is not numbered in the German edition.
63. 'Über Strategie', in Großer Generalstab (ed.), *Moltkes Militärische Werke*, 14 vols. (Berlin: E.S. Mittler, 1892–1912), II, Part 2, 33–40.
64. 'Über Strategie (1871)', in *Militärische Werke*, II, Part 2, 187 ff.
65. Bucholz, *Moltke and German Wars*, indicates that Bismarck only requested military assessments from Moltke.
66. 'Über Strategie', *Militärisches Werke*, IV, Part 2, 287–93; see also Daniel Hughes, *Moltke on the Art of War: Selected Writings* (Novato, CA: Presidio, 1993).
67. Bucholz, *Moltke and German Wars*, 18 ff.
68. Echevarria, *After Clausewitz*, chapter 7; on the *Gesamtschlacht* see Michael Geyer, 'German Strategy in the Age of Machine Warfare, 1914–45', in Paret (ed.), *Makers of Modern Strategy*, 532–3.
69. Robert M. Citino, *The German Way of War: From the Thirty Years War to the Third Reich* (Lawrence, KS: University Press of Kansas, 2005); Samuel J. Newland, *Victories Are Not Enough: Limitations of the German Way of War* (Carlisle, PA: Strategic Studies Institute, 2005).
70. This bifurcation persistently characterized the American way of war; see Colin Gray, 'The American Way of War: Critique and Implications', *Rethinking the Principles of War*, 13–40; Antulio J. Echevarria II, *Toward an American Way of War* (Carlisle, PA: Strategic Studies Institute, 2004); Eliot A. Cohen, 'Kosovo and the New American Way of War', in *War over Kosovo*, 38–62; Raymond B. Furlong, '*On War*, Political Objectives, and Military Strategy', *Parameters*, 13/4 (1984), 2–10; and the classic: Russel F. Weigley, *The American Way of War: A History of United States Military Strategy and Policy* (New York: Macmillan).
71. Brodie, *War and Politics*, 1.
72. Wayne P. Hughes, Jr, 'The Strategy–Tactics Relationship', in Colin S. Gray and Roger W. Barnett (eds.), *Seapower and Strategy* (Annapolis, MD: Naval Institute, 1989), 47.

73. John M. Collins, *Military Strategy: Principles, Practices, and Historical Perspectives* (Washington, DC: Brassey's, 2002), 3; Arthur F. Lykke, 'Toward an Understanding of Military Strategy', in *Military Strategy: Theory and Application* (Carlisle, PA: US Army War College, 1989), 3; Dennis M. Drew and Donald M. Snow, *Making Strategy: An Introduction to National Security Processes and Problems* (Maxwell Air Force Base: Air University, 1988), 13.
74. Gray, *Modern Strategy*, 17.
75. Betts, 'Is Strategy an Illusion', 5.
76. B. H. Liddell Hart, *Strategy* 2nd edn. (New York: Praeger, 1967), 335. Wylie, *Military Strategy*, 14, adds that strategy is a 'plan of action designed to achieve some end: a purpose together with a system of measure for its accomplishment'.
77. Michael I. Handel, 'Corbett, Clausewitz, and Sun Tzu', *Naval War College Review*, 53 (2000), 106–24; Kapt., a.d., Olaf Preuschoft, 'Clausewitz' Einfluss auf die Seemachtslehre', in *Clausewitz-Studien* (spring 1996), 1, 56–67; John E. Tashjean, 'Clausewitz: Naval War and other Considerations', *Naval War College Review*, 39/3 (May–June 1986), 51–8; and Hans Joachim Arndt, 'Clausewitz und der Einfluβ der Seemacht', in *Freiheit ohne Krieg?*, 203–19, discuss Clausewitz and sea power. Of course, Clausewitz could not have addressed those dimensions of warfare that were not recognized in his day, such as space, though authors have applied his ideas to them.
78. Mahan's and Corbett's principles regarding the importance of command of the sea relied on such familiar land–power concepts as central position, strategic lines, lines of communication, and concentration of force. Captain A. T. Mahan, *Naval Strategy Compared and Contrasted with the Principles and Practice of Military Operations on Land* (Boston, MA: Little & Brown, 1911); Mahan's principles appear throughout his classic work: *The Influence of Sea Power upon History, 1660–1783* (New York: Hill & Wang, 1890); Margaret Tuttle Sprout, 'Mahan: Evangelist of Sea Power', in *Makers of Modern Strategy*, 415–45, presents a summary of Mahan's views. Julian Corbett's revisions and amplifications of Mahan's principles appear in *Some Principles of Maritime Strategy* (Annapolis, MD: Naval Institute, 1911).
79. Kenneth Waltz, *Theory of International Politics* (Boston, MA: McGraw-Hill, 1979). Murielle Cozette, 'Realistic Realism? American Political Realism, Clausewitz and Raymond Aron on the Problem of Means and Ends in International Politics', *Journal of Strategic Studies*, 27/3 (September 2004), 428–53, argues that Clausewitz's views resemble the enlightened realism of Raymond Aron, rather than the more limited and cynical realism of Hans Morgenthau or the structural determinism of Waltz; however, the argument fails because the few political purposes Clausewitz discussed do not actually undermine the Morgenthauian argument that states ultimately pursue power for its own sake and because Clausewitz focused on the 'activity' of political interaction rather than the variety of purposes. Jan Willem Honig, 'Totalitarianism and Realism: Hans Morgenthau's German Years', *Security Studies*, 5/2 (winter 1995), 283–313, compares Morgethau's earlier views to his latter cynicism.

80. The technocratic view is represented by Harlan K. Ullman, 'On War: Enduring Principles or Profound Change?', in *Rethinking the Principles of War*, 79–94; Owens, *Lifting the Fog of War*; Arthur K. Cebrowski and John J. Garstka, 'Network-Centric Warfare: Its Origin and Future', *Proceedings of the U.S. Naval Institute*, 124/1 (January 1998), 28–35; David S. Alberts, John J. Garstka, and Frederic P. Stein, *Network Centric Warfare: Developing and Leveraging Information Superiority* (Washington, DC: Department of Defense, 1998); Robert J. Bunker, 'Technology in a Neo-Clausewitzian Setting', in *Clausewitzian Dictum*, 137–66; Andrew F. Krepenevich, 'Cavalry to Computer: The Pattern of Military Revolutions', *The National Interest*, 37 (autumn 1994), 30–42. The skeptics include: Colin Gray, *Another Bloody Century: Future Warfare* (London: Wiedenfeld & Nicholson, 2005); James Kurth, 'Clausewitz and the Two Contemporary Military Revolutions: RMA and RAM', in Bradford Lee and Karl Walling (eds.), *Strategic Logic and Political Rationality: Essays in Honor of Michael Handel* (London: Frank Cass, 2003); Williamson Murray, 'Clausewitz Out, Computer In: Military Culture and Technological Hubris', *The National Interest* (summer 1997), 57–64; Jeffrey R. Cooper, *Another View of the Revolution in Military Affairs* (Carlisle, PA: Strategic Studies Institute, 1994).
81. Handel, *Masters of War*, 3rd edn., 109–11.
82. This mission set is discussed in Huba Wass de Czege and Antulio J. Echevarria II, 'Toward a Strategy of Positive Ends', *National Security Studies Quarterly*, 8/1 (winter 2002), 1–26.
83. cf. United Nations Peacekeeping Operations, Background Note, dated February 28, 2006; http://www.un.org/depts/dpko/dpko/bnote.htm
84. Francis Fukuyama, *State-Building: Governance and World Order in the 21st Century* (Ithaca, NY: Cornell University Press, 2004); Stewart Patrick, 'Weak States and Global Threats: Fact or Fiction?', *The Washington Quarterly*, 29/2 (spring 2006), 27–53, calls into question assumptions concerning the threats posed by failed and failing states; Richard K. Betts, 'The Future of Force and U.S. National Security Strategy', *The Korean Journal of Defense Analysis*, 17/3 (winter 2005), 7–26.

# 7

## Principles of Strategy

This chapter discusses the major strategic principles Clausewitz uncovered in his search for objective knowledge, and their implications for contemporary war. Martial principles have assumed many names over time, passing for axioms, precepts, maxims, imperatives, or laws.[1] Military practitioners have developed principles for various levels and aspects of armed conflict, from strategy to operations to tactics, and so-called operations other than war. The individual principles themselves have changed along with knowledge of the art and science of war. Yet a certain canon of so-called classic or traditional principles has evolved and gained official sanction in most contemporary militaries: objective, offensive, mass, economy of force, maneuver, surprise, security, simplicity, and unity of command or effort.[2] Theorists continue to challenge this canon, and have introduced some innovative ideas.[3] Nonetheless, the canon appears largely unimpressed.

Contrary to conventional wisdom, Clausewitz did *not* reject martial principles, only prescriptive ones.[4] He took on a number of the assumptions of his day, and exposed their flaws, or the fact that they were based on a subjective rather than an objective basis, and urged his readers, above all, to consider all would-be principles critically. Indeed, he developed a number of patently subjective principles to encapsulate his two-year period of military instruction to the Prussian crown prince.[5] The examples Clausewitz used to illustrate each principle were drawn from his own period of warfare, and the purpose of these principles was to make the prince a competent military commander, rather than the author of a universally valid theory of war:

- Use all forces with utmost energy
- Concentrate maximum power where the decisive blow is to be struck
- Act quickly, use all available time
- Exploit all successes with the utmost energy

Universally valid principles are, in fact, products of, and evidence for, a sound theory. As Clausewitz said: 'Whenever concepts combine on their own to form a kernel of truth that we call a principle, and whenever they come together consistently enough to form a rule, theory should acknowledge the same.'[6]

*Principles of Strategy* 155

Kiesewetter's *Outline of Logic* defines a principle as 'a proposition that does not require being deduced from other propositions; it does not require a proof, but rather we discern its truth as soon as we grasp the principle itself'.[7] Book III 'On Strategy in General', in fact, examines a number of strategic principles which fit this description, and many are still considered valid today:

- Chapter 6, 'Boldness' ~ *Offensive*
- Chapter 8, 'Superiority of Numbers' ~ *Mass*
- Chapter 11, 'Concentration of Forces in Time' ~ *Mass*
- Chapter 12, 'Unification of Forces in Time' ~ *Mass*
- Chapter 7, 'Perseverance' ~ *Perseverance*
- Chapter 9, 'Surprise' ~ *Surprise*
- Chapter 14, 'Economy of Force' ~ *Economy of Force*
- Chapter 10, 'Cunning' ~ *Simplicity, Security, Surprise*[8]

As Clausewitz's discussion in the second chapter of Book II 'On the Theory of War' reveals, he originally considered strategy too complex to submit to principles. Instead, principles applied more to the realm of tactics because that was where 'theory could come closest to a positive doctrine' and, where principles could guide action most consistently.[9] However, as his undated note reveals, in the course of writing *On War*, he came across a number of strategic principles:

The theory of major wars, or strategy, has extraordinary difficulties, and we can rightly say that few people have an understanding of its specific elements, that is, have ideas derived from that which is necessary in terms of strategy's actual interconnections. In practice, most people follow only their own intuitive judgment (*Takt des Urteils*), which is only as effective as the degree of genius one possesses...

The great difficulties that attend a philosophical formulation of the art of war, and the many poor attempts that have been made at it, have brought most people to the conclusion that such a theory is impossible, since it concerns things that no permanent law can encompass. We would agree with this view and forgo any attempt to develop such a theory, but for the great number of propositions that can be made completely evident without difficulty: (1) that defense is the stronger form of fighting with a negative purpose, and that attack is the weaker form with a positive purpose; (2) that major successes help bring about minor ones; (3) that we can thus trace strategic effects back to certain centers of gravity; (4) that a demonstration is a weaker use of force than a real attack, and therefore must be given special consideration; (5) that victory exists not only in the occupation of the battlefield, but in the destruction of the enemy's physical and psychological forces, and that these usually are attained during the pursuit after a successful battle; (6) that success is always greatest where a victory has been won, and that, therefore, changing from one line of battle or direction of advance to another can only be regarded as a necessary evil; (7) that the justification for an envelopment can be made only by the general superiority of our forces or of our lines of communication and retreat with respect to those of the enemy; (8) that flank-positions, thus, are also to be considered in the same way; (9) that every attack weakens as it advances.[10]

It is clear from the above passage that Clausewitz had changed his views: he now believed that it was possible to uncover laws or principles governing strategy, and he thought he had already discovered several. What the undated note does not make clear, however, is whether he considered one of the propositions predominant, the organizing principle for strategy itself. Clearly, he had yet to work this change of views into Book II 'On the Theory of War' and Book III 'On Strategy in General'. Still, the undated note shows that he accepted the possibility of discovering laws and principles for strategy.[11]

As we have seen, *On War* is a search for objective knowledge, and if that existed, then principles, as deductions from that knowledge, can also exist. Principles spring, or should, from underlying cause-and-effect relationships, which create discernable patterns over time. Such patterns, in turn, make scientific analysis possible. Otherwise, only a vast number of separate parts—a rhapsody—would exist without any sense of how, or whether, the parts were related. The existence of laws and principles makes it possible to draw conclusions, learn lessons, and practice deductive reasoning. Without them, anything is as possible as anything else. Rolling the dice would prove just as effective as following the insights of genius. In other words, Clausewitz needed principles, just as he needed laws and other verifiable truths to construct a scientifically valid theory of war, an ordered body of knowledge.

Nonetheless, the application of principles required skilled judgment, the culmination of pure and practical reasoning. The absence of that ingredient, in short, had been the problem with the principles of Bülow, Lloyd, and Jomini, which had been portrayed as applicable regardless of the situation, without the need for judgment, when in fact they were not. Throughout *On War*, Clausewitz stressed the importance of grasping the meaning behind principles, instead of treating them as rigid rules. Applying principles was, in his mind, a matter of experienced judgment, and required a certain sensibility, or tact. Unfortunately, the tendency in highly stressful situations, such as war, is to reach for checklists that prescribe action, rather than to exercise judgment. The British theorist, J.F.C. Fuller, purportedly abandoned his quest to develop principles of war because the British army began treating them as prescriptive rules.[12] That tendency turns principles into immutable laws which must be followed regardless of the aim, and is antithetical to Clausewitz's approach.

However, he encountered another problem, mentioned in the last chapter of Book VI and again in Book VIII, namely, that principles did not appear to exist for wars in which a decision was not sought, or at least he had not found any to that point.[13] Wars aiming at a decision by battle were perhaps rarer in history, but their principles were easier to discern and understand. Wars where such a decision was not sought, in contrast, varied so greatly that each case had to be judged according to its particular circumstances. He settled on caution and common sense as the chief principles, or guides, for these types of wars. However, we get the sense that this measure was merely a temporary solution:

> That any theory of war, if it desires to be and to remain based on philosophical proofs, now finds itself in a bind, is clear. Everything which relies on the law of necessity in the concept of war appears to fly from it, and the concept itself is in danger of being dispossessed of every point of support. However, the obvious solution soon shows itself. The more a moderating principle enters into the violent act, or rather, the weaker the motive for action becomes, the more the action tends toward inaction, the less it needs to do, and the less it needs guiding principles. The entire art of war thus transforms itself into mere caution, and this caution will be primarily directed at ensuring that this dubious equilibrium is not suddenly upset to our disadvantage, and that the half-war not become a whole one.[14]

Clausewitz did realize, as we mentioned earlier, that the underlying law of combat, or rather its threat, remained valid. Even if no fighting occurs, it is the threat of combat that causes events to happen as they do. Hence, the laws were not in jeopardy so much as the principles.

## DEFENSE AND ATTACK

Clausewitz maintained throughout *On War* that the defense was the stronger form of war.[15] This argument, he realized, contradicted the rather fiercely held assumption—which many still consider valid today—that the attack was stronger than the defense. If the attack were truly stronger, he asked, would not both parties opt for the offensive directly at the outset of a conflict? Why would either party opt to defend rather than attack? If the defense did not offer intrinsic advantages, which at least partially offset a deficiency in military strength, it would be a pointless undertaking.

### Defense

Clausewitz defined the concept (*Begriff*) of the defense as 'warding off (*Abwehren*) of a blow', and identified the distinguishing characteristic of the defense as 'awaiting the blow'.[16] In examining this concept, Clausewitz applied the same method, albeit somewhat cruder here, he used in Book I regarding the concept of war; failure to appreciate that has led to a great deal of misunderstanding.[17] When he examined the concept of defense from a purely logical standpoint, he found that it offered three major advantages over the attack. First, it was easier to carry out, since the purpose of the defense was merely to preserve or maintain (*erhalten*), and preserving is less difficult than conquering or capturing (*erobern*), which is the purpose of the attack; in short, the defender can achieve success simply by avoiding the aim of the attacker, while the attacker cannot succeed unless he subdues the defender. Second, time favored the defense; any delay or hesitation on the part of the attacker benefited the defender because the defense tended to grow stronger over time, while the attack usually became weaker. Third, the defense offered the advantage of position; the defender in most cases chose the terrain for the battle.[18] These advantages held true, Clausewitz believed, in tactics as well as strategy, though in subsequent chapters he modified those advantages.

With regard to tactics, for instance, only three things produced decisive advantages in Clausewitz's view: (*a*) surprise, or suddenly confronting one's adversary with more troops than he expected; (*b*) familiarity with the area; and (*c*) assault from multiple sides.[19] The attacker can take advantage of only the first and third factors, and then only partially, while the second clearly favors the defender, who can also make some use of the first and third. Clausewitz also conceded that the attacker had an advantage in that he could strike at any point along the line of defense, and could achieve local superiority at that point. He felt, however, that the defender could more than compensate for this advantage by surprising his opponent with the strength and direction of his counterattacks. Thus, tactically, the defense offered more advantages than the attack.

Concerning strategy, Clausewitz identified six conditions or factors that contributed to success: (*a*) surprise, (*b*) familiarity with the area, (*c*) advancing from multiple sides, (*d*) fortresses, (*e*) support of the population, and (*f*) the exploitation of major psychological forces.[20] The first three were essentially the same as in tactics, though their influence was often greater at the level of strategy. The strategic initiative the attacker possessed could, for instance, bring any war to a rapid conclusion, if properly employed, and if the defender obliges the attacker by making mistakes in planning and execution.

The only other factor that favored the attack, in Clausewitz's view, was that of falling on the enemy from multiple directions. The attacker could accomplish that feat much more easily than the defender. Circumstances might tip the balance one way or the other: if, for example, the defender was fighting on ground he had conquered, he could not necessarily count on the support of the population. However, in general, the majority of these factors favored the strategic defense. Hence, even at the strategic level, the defense was the stronger form of war.

Clausewitz claimed that historical study and personal experience showed that, in most cases, the weaker party opted to defend, even if by its customs or traditions it would have preferred to attack. The stronger party, by comparison, almost never chose to defend. Commanders, in other words, understood, even if they did not want to admit, that the advantages of the defense outweighed those of the attack, and thus helped offset the military superiority of the attacker. Therefore, if the defense were chosen by the weaker opponent and this choice resulted in some approximation of parity, the defense must be the stronger form of war.[21]

Clausewitz also noted that the defense, though stronger, had a passive or negative purpose since its aim from the standpoint of pure logic, was merely to preserve or maintain. The attack, on the other hand, had a positive purpose since it sought to acquire something—territory, treasure, or something else. Yet, precisely because the defense had a negative purpose, Clausewitz felt that, in practice, we should use it only on a temporary basis, that is, until a favorable balance of strength occurred that would enable us to assume the offensive, and thus to pursue a positive aim. Indeed, he concluded that beginning on the defensive and transitioning to the offensive was the natural course in war.[22] Not only did he find it prudent to finish off an attacker by means of a counterattack, which thereby prevented a renewal of the attack, he actually found this approach more likely to result in major successes:

We maintain...candidly that in the form of war we call defense not only is victory more likely, but also that the extent and effectiveness achieved can be the same as with the attack, and that this is the case not only in the sum of the successes of all the battles that make up a campaign, but also as regards the individual battles....[23]

His personal experiences in Europe's wars against Napoleon seemed to validate this view; the Russians, for instance, had defeated the French with a defensive campaign in 1812–13, but then had to follow up with a counterattack in order to destroy the *Grande Armée*.[24]

Clausewitz repeatedly stressed the importance of the counterattack as an integral part of the defense:

Whenever a victory achieved by the defensive form of war is not exploited in some manner by further military action, it is a great mistake. The rapid, forceful transition to the attack—the swift sword of vengeance—is the crowning moment for the defense.[25]

The idea of the counterattack, he argued, had to be in the defender's mind from the outset: 'the defense cannot be thought of without the counterattack.'[26] The problem with this emphasis, however, is that it shifted his pure concept from merely preserving oneself or one's territory toward that of conquest. Accordingly, as the aim of the defender moved toward that of the attacker, the former would necessarily assume many of the burdens originally associated with the latter. In other words, Clausewitz's emphasis on the counterattack as an inseparable part of the defense undermined, to a certain extent, his argument that, in a purely logical sense, the defense was easier to execute than the attack. The key difference under this formulation is that the defender no longer *awaits* the attack, but instead must *anticipate* it, which is much more difficult. In practice, anticipation requires well-developed skills on the part of commanders and their staffs, who must correctly analyze avenues of approach into their country, deduce the attacker's likely courses of action, and properly dispose their forces in advance. Hence, Clausewitz downplayed somewhat the practical difficulties facing the defense.

Clausewitz also believed that thinking in strictly defensive terms, that is, of merely awaiting the blow, ran counter to the pure concept (*Begriff*) of war. Even a defensive war was not purely defensive, per se, that is, wholly passive: a defensive war could be fought with offensive campaigns, a defensive campaign could involve offensive battles, and a defensive battle could include offensive tactics.[27] Hence, neither form of war existed wholly independent of the other: the attack included elements of the defense and the defense elements of the attack. Again, the principal characteristic that distinguished defense from attack was that the former awaited—indeed anticipated—the blow, while the latter decided where and when to deliver it.

Yet, by the same logic, the attacker could also anticipate where the defender might attempt a counterblow, and prepare accordingly. Clausewitz's logic, thus, begins to break down as he introduces the counterattack into the concept of the defense. In any case, as van Creveld points out, the purpose of the Prussian theorist's overall argument was merely to show that 'the defense as such is stronger than the attack as such'.[28] In other words, Clausewitz merely sought to, and to a certain extent succeeded in, correcting many of the myths surrounding the purported the superiority of the attack.

Although Clausewitz was clearly not arguing that the best strategy is a defensive one, the defense is nonetheless an important concept in his overall theory of war. He argued, in fact, that, contrary to popular belief, war did not originate with the attack, but with the defense:

Admittedly, the conqueror decides upon war before the defender, who lacks any hostile intentions...yet, war is more with the defender than the conqueror since it is first brought into being by the defense...the conqueror would prefer to enter our country unopposed; if we do not want him to do so, then we must make war.[29]

When we consider the origin of war logically, the actual concept of war arises not with the attack—because this form of war has possession more than fighting as its absolute purpose. Instead, it arises first with the defense—because the defense has fighting as its immediate purpose since fighting and warding off essentially amount to the same thing... it is therefore at the heart of the matter that the side that first brings the element of war into question, from whose perspective it is first possible to think of opposing wills, and also establishes the initial contours of the conflict—is the defense.[30]

In other words, war cannot occur without the idea of resistance, without the existence of an opposing will. It is the clash of wills that lies at the root of war, and that clash cannot occur unless one side opts to defend itself against the encroachment of the other. The defense is thus the first evidence that an opposing will exists.

## Attack

Clausewitz's chapters concerning the attack generally mirror what he wrote about the defense. As he said in the introductory chapter of Book VII 'Attack' when 'two concepts form a logical contradiction, the one thus complements the other, and so the one brings to light the other'.[31] What he said about defense, in other words, also revealed important truths concerning the attack. Hence, his discussion of attack focused on bringing further clarity to those points not sufficiently emphasized in his treatment of defense.

In his discussion of the attack, Clausewitz reiterated that neither the attack nor the defense were mutually exclusive concepts. Each included important elements of the other: 'There is thus in the act of the attack, especially as regards strategy, a constant variation and linkage between attack and defense.'[32] An attacker often had to employ defensive measures in order to maintain his advance; the defense, of course, was nothing without the counterattack.

Each attack, Clausewitz added, must end in either peace, or defense.[33] An attacker, on the whole, could expect the force of his attack to lose momentum as it progressed. He listed seven factors that caused the attacker's strength to diminish: (*a*) occupation of the enemy's country, (*b*) the need to secure lines of communication, (*c*) losses incurred through combat and illness, (*d*) the greater distance replacements had to travel, (*e*) the investment of sieges and fortresses, (*f*) moral and physical reduction of effort, and (*g*) the defection of allies.[34] The attacker, in a word, had the burden of defending whatever he conquered, while his reinforcements and supplies would have ever greater distances to travel. Clausewitz thus concluded that most attacks did not lead directly to the end of hostilities, but instead reached a culminating point at which the 'superior strength of the attack... is just enough to maintain a defense and wait for peace'.[35]

The defender, on the other hand, could expect to gain strength as he fell back on his bases and his lines of communication and supply. Moreover, the defender could expect support from the (presumably friendly) indigenous population, whereas the attacker could expect to encounter increasing resistance, unless he was arriving as a liberator. Finally, the defender stood a reasonable chance of having allies come to his aid in an effort to maintain a balance of power, while the attacker usually had little external aid.[36]

Clausewitz believed that proceeding beyond the culminating point of the attack merely invited disaster, for it was wrong to assume 'that so long as an attack progresses there must still be some superiority on its side'.[37] It was thus important for both sides to calculate the culminating point of the attack correctly when planning a campaign. The attacker needed to do so to avoid taking on more than his forces could manage; while the 'defender must be able to recognize this error if the enemy commits it, and exploit it to the full'.[38]

All of these factors not only underscored once again the general superiority of the defense, they also highlighted some particular characteristics of the attack. First, every attack gradually diminished in strength as it progressed; at times this reduction was offset by greater losses on the part of the defense. So, the attacker's loss of strength had to be considered in relation to that of the defender. Nonetheless, the inevitable loss of strength by the attacker had to be accounted for in any war plan. Second, any attack that did not end in peace must eventually grind to a halt, since the strength of the attacker spends itself until it is no longer sufficient to overcome the defense; at that point the attacker must transition to the defense. Clausewitz referred to this as the culminating point of the attack (discussed below).[39] Third, it is a special shortcoming of the attack, that whenever it does not end in peace, it leaves the attacker in the position of having to shift to an ill-prepared defense, unless this eventuality was planned for in advance.[40]

Throughout Books VI and VII Clausewitz considered both forms of war in terms of the situations and circumstances likely to affect them, and be affected by them, such as types of resistance, operations on a flank, fortresses, fortified positions, mountains, rivers, forests, swamps, billets, cordons, and convoys, etc. Space does not permit a complete discussion of them, however. Again, readers will find that Clausewitz's methodology follows the same outline discussed earlier: the general concept itself is first discussed in theoretical terms, then considered with respect to the material world.

## SUPERIORITY OF NUMBERS

Clausewitz wrote that bringing the greatest possible number of troops into action at the decisive point was the 'first principle of strategy'.[41] Strategy, he explained, determined the place, the time, and the forces with which the battle was to be fought, and strategy's role was, therefore, to calculate space and time so as to have a preponderance of force at the decisive point. His historical observations, which ranged from ancient times to his own day, revealed that numerical superiority was the 'most common' element in tactical and strategic victory, though it was never the only factor. Others included the purpose of the engagement, the means used, circumstances of terrain and weather, the skill of the commander, and the fighting value of the troops.

Numerical superiority, he noted, always varied in degree—ranging from 'two to one, or three or four to one, and so on'—so that its influence on victory, too, was one of degree.[42] If the degree was great enough, numerical superiority can overcome all other circumstances and prove decisive. The fundamental goal was, once again, to strive for the greatest degree of superiority of numbers at the decisive point, superiority alone did not guarantee victory. Conversely, the lack of numerical superiority did not mean imminent defeat.

## CONCENTRATION OF FORCES IN SPACE AND TIME

In Clausewitz's view, military commanders should divide their forces only on rare occasions.[43] He railed against the customary practice of dividing and subdiving one's forces in the field and sending them off to perform ancillary tasks. Instead, the purpose of the campaign and the nature of the means to be used should dictate the extent to which we might divide our forces. Moreover, he urged that, since the best strategy was always to be strong at the decisive point, commanders should commit their forces simultaneously rather than sequentially.

Clausewitz argued that in tactics it made sense to commit one's forces sequentially, that is, to keep a reserve of fresh troops to throw into the battle in its final stages, when our opponent's divisions were psychologically exhausted and physically depleted. As a rule, the longer troops were exposed to combat, the less effective they became. Therefore, committing fresh troops to the fight in its final stages could tip the scales in our favor. Exposure time was thus a key factor in tactics. In strategy, however, only a simultaneous commitment of forces made sense. Tactically, we could not carry out an effective sequential commitment of forces—one that outlasted the enemy—unless our strategy had made the maximum number of forces available to us on the battlefield. Strategically, a sequential commitment of forces would only undermine our ability to employ a sequential commitment of troops in tactics, thereby forfeiting an important advantage to our opponent.

Moreover, the mere presence of all possible friendly forces on the field of battle, or in close proximity to it, can influence the outcome in our favor because they will certainly have an effect on the enemy's decisions, even if only a portion of those forces are actually involved in the fighting. The larger the number of friendly troops available for the fight, in other words, the less impact any tactical loss was likely to have on the total force.

Clausewitz also argued that the same logic held true for losses incurred through illness, fatigue, and privation. The larger the force, he reasoned, the greater its ability to address challenges posed by disease, sustenance, and shelter. For instance, a larger army would have more medical facilities at its disposal to combat illness and disease, and it would cover a greater area and thus have access to more forage and shelter. He thus proved the law (*Gesetz*), to his own satisfaction at least, that in strategy one can never be too strong, and that all forces earmarked for a particular strategic purpose 'must be applied to it *simultaneously*'.[44] Moreover, the more we can apply these forces in a single act and at a single moment in time, the better.

## STRATEGIC RESERVE

Clausewitz argued that, in general, the idea of a strategic reserve was a good one. Just as in tactics, a reserve acted as a hedge against uncertainty, as a way to offset unforeseen and unfavorable results. However, he insisted that we should maintain a strategic reserve only in situations in which uncertainty was high. Otherwise, it reduced one's chances of achieving a desirable outcome in the decisive battle. The larger the forces involved, the more difficult it was to conceal their movements. If we can observe our enemy's major movements, then we can reasonably estimate his intentions. The more we move from the realm of tactics toward that of politics, he added, the more certainty we enjoy. Interestingly, this statement contradicts what he argued in Book II, namely, that uncertainty was greater in strategy than tactics. In any case, judgment was again the key. Clausewitz thus concluded that, as a rule, strategy should renounce the use of a reserve.

## ECONOMY OF FORCE

Clausewitz used the phrase economy of force literally—meaning to get the most out of one's forces. 'We must always keep in mind', he warned, 'that no part of one's forces should be idle.'[45] We should not waste forces by sending them on trivial missions, and we should have as many forces engaging our opponent as possible. Nor should we allow the enemy to tie down a large number of our forces with a minimum number of his own. In other words, for Clausewitz this principle was the converse of its modern counterpart.

## SURPRISE

Clausewitz maintained that this principle underpinned all military activity, for without it, one could not achieve superiority at the decisive point.[46] He saw surprise as one of the 'means' by which superiority was attained, and because of the 'psychological effect' it created, which tended to compound material superiority, surprise ranked as a principle in its own right. In his view, surprise was best achieved through secrecy and speed of execution; indeed, in the following chapter, 'Cunning' (*Der List*), he added that surprise owed itself to at least some degree of deception or use of a ruse.[47] He also stressed that only large-scale surprises brought about major results, but cautioned that basic friction made it difficult to achieve large-scale surprise consistently. The greater the intended surprise, the more difficult it was to accomplish.

Overall, he felt that cunning was less important to a commander than genuine understanding and penetrating insight. History did not show cunning to be a significant trait. Nor did it show surprise to be strategically significant, as a rule. Both can aid an inferior force. In desperation one might resort to a ruse or to the use of surprise to compensate for one's weaknesses. In the real world, surprise can create a psychological effect great enough to overshadow weaknesses in one's forces or dispositions. Thus, an inferior combatant lacking in sound knowledge of war can defeat a foe that is superior, and well trained.

## PERSEVERANCE

For Clausewitz, perseverance meant a commander's ability to remain psychologically steadfast in battle, even when inundated by a multitude of negative impressions.[48] High 'courage and stability of character', the principal components of perseverance, were thus essential qualities for any commander.

Clausewitz's principle of perseverance thus concerned only the mind of the commander.

## TURNING MOVEMENTS AND FLANK POSITIONS

The fundamental definitions of turning movements, envelopments, and flanking positions have changed little since Clausewitz's day. Envelopments are maneuvers around an opponent's position, so as to avoid his strength and strike at his flanks and rear. A turning movement is a form of envelopment where an attacker avoids the defender's position entirely in order to seek critical terrain deep in an adversary's rear areas and along his lines of communication, the occupation of which would force the defender to abandon his position.[49] 'The enveloping or turning movement', Clausewitz explained, 'may have two objectives. It may aim at disrupting, or cutting, communications, causing the army to wither and die, and thus be forced to retreat; or it may aim at cutting off the retreat itself.'[50] However, since envelopments tend to expose an attacker's lines of communication to counterattack, Clausewitz argued that they were rarely practicable, being 'imminently more appealing in books than in actual life' and were a threat only to extended lines of communication; even the threat of being cut off and surrounded, he added, should not be overrated, since disciplined troops and bold commanders were more likely to breakout than be trapped.[51]

Clausewitz defined a flank position as any point or location meant to be held after an attacker passed it by, so that it remained a threat to the attacker's strategic flank. Such locations included fortified and unfortified positions, whether perpendicular or parallel to an attacker's line of advance. Flank positions could prove effective, he pointed out, if they forced the attacker to delay his advance; however, they were risky if the attacker was not checked, since the defender essentially forfeited his chances of retreat. As he pointed out, the Prussian army's position on the Saale River during Napoleon's advance in 1806 could have been an effective flanking position.[52]

Rather than treat the act of falling on the enemy's rear as a formula for success, Clausewitz argued that flanking operations in general were most effective only under the following conditions: (*a*) while on the strategic defensive; (*b*) toward the end of a campaign, when the enemy's lines of communication have been extended; (*c*) especially during a retreat into the interior of the country; and (*d*) in conjunction with armed insurrection.[53] All of these conditions, save the last, were present in MacArthur's famous landing at Inchon during the Korean conflict, a classic turning movement that saved UN forces from defeat. As the lethality of the battlefield continues to increase, envelopments (including those vertical in nature) and turning movements are likely to gain even greater significance as forms of maneuver.

## THE CULMINATING POINT OF VICTORY

Clausewitz determined that the moral and physical superiority gained through a victory generally augmented the strength of the victor, adding to his superiority, but only to a point, and this he called the culminating point of victory.[54] This fact, he pointed out, was particularly evident in wars in which it was not possible for the victor to completely defeat his opponent. The same factors that contributed to reducing the strength of the attacker also played a role in diminishing the moral and material superiority that a military force gained through victory:

> ... the use of a victory, the further advance in an offensive war in general, will consume the superiority with which one began or which was obtained by the victory.... This culminating point of victory is thus to be the result in every war where the destruction of the enemy cannot be the military aim, and that will be the case in most wars. The point at which attack becomes defense is, thus, the natural aim of all campaign plans.[55]

## PURPOSE

As we have seen, for Clausewitz, the purpose of the war determined the character of the conflict at every level:

> Since war is no act of blind passion, but rather is subordinated to its political purpose, the value of that purpose must determine the extent of the sacrifices to be made for it. This is not only the case for the *magnitude* of the war, but for its *duration* as well.[56]

If sacrifices begin to exceed the value of the original purpose, we must renounce the purpose and seek peace. 'The original political views', Clausewitz added, 'can change greatly and in the end become something entirely different, *since they are shaped by events and their probable consequences.*'[57] The military aim (*Ziel*), in contrast, should flow from both the nature of the purpose as well as the limitations of the means. Both Clausewitz's concept and the modern principle stress the importance of balancing focus on the objective, on the one hand, and the requirement to adapt appropriately when the situation changes, on the other hand; the key is judgment, which must appreciate *whether*, *when*, and *how* the objective should change.

CONCLUSIONS AND IMPLICATIONS

Although Clausewitz rejected prescriptive theories and doctrines, he clearly believed certain truths, in the form of laws and principles, existed for the conduct of war. Principles emerged from war's underlying cause-and-effect relationships, its laws, and judgment determined how they should be applied. As mentioned previously, many of the principles Clausewitz discussed in *On War* have become part of the canon of official principles now in service with a number of contemporary militaries: objective, offensive, mass, economy of force, maneuver, surprise, security, simplicity, and unity of command or effort.[58] Indeed, these so-called traditional principles hardly advanced beyond his. When we add the other principles he discovered—perseverance, envelopments, and culminating points—we find little indeed that is new in contemporary doctrine.

Despite the emergence of a canon of martial principles, mastering them seems neither sufficient nor necessary for military victory. Mass, maneuver, offensive, and surprise, for instance, did not break the deadlock of trench-warfare in World War I, and might actually have contributed to prolonging the stalemate. So, while some strategists argue the historical 'record shows that winners, by and large, took heed of the Principles', while the losers, 'by and large did not', there is clearly more to the problem.[59] Apparently, not all principles are created equal. Some, depending on circumstances perhaps, trump the rest, either alone or in combination with others. Woe to the strategist who is unable to find the right combination.

Of course, the problem is that principles, by definition and design, simplify, or rather oversimplify, cause-and-effect relationships in the physical world. As Clausewitz warned, practitioners must balance pure principles against material circumstances, a task requiring skilled judgment derived from knowledge and experience. Mastering the principles of war can create a mental 'box' that will both facilitate and impede creative thinking. It is the quality of our judgment, not our mastery of the principles that saves us from becoming confined in the latter. Practitioners can also benefit from the activity—as per Clausewitz's method—of discovering, proving, or revising principles and underlying laws, which can lead to a deeper understanding of war itself.

Nonetheless, some of Clausewitz's principles are more appropriate for a linear than a nonlinear battlefield, one without frontlines. For instance, his culminating point of victory and ideas concerning turning movements and flank positions apply best in linear context, where progress can be measured in terms of territory taken or lost.[60] However, his principles of mass (superiority of numbers, concentration of forces in time and space, and strategic reserve) economy of force, attack and defense, surprise, cunning (simplicity and security), and perseverance, though developed with Napoleonic engagements in mind, would still apply in a nonlinear environment where the aim is to convince more than to destroy.

With the advent of weapons of mass destruction, military doctrine modified the principle of mass—concentrating forces to maximize combat power at the point of decision—to mean the massing of effects, and to accommodate the need for greater dispersion.[61] The tension between concentration and dispersion has been present since the nineteenth century with improvements in firearms. Yet concentration of forces still occurs, though it does so on a larger geographic, if not global, scale; this is true despite attendant claims that the advent of precision-guided munitions obviates the need to concentrate firepower.[62] In Operation Iraqi Freedom, six of twelve American carrier battle groups deployed to the Persian Gulf and the Mediterranean Sea, making them unavailable for use in other theaters, a concentration of forces when viewed globally. Massing effects, thus, still requires some massing of force.

For Clausewitz, economy of force meant principally using all one's combat power to best effect, not leaving troops out of a major battle, or spending one's resources on low-payoff activities. Today, economy of force merely complements mass; achieving the former in one location enables the latter to occur elsewhere. Operation Iraqi Freedom was an example of an attempt to supplant mass with economy of force—or more precisely—to replace the idea of maximizing force with that of minimizing it through greater use of precision, speed of movement, and intelligence.[63] That attempt succeeded well enough in the initial phases of the conflict. However, it failed completely when the conflict morphed into a form of insurgency, and military operations shifted from combat toward providing security (still a form of combat) for reconstruction efforts.[64] Economy of force thus proved inadequate for maintaining control over key people and places. Perhaps security, a core mission in such operations, is also the primary principle that should drive activity in the reconstruction phase of a conflict.

With respect to attack and defense, contemporary military doctrine generally agrees with Clausewitz's view that these concepts are not mutually exclusive.[65] It also stresses that the defense is only a temporary measure, and not decisive. However, contrary to Clausewitz, military doctrine sees more advantages in the attack than in the defense, the most common of which is retaining the initiative. Yet this advantage is more subjective than objective. In martial arts, a defender can take advantage of an attacker's momentum (initiative) to throw him off balance and render him vulnerable, thereby turning a presumed advantage into a disadvantage. Similarly, the term initiative is often confused with having the upper hand; it means simply having the power to force one's opponent to react, but that can apply equally to the defense as well as the attack. When the attacker's actions play into the hands of the defender, as they often do in martial arts, it is the defender who actually has the upper hand, even though he is merely reacting to the blows of the attacker.

The defense does have political advantages: the international community is sometimes slow to respond to crises, but it is more likely to intervene on behalf of a state that has been invaded. However, an overly aggressive counterattack can rapidly undermine those advantages. Operationally and tactically, the advantage appears to rest with the attacker; suicide bombers, car bombs, and improvised explosive devices are just some of the means terrorists have used to attack open societies.[66] Globalization has enhanced the mobility and communication capabilities of nonstate actors, while at the same time increasing the costs of providing security.[67] Attackers may now, for perhaps the first time in history, be limited only by their imaginations.

Today, as in Clausewitz's day, surprise is the use of unexpected means to gain a psychological or physical advantage over an opponent.[68] The means, of course, need not be physical violence; information, or psychological violence, has recently become the weapon of choice, considered by some to be more powerful than physical force. Indeed, 'war of ideas' has become the phrase of choice.[69] Unfortunately, some of history's bloodiest wars have been wars of ideas. Another use of information, deception, has taken the place of cunning in most military literature, and a great deal has been written about it of late.[70] It is, of course, as old as war itself. Nonetheless, the essential and perhaps expanding role of information in conflict is best understood within the context of Clausewitzian theory.[71]

Perseverance for Clausewitz concerned the commander's ability to withstand the stresses and strains of battle, which today is often referred to as psychological resilience. In contrast, contemporary military literature regards perseverance as the ability of officers and soldiers to remain committed to their missions, and to prepare themselves for the possibility of a long struggle. However, in this sense, perseverance is less about will power than it is about suitability, or aptness. A military force is more suitable when it has the capability to communicate with the indigenous population, for instance, and is prepared to help build institutions, not just destroy them.[72]

Perhaps the most serious weakness in contemporary principles and their Clausewitzian antecedents, however, is that they pertain to military operations or battles more than wars, that is, they have a battle-focus rather than a war-focus.[73] A battle-focus differs from a war-focus in that it concentrates on subduing one's adversary more than, and sometimes at the cost of, accomplishing one's political objectives. A war-focus, in contrast, begins with the principal political objective and plans backward from it, and arranges its means accordingly. Surprise, offensive, mass, economy of force, for instance, all have a battle-focus: they are only useful when the military aim is to take down the military forces of one's opponent. In terms of translating military victories into political successes, they avail little. A number of authors have recently tried to develop principles that might help close this gap.[74]

Only objective and maneuver seem to have potential for a war-focus, but they require some modification. Contemporary US doctrine, for instance, states that 'the purpose of objective is to direct every military operation toward a clearly defined, decisive, and attainable objective'.[75] Not only is this definition a tautology, it addresses only the military aim (*Ziel*) of the war, as if the political purpose (*Zweck*) were irrelevant. The purpose sets the aim and determines the desired results. Doctrine would do well, therefore, to distinguish between purpose and aim as Clausewitz did, and not to assume decisive victory always serves the purpose. Of course, in military doctrine, the military aim typically displaces the political purpose, but this only pushes war into the realm of logical necessity, which as we have seen is not reflective of reality.

Doctrine would also do well to include a discussion of political maneuver, placing one's opponent in a position of disadvantage politically, which must occur before, during, and after operational maneuver. It is best to see operational maneuver as embedded in and subordinate to political maneuver, rather than attempting to follow a logic of its own. So, even if not all of Clausewitz's principles remain valid in the context of contemporary war, his underlying laws do, and they provide a basis for developing martial principles appropriate for today.

## NOTES

1. Alger, *Quest for Victory*, 4.
2. Department of Defense, *Doctrine for Joint Operations: Joint Publication 3-0* (Washington, DC, 2006), Appendix A. It is not in the scope of this chapter to compare the principles of war of every major military to those of Clausewitz; instead, I use those outlined in US joint doctrine as representative since they are the most recent, and because as Zvi Lanir, 'The "Principles of War" and Military Thinking', *The Journal of Strategic Studies*, 16/1 (March 1993), 1–17, reveals, the

principles of major Western and non-Western militaries have been more similar than not. The most recent British principles (2001), for instance, revert 'back to the wording used in a version produced shortly after the Second World War and promulgated by the likes of Montgomery and Slim'. Maj. Gen. A. A. Milton, 'British Defense Doctrine & the British Approach to Military Operations', *RUSI Journal*, 146/6 (December 2001), 41–4, here 42.
3. A major effort in this regard recently concluded; compare: Anthony D. McIvor (ed.), *Rethinking the Principles of War* (Annapolis, MD: Naval Institute, 2005), a collection of twenty-nine essays concerning various aspects of and recommendations for the canon; Robert Leonhard, *Principles of War for the Information Age* (Novato, CA: Presidio, 1998); Russell W. Glenn, 'No More Principles of War?', *Parameters*, 28/1 (spring 1998), 48–66; William T. Johnsen, Douglas V. Johnson II, James O. Kievit, Douglas C. Lovelace, Jr, and Steven Metz, *The Principles of War in the 21st Century: Strategic Considerations* (Carlisle, PA: Strategic Studies Institute, 1995), suggest revising the principles of initiative, unity of effort, and security, and adding focus, orchestration, and clarity.
4. For the conventional wisdom, see Brodie, *War and Politics*, 446; and Alger, *Quest for Victory*, 186.
5. Carl von Clausewitz, *Die wichtigsten Grundsätze des Kriegführens zur Ergänzung meines Unterrichts bei Sr. Königlichen Hoheit dem Kronprinzen*. Reprinted in *Vom Kriege*, 1047–86.
6. *Vom Kriege*, VIII/1, 951; *On War*, 578.
7. Kiesewetter, *Grundriss*, I, 491.
8. Respectively: *Vom Kriege*, III/6 'Die Kühnheit'; III/8 'Überlegenheit der Zahl', III/11 'Sammlung der Kräfte im Raum', and III/12 'Vereinigung der Kräfte im Zeit'; III/7 'Beharrlichkeit', III/9 'Die Überraschung', and III/14 'Ökonomie der Kräfte'; III/10 'Die List'. One could even take his chapters on psychological forces—III/3 'Moralische Größen' (Moral Forces); III/4 'Die Moralische Hauptpotentzen' (Principal Moral Elements); and III/5 'Kriegerische Tugend des Heeres' (Military Virtues of the Army)–and equate them to what some called another principle of war, morale. Thomas B. Vaughn, 'Morale: The 10th Principle of War', *Military Review*, 63 (May 1983), 29.
9. *Vom Kriege*, II/2, 289–92, II/4, 307; *On War*, 140–1, 152.
10. *Vom Kriege*, 182–3; *On War*, 71; enumeration added for clarity. The second principle, concerning the relationship between 'major and minor successes', underpins Clausewitz's concept of the center of gravity, and so is discussed in Chapter 8. He wrote time and again about the interdependence of events in war: 'small things always depend on great ones, the unimportant upon the important, and the incidental upon the essential'. For example, the defeat of the main Prussian army at Jena-Auerstadt in 1806 led to a number of smaller garrisons and depots falling rather quickly into French hands. *Vom Kriege*, VIII/4, 976; *On War*, 596.
11. Clausewitz initially avoided discussing strategic principles, but offered the following examples of tactical principles: we must not use cavalry against

unbroken infantry, except in emergencies; we should not discharge firearms until the foe is within effective range; one should hold back as many troops as possible for the final phase of the fight. *Vom Kriege*, II/4, 307; *On War*, 152.
12. Alger, *Quest for Victory*, 122–3.
13. *Vom Kriege*, VI/30, 858–9; *On War*, 516–17.
14. *Vom Kriege*, VIII/6, 989; *On War*, 604.
15. The defense receives special attention in *Vom Kriege*, Book VI 'Defense' chapters 1–5; see also, Book I, chapter 1; Book VII 'Attack' chapters 1–2; and Book VIII 'The Plan of War' chapter 8.
16. *Vom Kriege*, VI/1, 613, VI/8, 647; *On War*, 357, 379.
17. Azar Gat, 'Clausewitz on Defense and Attack', *Journal of Strategic Studies*, 11/8 (March 1988), 20–6, makes this error, and thus confuses Clausewitz's analysis of defense from the standpoint of pure logic with his observations of the defense in a practical sense.
18. *Vom Kriege*, VI/1, 614; *On War*, 358.
19. *Vom Kriege*, VI/2, 618; *On War*, 360.
20. *Vom Kriege*, VI/3, 622–3; *On War*, 363.
21. *Vom Kriege*, VI/1, 619; *On War*, 359.
22. *Vom Kriege*, VI/8, 649; *On War*, 379.
23. *Vom Kriege*, VI/9, 669; *On War*, 392.
24. Herberg-Rothe, *Rätsel Clausewitz*, 39–43.
25. *Vom Kriege*, VI/5, 633–4; *On War*, 370.
26. *Vom Kriege*, VII/2, 871; *On War*, 524.
27. *Vom Kriege*, VI/1, 615, 613; *On War*, 357.
28. Creveld, 'Eternal Clausewitz', 44.
29. *Vom Kriege*, VI/5, 634; *On War*, 370; George H. Quester, *Offense and Defense in the International System* (New Brunswick, NJ: Transaction, 2003), attempts to examine the relative strengths of attack and defense from the standpoint of capabilities, and concludes 'Offenses produce war and/or empire; defenses support defenses and peace', 208; whereas, for Clausewitz, war begins with defense.
30. *Vom Kriege*, VI/7, 644; *On War*, 377.
31. *Vom Kriege*, VII/1, 869; *On War*, 523.
32. *Vom Kriege*, VII/2, 871; *On War*, 524.
33. *Vom Kriege*, VII/(22), 943–4; *On War*, 572.
34. *Vom Kriege*, VII/4, 877; *On War*, 527.
35. *Vom Kriege*, VII/5, 880; *On War*, 528.
36. *Vom Kriege*, VII/2, 873–4, VII/(22), 942; *On War*, 524–5, 570–1.
37. *Vom Kriege*, VII/(22), 942; *On War*, 571.
38. *Vom Kriege*, VII/(22), 943–4; *On War*, 572.
39. *Vom Kriege*, VII/5, 879; *On War*, 528.
40. *Vom Kriege*, VII/(22), 944; *On War*, 572.
41. *Vom Kriege*, III/8, 374; *On War*, 195.
42. *Vom Kriege*, III/8, 374; *On War*, 194.

43. *Vom Kriege*, III/11, 388; *On War*, 204.
44. *Vom Kriege*, III/12, 395–6; *On War*, 207; emphasis original.
45. *Vom Kriege*, III/14, 401; *On War*, 213.
46. *Vom Kriege*, III/9, 379; *On War*, 198.
47. *Vom Kriege*, III/10, 386; *On War*, 202.
48. *Vom Kriege*, III/7 'Beharrlichkeit' 371; *On War*, 193.
49. *Vom Kriege*, V/16 'Verbindungslinien' (Lines of Communication) discusses turning movements; VI/14 'Flankenstellungen' (Flank Positions), and VI/24 'Flankenwirkung' (Operations on a Flank) discuss their namesakes in some detail.
50. *Vom Kriege*, V/16, 600; *On War*, 346–7.
51. *Vom Kriege*, V/16, 600; *On War*, 347.
52. *Vom Kriege*, VI/14, 704–5; *On War*, 415–16.
53. *Vom Kriege*, VI/24, 776–7; *On War*, 465.
54. *Vom Kriege*, VII/(22), 935; *On War*, 566.
55. *Vom Kriege*, VII/(22), 940–2; *On War*, 570.
56. *Vom Kriege*, I/2, 217, emphasis original; *On War*, 92.
57. *Vom Kriege*, I/2, 217–18, emphasis original; *On War*, 92.
58. The British army, at the urging of J.F.C. Fuller, was evidently the first to codify an official list of principles, which it did in 1920; the US Army followed one year later. Alger, *Quest for Victory*, 115–16, 122–5. Fuller believed martial principles were 'eternal, universal, and fundamental', though his list of 'eternal' principles varied from one manuscript to another. Still, the British army's official 'Principles of War' have survived, albeit in modified form, to the present. Ironically, Fuller's influence also played a part in the later abandonment of official principles, albeit temporarily, as criticism of his book, *Foundations of the Science of War*, and his political views mounted, and caused him to fall from public favor. Alger, *Quest for Victory*, 125–6, 186.
59. John M. Collins, *Grand Strategy: Principles and Practices* (Annapolis, MD: Naval Institute, 1973), 28.
60. Some military doctrine formally recognizes the idea of culminating points as a key concept of operational design: 'The art of attack at all levels is to achieve decisive objectives before the culminating point is reached. Conversely, the art of defense is to hasten the culmination of the attack.' FM 100–5, pp. 6–8 (1993). See also George M. Hall, 'Culminating Points', *Military Review* (July 1989), 79–86.
61. JP 3–0, A–1. Leonhard, *Principles of War*, 94–7, argues that, from the standpoint of kill ratios, mass has never been a valid principle.
62. Stephen D. Biddle, 'Allies, Airpower, and Modern Warfare: The Afghan Model in Afghanistan and Iraq', *International Security*, 30 (winter 2005–6), 161–76; Paul Murdock, 'Principles of War on the Network-Centric Battlefield: Mass and Economy of Force', *Parameters*, 32/1 (spring 2002), 86–95. Gen. Gordon R. Sullivan and Col. James M. Dubik, U.S. Army, 'Land Warfare in the 21st Century', *Military Review* (September 1993), 22, traces the expansion of the

battlefield through the 1991 Gulf War. Lt. Col. Edward Mann, 'One Target, One Bomb: Is the Principle of Mass Dead?', *Military Review* (September 1993), 33–41.

63. Summary of Lessons Learned, Prepared Testimony by Secretary of Defense Donald H. Rumsfeld and General Tommy R. Franks, presented to the Senate Armed Services Committee, July 9, 2003; Harlan K. Ullman and James P. Wade, *Shock and Awe: Achieving Rapid Dominance* (Washington, DC: National Defense University, 1996).
64. Max Boot, 'The Struggle to Transform the Military', *Foreign Affairs*, 84/2 (March–April 2005), 103–18.
65. JP 3–0, A–1. Leonhard, *Principles of War*, 80–5, challenges the primacy of the offensive in military thinking, and maintains it has never been a valid principle of war, and cannot be separated from defense.
66. An interesting but controversial analysis of the tactic and motives behind suicide bombing is Robert A. Pape, *Dying to Win: The Strategic Logic of Suicide Terrorism* (New York: Random House, 2005), who contends that it is motivated by the political aim of forcing an 'occupier' to leave, rather than by religious fundamentalism. Andrew Silke, 'The Role of Suicide in Politics, Conflict, and Terrorism', *Terrorism and Political Violence*, 18 (spring 2006), 35–46.
67. Antulio J. Echevarria II, 'Globalization and the Clausewitzian Nature of War', *The European Legacy*, 8/3 (June 2003), 317–32; and Herfried Münkler, 'Ist Terrorismus eine neue Form der Kriegführung? Einige Überlegungnen im Anschluss an Clausewitz', in Berlin Colloquium 2003, 'Kampf gegen den Terrorismus', Clausewitz-Gesellschaft, e.v., Heft 4, 24–34.
68. JP 3–0, A–1. Leonhard, *Principles of War*, 182–93, rightly contends that surprise will only increase in importance in future warfare; Col. B. R. Isbell, 'The Future of Surprise on the Transparent Battlefield', in *Science of War*, 149–63, expresses similar views.
69. US Secretary of Defense, Donald H. Rumsfeld, recently stated: 'If I were grading I would say we probably deserve a 'D' or a 'D-plus' as a country as to how well we're doing in the battle of ideas that's taking place in the world today.' http://www.cbsnews.com/stories/2006/03/27/terror/main1442811.shtml.
   Zeyno Baran, 'Fighting the War of Ideas', *Foreign Affairs*, 84/6 (November/December 2005), 68–78; Robert Satloff (ed.), *The Battle of Ideas in the War on Terror: Essays on US Public Diplomacy in the Middle East* (Washington, DC: Washington Institute for Near East Policy, 2004).
70. Department of Defense, *Joint Doctrine for Military Deception, Joint Publication 3-58* (Washington, DC, 1996), identifies five types of deception: strategic, operational, tactical, service, and that related to operational security. See Roy Godson and James J. Wirtz, 'Strategic Denial and Deception', *International Journal of Intelligence and Counterintelligence*, 13/4 (winter 2000), 424–36; James F. Dunnigan and Albert A. Nofi, *Victory and Deceit: Dirty Tricks at War* (New York: William Morrow, 1995).

71. This is the point of Robin Brown, 'Clausewitz in the Age of Al-Jazeera: Rethinking the Military–Media Relationship', August 28, 2002; http:\\www.clausewitz.com
72. David H. Petraeus, 'Learning Counterinsurgency: Observations from Soldiering in Iraq', *Military Review*, 86 (January–February 2006), 2–12.
73. Antulio J. Echevarria II, 'Principles of War or Principles of Battle?', in *Rethinking the Principles of War*, 58–78.
74. Bathsheba Crocker, John Ewers, and Craig Cohen, 'Rethinking and Rebuilding the Relationship between War and Policy: Post-Conflict Reconstruction', and Mary H. Kaldor, 'Principles for the Use of the Military in Human Security Operations', in *Rethinking the Principles of War*, 360–87, 388–400, respectively.
75. JP 3–0, A–1. Leonhard, *Principles of War*, suggests replacing objective with 'options', 138–61, but this solution has numerous political implications.

# 8

# Center of Gravity

The term center of gravity, which Clausewitz defined as the 'focal point of force and movement, upon which the larger whole depends', appears more than fifty times in *On War*.[1] He clearly considered it important. It also figures large in contemporary military doctrine. However, a number of theorists and practitioners actively question the value of a concept developed nearly two centuries ago, within a now distant culture, by a theorist who was equipped with very different conceptual tools.[2] After all, Clausewitz's thinking was obviously influenced by his experiences in the industrial-age wars of Napoleon, who typically sought to amass superior forces for a decisive battle.

As we have seen, concentration of forces is no longer considered a valid principle of war, and in today's globalized world, the trend is toward noncontiguous operations; in any case, terrorists, insurgents, and other nonstate actors seem to have no physical center to attack. Moreover, the concept of center of gravity smacks of linear thinking.[3] That does not sit well in an age that desires to embrace the nonlinear, the complex, and the chaotic. These issues notwithstanding, the concept's advocates have perhaps been too optimistic, and its critics too skeptical. Clausewitz's center of gravity remains valid today, but before applying it we need to gain a better understanding of his original concept, and appreciate its limitations.

## COMPETING DEFINITIONS

Since the Clausewitzian renaissance of the 1980s, military theorists and practitioners have wrestled with defining centers of gravity, which US doctrine once upheld as the keys to 'all operational design'.[4] In the process, the concept acquired a broad range of meanings. For instance, the concept appealed to maneuver theorists of the 1980s and 1990s, who defined it as the element—an enemy force, important terrain features, boundaries between army groups, or lines of communication–which, if destroyed or neutralized, would result in a rapid, blitzkrieg-style victory.[5] In a similar vein, airpower theorists, such as John Warden, claimed that striking an opponent's various centers of gravity simultaneously would force him into a sort of strategic paralysis.[6] Other military theorists, such as J.C. Wylie, argued that centers of gravity equated to the 'critical aspects' of the particular kind of conflict (continental, maritime, air, guerilla, etc.), the control of which could compel an opponent to comply with one's strategic objectives.[7] Similarly, counterinsurgency experts like Andrew Krepinevich held that the center of gravity for those kinds of conflicts was 'the target nation's population'.[8] Key US decision-makers apparently agree; as Secretary of Defense Donald Rumsfeld stated, 'We are fighting a battle where the survival of our free way of life is at stake and the center of gravity of that struggle in not simply on the battlefield overseas; it's a test of wills, and it will be won or lost with our publics, and with the publics of other nations.'[9] Other authors suggested that centers of gravity might lie more in the so-called aftermath of war, in 'governance operations', those activities related to political and economic reconstruction; indeed, it may be in the so-called aftermath where one's political objectives are finally attained.[10]

Official military doctrine was hardly more consistent; each of the services developed different interpretations, ranging from key vulnerabilities to sources of strength.[11] As a result, some military writers complained, and with justification, that service definitions had collectively stretched the meaning of center of gravity beyond the point of practical utility; the term had come to mean virtually 'anything worthy of being attacked'.[12] Centers of gravity thus resembled Jomini's decisive points—anything that, if captured or destroyed, 'would imperil or seriously weaken the enemy'.[13]

When US Joint doctrine arrived in the mid-1990s, it only added to the confusion. Joint Publication 3-0, the doctrinal foundation of US operations, declared that the essence of the operational art was the massing of effects against an enemy's sources of power, or centers of gravity, to gain a decisive advantage; it defined centers of gravity as the 'characteristics, capabilities, or locations from which a military force derives its freedom of action, physical strength, or will to fight'.[14] It went on to state that, from a strategic perspective, centers of gravity might include a military force, an alliance, national will or level of public support, a set of critical capabilities or functions, or a belligerent's national strategy itself. From an operational perspective, centers of gravity might be the principal element of combat power, such as an armored reserve, that can either assure, or prevent, the accomplishment of one's objectives. The current (2006) incarnation of that doctrine defines centers of gravity essentially as sources of strength, though the examples it offers often do not accord with this definition.[15]

## UNDERSTANDING THE PURE CONCEPT

This approach contrasts markedly with that of Clausewitz, who saw a center of gravity as the thing that, if struck, would lead one to decisive victory. His development of the concept was evidently inspired by the lectures of German physicist Paul Erman, a professor at the University of Berlin and the War College, and a member of the Royal Academy of Sciences. We know Clausewitz and Erman had at least a cordial relationship, with the former purportedly attending the latter's lectures for an entire year without missing any.[16] Indeed, Clausewitz's definition is consistent with how the concept is represented in elementary physics.

Physicists describe a center of gravity as the point where gravitational forces converge within an object; accordingly, taking the center of gravity away, should cause the object or individual to collapse. As Clausewitz explained:

> ... it is against that part of the enemy's forces where they are most concentrated that, if a blow were to occur, the effect would emanate the farthest; furthermore, the greater the mass our own forces possess when they deliver the blow, the more certain we can be of the blow's success. This simple train of thought lends itself to an analogy that enables us to grasp the idea more clearly, namely, the nature and effect of a center of gravity in the mechanical sciences.[17]

The center of gravity may not be the most economical or practical point against which to strike an object, however.

According to the laws of physics, we can think of an object in two ways: as a composite of many smaller particles, each of which is acted on by gravity; or as a single object, which is acted on by gravity only at a single point.[18] Understandably, physicists prefer the latter, since it makes calculating the interaction of force and matter that much easier. However, they also acknowledge that a center of gravity amounts to little more than a mathematical approximation, since gravity acts on *all* the points in an object simultaneously.

Calculating a center of gravity for a simple, symmetrical object—a ruler, a rock, a boomerang—is not difficult. The center of gravity for a ruler is located at its midpoint. The center of gravity for a sphere lies at its geometric center. Interestingly, the center of gravity for a boomerang, though not difficult to calculate, does not lie on the object itself, but in the space between the V.[19] So, striking at the center of gravity of a boomerang will do the instrument little harm. We would need to strike at one of the legs of the V.

However, calculating the center of gravity for a complex object, such as a bolos or a human being with multiple moving parts, is more difficult. Such objects must be artificially frozen in time and space. When a complex object changes the distribution of its weight, its body position, or if external mass is added, or subtracted, the center of gravity shifts. For example, the center of gravity of a wrestler standing erect would be at a spot roughly behind his navel. If the wrestler raises his arms, he also lifts his center of gravity to a point somewhere above his navel. If he moves about rapidly, his center of gravity changes just as rapidly. If he becomes locked in hand-to-hand contest with an opponent, as in Clausewitz's metaphor of two wrestlers, the gravitational forces acting on both bodies will affect the centers of gravity of each. A physicist might treat both masses as one and calculate a common center of gravity for the total mass. However, if the struggle continues at a quick pace, the centers of gravity will naturally change faster than is possible to calculate.

Strictly speaking, therefore, an individual's center of gravity is *not* a source of strength, though balance, weight, and leverage certainly matter in wrestling. Rather, it represents the point of confluence where gravitational forces come together. A combatant's strength, for instance, might derive from his muscles, his brains, or his weapons, or any combination of them. They relate to his center of gravity only so far as he needs *balance* to use them.

Nor is a center of gravity necessarily a weakness. A combatant might be physically weak, intellectually challenged, or in need of weapons. While these deficiencies would obviously equate to weaknesses in a combat situation, they have little to do with the soldier's center of gravity. A center of gravity is not a weakness, per se, though it can be weak, or vulnerable if it is exposed.

## UNDERSTANDING THE APPLIED CONCEPT

Clausewitz added that the center of gravity concept applies wherever a certain 'unity' (*Einheit*) and 'connectivity' or 'interdependence' (*Zusammenhang*) exist with respect to an adversary's forces and the space they occupy.[20] The type and number of his centers of gravity will thus depend on the degree of connectivity, or overall unity, that his forces possess:

Just as the center of gravity is always found where the mass is most concentrated, and just as every blow directed against the body's center of gravity yields the greatest effect, and—more to the point—the strongest blow is the one delivered by the center of gravity, the same is true in war. The armed forces of every combatant, whether an individual state or an alliance of states, have a certain unity and thus a certain *interdependence* or *connectivity* (*Zusammenhang*); and where such interdependence exists, we can apply the center of gravity concept. Accordingly, there exist *within* these armed forces certain centers of gravity which, by their movement and direction, exert a decisive influence over all other points; and these centers of gravity exist *where* the forces are most concentrated. However, just as in the world of inanimate bodies where the effect on a center of gravity is at once limited and enhanced by the interdependence of the parts, the same is true in war [Emphasis added].[21]

It is important to point out that Clausewitz's statement that the center of gravity is found 'where the forces are most concentrated' refers less to the forces, than to what concentrates them. As in physics, his center of gravity concept acts as a *focal point*: a nucleus where forces of power and movement come together.

Clausewitz's critique of Napoleon's actions during the so-called brilliant February campaign of 1814 illustrates the point. Napoleon, with about 70,000 men, confronted advancing Prussian and Austrian armies numbering about 200,000 men; Bonaparte first defeated Marshal Blücher's Army of Silesia (75,000) in successive engagements, then turned to face General Schwarzenberg's Army of Bohemia (125,000), and drove it back as well. However, Napoleon failed to achieve a truly decisive victory against either of his foes; both regrouped and resumed their advance on Paris, eventually resulting in Bonaparte's abdication in April 1814, and his exile to the island of Elba one month later.[22]

Clausewitz argued that Napoleon should have continued hammering away at Blücher until the Army of Silesia was crushed, rather than battling two opponents successively and achieving only incomplete victories: 'Blücher, though numerically weaker than Schwarzenberg, was nonetheless the more important adversary due to his enterprising spirit; hence, the center of gravity lay more with him, and it pulled the rest of the allied forces in his direction'.[23] In other words, defeating Blücher decisively would have caused the Austrians to withdraw; Blücher was, therefore, the allies' center of gravity, even though he had fewer forces than Schwarzenberg.

For Clausewitz, then, the term center of gravity refers less to the concentrated forces than to the actual element that causes them to concentrate and gives them purpose and direction. Arguably, Blücher's personal enmity toward the French, which was apparently legendary, was the ultimate focal point. Regardless, the point remains that centers of gravity are more than concentrations of combat forces. Moreover, Clausewitz attributed 'spheres of effectiveness', or influence, to centers of gravity: the 'advance or retreat' of such centers can affect other forces.[24] Accordingly, as focal points, such as Blücher, advance or withdraw across the battlefield they tend to draw friendly forces with them. In short, Clausewitz's centers of gravity draw energy and resources to themselves, and then redirect them elsewhere: they possess centripetal or inward-moving force, which they can convert into a centrifugal or outward-moving power.

In Book VI, Clausewitz's concept adheres rather closely to the physics' analogy; in Book VIII, he addresses its applicability to planning a war:

What theory can admit to thus far is the following: everything depends upon keeping the dominant characteristics of both states in mind. From these emerge a certain center of gravity, a focal point of force and movement, upon which the larger whole depends; furthermore, it is against the enemy's center of gravity that we must direct the collective blow of all of our power.

Small things always depend on large ones, the unimportant on the important, the incidental on the essential. This relationship must guide our thoughts.

Alexander the Great, Gustavus Adolphus, Charles XII, and Frederick the Great each had their centers of gravity in their respective armies. If their armies had been destroyed, these men would have been remembered as failures. In states with many factions vying for power, the center of gravity lies mainly in the capital; in small states supported by a more powerful one, it lies in the army of the stronger state; in alliances it lies in the unity formed by common interests; in popular uprisings it lies in the persons of the principal leaders and in public opinion. The blow must be directed against these things. If the enemy loses his balance after such a blow, he must not be allowed to regain it; blows must rain down on him continuously. In other words, the victor must direct all of his blows in such a way that they will strike at the whole of the enemy, not just a part of him.[25]

In other words, the center of gravity can be discussed only after we consider our opponent holistically, that is, after we analyze the connections among his various elements and determine what, if anything, holds them together. In this sense, the armies of Alexander, Gustavus, Charles XII, and Frederick II were significant *not* because they were sources of power, but because they formed centers of power that enabled these leaders to hold their states together. In each of these cases, the actual sources of power consisted of (*a*) the population base for the conscription of soldiers, (*b*) the manufacturing base for producing arms, and (*c*) the economic base for financing the overall effort.[26]

Put differently, these sources supplied the raw power that came together in the form of organizations called armies, which were in turn controlled with discipline, punishments, rewards, incentives, and other measures, and made to serve as instruments of the state. Hence, it is more accurate to think of military organizations as focal points where different kinds of power come together, rather than as sources of power.

Under some circumstances, as Clausewitz pointed out, the personalities of key leaders, a state's capital, or its network of allies and their community of interests might perform the centripetal or centralizing function of a focal point.[27] Certainly, his ideas accord with current counterinsurgency theories, which hold that the centers of gravity for popular uprisings are the personalities of the principal leaders and public opinion.[28]

Clausewitz reinforced this point in Book VIII, chapter 9, 'Plan of a War Designed to Lead to the Total Defeat of an Enemy', where he explained that finding a center of gravity depends: 'first, upon the [opponent's] political connectivity (*Zusammenhang*) or unity' and 'second, upon the situation in the theater of war itself, and which of the various enemy armies appear there.'[29] The criterion once again is the extent to which we could regard the enemy's forces as a single entity. Napoleon could well have looked for one center of gravity for his war in Spain, and quite another one for his campaigns in eastern Europe; the allied efforts in each case were separated enough politically and geographically to be regarded as two different wars. Hence, the unity, or lack of it, formed by political–military forces and the geographical spaces they occupy can create more than one center of gravity.

Clausewitz advised tracing these back to a single one whenever possible. Yet he also allowed for the possibility that an adversary might lack the unity necessary to have a specific center of gravity; units which have lost their leaders and cohesion, and unorganized rabble, for instance, would probably not have centers of gravity. The key, then, is whether the separate elements of an adversary are 'connected' sufficiently so that actions against him in one area will affect him appreciably in others.

In this same chapter of *On War*, Clausewitz outlined two war-planning principles, the first of which involves the center of gravity:

The first principle is: To trace the full weight (*Gewicht*) of the enemy's power (*Macht*) to as few centers of gravity as possible, when feasible, to one; and, at the same time, to reduce the blow against these centers of gravity to as few major actions as possible, when feasible, to one. And, finally, to keep all subordinate actions as subordinate as possible. In a word, the first principle is: To act with the utmost concentration. The second principle is: To act as rapidly as possible, permitting no delay or detour without substantial justification.[30]

Notably, he did not offer similar principles for wars of limited purposes and aims, though that is common practice today. Centers of gravity, he observed, were more 'operative' (*wirksame*) the more we tend toward campaigns or wars designed to defeat an adversary completely.[31] Otherwise, the psychological and material forces engaged are not strong enough to bring centers of gravity to the surface. Indeed, as we saw in Chapter 7, he was not altogether sure he could find any laws or principles for operations where a decision was not sought: prudence and common sense seemed to offer the only valid guidelines, though as the last chapter of Book VI suggests, he remained unsatisfied with this conclusion.[32]

184   *Strategy, Balancing Purpose, and Means*

Clausewitz's concept has been called linear because his description seemingly implies a relationship based on directly proportional effects: a center of gravity attacks a center of gravity to produce a decisive result. Yet, in some respects, his concept implies a nonlinear relationship as well, because the embattled centers of gravity are not always similar; an army versus public opinion, for example, pits a physical mass against an attitude, which might easily generate disproportionate results. Similar results can also occur when attacking something intangible, such as an alliance's community of interests, or something relatively small, such as a political or military leader, which can bring down an entire state or coalition.

## CONCLUSIONS AND IMPLICATIONS

In summation, Clausewitz's center of gravity is best thought of as a focal point, rather than as a source of strength, or a specific strength or weakness. Centers of gravity only exist where an adversary's separate parts are connected enough to form a single entity; they can be said to possess centripetal forces of a sort, which act to hold systems or structures together. Striking or neutralizing the focal points, therefore, should cause the systems to collapse.

Moreover, in Clausewitz's view, centers of gravity only become truly evident in wars in which a decision is sought; such conflicts unleash powerful forces, and competition between military aims and political purposes is minimal. In wars where a decision is not sought, collapsing an opponent's entire system or structure might not serve one's political purposes, and might indeed run counter to them. For instance, the First Iraq War (1990–1) was a limited conflict in which the center of gravity concept should not applied. Translating the war's strategic objectives—(*a*) withdrawal of Iraqi forces from Kuwait, (*b*) restoration of legitimate government in Kuwait, (*c*) assuring security and stability of the Persian Gulf region, and (*d*) protecting American lives—into operational and tactical objectives should have given coalition forces everything they needed to focus their efforts in order to achieve success.[33]

However, the US combatant commander, General Norman Schwartzkopf, and his air component commander, General Charles Horner, developed competing ideas of the Iraqi centers of gravity. Schwarzkopf saw three distinct centers of gravity: Saddam Hussein; the Republican Guard; and Iraqi chemical, biological, and nuclear capabilities. Horner, whose thinking was evidently influenced by some of the tenets of airpower theory, identified twelve 'target sets' ranging from national leadership and command and control to railroads, airfields, and ports—each of which in his view corresponded to a center of gravity. Consequently, and quite needlessly, the planning staff at US Central Command spent too much time trying to determine what the centers of gravity were rather than what to do about them.[34]

Unless our military aim is to render the enemy defenseless, inserting the concept of center of gravity into the strategic planning process is unnecessary, and possibly harmful. Regrettably, military doctrine generally fails to appreciate this point, asserting that centers of gravity exist for all kinds, and at all levels, of war. Defeating tactical centers of gravity is assumed in all cases to facilitate the accomplishment of tactical objectives, which, in turn, contribute to the defeat of operational centers of gravity, which likewise assist in accomplishing operational objectives, and so on.[35]

Yet this rationale inevitably leads to overuse of the term. Certainly, we can search for, and likely find keys to 'winning' wars where decisions are not sought; however, we ought to refrain from referring to these as centers of gravity, as that would only dilute the term. If everything is a center of gravity, nothing is. In military doctrine, the purpose of identifying centers of gravity is to assist practitioners to focus their efforts and resources. As one former US Army general explained, approaching a military problem 'from the perspective of a center of gravity leads you to see very quickly that some vulnerabilities are interesting but a waste of resources because they do not lead anywhere useful in the end'.[36] We should restrict our use of centers of gravity to wars where the complete defeat of an opponent is sought; if the term is overused it will lose its value. Should that occur, one might ask why bother identifying them at all.[37]

Centers of gravity are more than critical capabilities. They are points which, if attacked or neutralized, would bring about the complete collapse of an opponent. At present, the war against al-Qaeda is limited only by the means employed, rather than the purposes at stake. Hundreds of Islamist leaders and clerics have purportedly declared a 'defensive jihad' that requires every Muslim to participate, either by taking up arms, providing financial donations, or safe havens: 'complete victory over the infidels is a goal that "is not subject to discussion", and permits "no half-solutions" and "no bargaining"'.[38] Hence, it is the kind of conflict where political purposes are completely in alignment with attacking an opponent's center of gravity, though history tells us that such wars do not necessarily end in the political annihilation of one side or the other.[39]

By comparison, the Iraq War of 1990–1 was not such a conflict, even though, to use Clausewitz's framework, the physical and psychological forces engaged were sufficient to cause centers of gravity to emerge. NATO's interventions in Bosnia or Kosovo where, by all accounts, political consensus was rare or nonexistent, were also not appropriate for the use of centers of gravity.[40] Many factors contributed to Slobodan Milošović's decision to accept NATO's terms for settling the Kosovo conflict, for instance; to single out any one of them as the center of gravity oversimplifies the problem.[41]

Jihadist organizations, such as al-Qaeda, might well have decentralized cells and other sympathetic organizations operating globally, if somewhat autonomously. Nonetheless, a certain political unity can be found in their avowed hatred of apostasy and secularism.[42] This unity thus reveals an obvious focal point. The center of gravity of such groups is thus more political and ideological than physical in nature.[43] In any case, reducing the ideological appeal of, if not the empathy toward, the jihadist movement overall would, in turn, help reduce the groups' ability to recruit and regenerate themselves.[44]

Such measures would, of course, require large-scale social, political, and economic efforts to address the root causes of terrorism.[45] A major portion of these efforts, of course, is the so-called 'war of ideas'. Yet, contrary to teaming rhetoric concerning this topic, we seem to know little about what wars of ideas are, or how they end.[46] Winning such wars requires spending more diplomatic than military capital; however, a relationship exists between the two that is not widely understood.

Moreover, given the potential for further proliferation of weapons of mass destruction, we must assume that defeating our opponent's center of gravity will not suffice to prevent an attempt, by one of his severed tentacles, to inflict a retaliatory blow. Proliferation of weapons of mass destruction, particularly in today's globalized environment, could well make the center of gravity concept academic: we might have to strike multiple cells of a global network virtually simultaneously to prevent retaliation. In other words, considering each of our adversary's many parts may become just as important as thinking about the sum of those parts.

Clausewitz's center of gravity aims at a specific effect. It is, therefore, an effects-based concept, rather than a capabilities-based one. It should, therefore, encourage more thorough thinking, on the part of policymakers as well as commanders, regarding the ends we wish to achieve. Estimating an opponent's center of gravity requires exercising 'strategic judgment' (*strategische Urteil*), which must be honed through experience, and by internalizing objective knowledge.[47] Although the center of gravity has important limitations, it remains valid even in the mixed context of contemporary war. Misapplying it is, however, a very real possibility, especially in today's globalized environment in which minor elements can operate nearly autonomously and yet with truly devastating destructive power.

## NOTES

1. *Vom Kriege*, VI/27, 810. This chapter is based in part on Antulio J. Echevarria II, 'Clausewitz's Center of Gravity: It's *Not* What We Thought', *Naval War College Review*, 56/1 (winter 2003), 71–8.
2. Compare: T. M. Kriwanek, 'The Operational Center of Gravity' (Ft. Leavenworth, KS: School of Advanced Military Studies, 1986), 20–1, who argues that Clausewitz's concept is rooted in industrial-age warfare; Steven Metz and Frederick M. Downey, 'Centers of Gravity and Strategic Planning', *Military Review*, 68/4 (April 1988), 22–33, urge that it can be useful, but might require too much effort to make it work.
3. Beyerchen, 'Nonlinearity', 87, describes the center of gravity as a linear concept.
4. Department of the Army, *Operations: FM 100–5* (Washington, DC, 1986); FM 3-0. One popular attempt was the CG–CC–CR–CV (center of gravity–critical capabilities–critical requirements–critical vulnerabilities) model of Joe Strange, *Centers of Gravity and Critical Vulnerabilities: Building on the Clausewitzian Foundation So That We Can All Speak the Same Language*, Perspectives on Warfighting Series, no. 4 (Quantico VA: US Marine Corps Association, 1996). It suggests that CGs have critical capabilities (CCs), which, in turn, have critical requirements (CRs)—such as open lines of communication—which enable CCs to function; inadequately protected CRs create critical vulnerabilities (CV), which can be attacked to defeat CGs. This method, thus, defined centers of gravity as critical capabilities. Other methods include the Strategic Helix, which entailed attacking all potential centers of gravity until the real one is hit; it is a 'recon by destruction' approach that assumes unlimited resources; Seow Hiang Lee, 'Center of Gravity or Center of Confusion: Understanding the Mystique', Wright Flyer Paper no. 10 (Maxwell, AL: Air Command and Staff College, 1999), 27–8. The Onion Method amounts to eating one's way through multiple layers of an adversary's national power to get at the center of gravity; Colin Agee, *Peeling the Onion: The Iraqi's Center of Gravity* (Ft. Leavenworth, KS: School of Advanced Military Studies, 1992), 26–7. Both assume the center of gravity lies within the Helix or the Onion.
5. Two works represent the canon of maneuver warfare theory: Robert R. Leonhard, *The Art of Maneuver: Maneuver-Warfare Theory and AirLand Battle* (Novato, CA: Presidio, 1991); William S. Lind, *Maneuver Warfare Handbook* (Boulder, CO: Westview, 1985).
6. John A. Warden III, *The Air Campaign: Planning for Combat* (Washington, DC: National Defense University, 1988), 9–10; and 'The Enemy as a System', *Airpower Journal*, 9/1 (spring 1995), 40–55; see also Phillip Meilinger (ed.), *10 Propositions Regarding Air Power* (Washington, DC: Air Force History and Museums, 1995).
7. Admiral J. C. Wylie, *Military Strategy: A General Theory of Power Control* (Annapolis, MD: US Naval Institute, 1967/1989, 77–8.

8. Krepinevich, 'War in Iraq', 1, 4–6; and *The Army in Vietnam* (Baltimore, MD: Johns Hopkins University Press, 1986), 9 ff.; he also explained that if an external power, such as the United States, provides the bulk of the counterinsurgent forces, then its own population (the home front) becomes a center of gravity as well.
9. SGT Sara Wood, 'Secretary Rumsfeld: U.S. Must Outdo Terrorists in Public Opinion Battle', USA American Forces Press Service, February 18, 2006.
10. Nadia Schadlow, 'War and the Art of Governance', *Parameters*, 33/3 (autumn 2003), 85–94.
11. The US Marine Corps, for instance, tended to define centers of gravity as key vulnerabilities; see Department of the Navy, *Warfighting: Marine Corps Doctrinal Publication 1* (Washington, DC, 1997), 45–7. The US Air Force equated centers of gravity to 'critical points', or nodes, that one could 'surgically' destroy with long-range precision munitions, or other bombing assets; see Department of the Air Force, *Air Force Doctrine Document 1* (Washington, DC, 1997), 79. The US Army came to regard the center of gravity as a 'source of strength', and tended to search for a single one, normally the principal 'characteristic, capability, or locality' that stood in the way of mission accomplishment; see Department of the Army, *Operations: FM 100–5* (Washington, DC, 1993), 6–13. The US Navy amplified this view, defining a center of gravity as 'something the enemy must have in order to continue military operations—a source of strength, but not necessarily strong or a strength in itself'. See Department of the Navy, *Naval Warfare: NDP 1* (Washington, DC, 1994), 35.
12. James Schneider and LTC Lawrence Izzo, 'Clausewitz's Elusive Center of Gravity', *Parameters*, 17/3 (September 1987): 49; William Lind, 'The Operational Art', *Marine Corps Gazette*, 72/4 (April 1988), 45.
13. Jomini, *Summary*; Shy, 'Jomini', *Makers of Modern Strategy*, 152–4.
14. Department of Defense, *Doctrine for Joint Operations: Joint Pub 3-0* (Washington, DC, 1995), GL-4.
15. JP 3-0 (2006) defines a center of gravity as 'the source of moral and physical strength, power, and resistance' that 'provides freedom of action, physical strength, and will to fight', chapter IV, p. 10.
16. Paret, *Clausewitz*, 310–1.
17. *Vom Kriege*, VI/27, 810; *On War*, 485. Most sources citing Clausewitz's definition draw from one of two passages in the Howard–Paret translation: 'the center of gravity is...always found where the mass is concentrated most densely, that it is *the hub of all power and movement*, on which everything depends', and that it emerges from the 'dominant characteristics of both belligerents. The first principle is that the ultimate substance of enemy strength must be traced back to the fewest possible *sources*, and ideally to one alone. The attack on these sources must be compressed into the fewest possible actions—again, ideally, into one. The task of reducing the *sources* of enemy strength to a single center of gravity will depend on: 1. The distribution of the enemy's political power...2. The situation in the theater of war where the various armies are operating' *On War*,

VI/27, 485–6; VIII/4, 595–6. However, this translation strips away the physics' metaphors Clausewitz used to describe the concept, metaphors essential for understanding it. It also creates the impression that a center of gravity derives from a source of strength, or that it is an actual strength. Howard and Paret admit that their translation is more interpretive than literal; also, they surely could not have foreseen the extent to which the US military would adhere to their interpretation literally. The German text reveals that Clausewitz never used the word 'source' (*Quelle*) when describing the concept; nor did he equate the term center of gravity to 'strength' or 'a source of strength'.

18. Geoff Jones, Mary Jones, and Phillip Marchington, *Cambridge Coordinated Science: Physics* (Cambridge: Cambridge University Press, 1993), 52–5.
19. Jones, et al., *Physics*, 53.
20. *Vom Kriege*, V/9, 453.
21. *Vom Kriege*, VI/27, 810–1; *On War*, 485.
22. David G. Chandler, *Campaigns of Napoleon* (New York: Macmillan, 1966), 945–76.
23. *Vom Kriege*, II/5, 324; *On War*, 163.
24. *Vom Kriege*, VI/27, 810–11; *On War*, 485.
25. *Vom Kriege*, VIII/4, 976–7; *On War*, 596.
26. Michael Howard, *War in European History* (Oxford: Oxford University Press, 1979), stresses the importance of each in the evolution of war and armies in Europe.
27. Col. Richard M. Swain, 'Clausewitz, FM 100-5, and the Center of Gravity', *Military Review* (February 1988), 83, and Schneider and Izzo, 'Clausewitz's Elusive Center of Gravity', 49, argue that Clausewitz carried the analogy 'too far' in going beyond concentrations of forces.
28. Hahlweg, 'Clausewitz and Guerrilla Warfare', 127–33; 'Vorlesungen über den kleinem Krieg', *Schriften–Aufsätze–Studien–Briefe*, 208–599.
29. *Vom Kriege*, VIII/9, 1009–10; *On War*, 617.
30. *Vom Kriege*, VIII/9, 1009; *On War*, 617; the word 'source' (*Quelle*) does not appear.
31. *Vom Kriege*, VI/28, 813; *On War*, 488.
32. *Vom Kriege*, VI/30, 857–8; *On War*, 516.
33. Eliot Cohen, et al., *Gulf War Air Power Survey*, 5 vols., Vol. I: *Planning and Command and Control* (Washington, DC: Government Printing Office, 1993), 83–4.
34. cf. Lee, 'Center of Gravity or Center of Confusion', 18–19.
35. JP 3-0, chapter IV, 11.
36. Gen. (Ret.) Huba Wass de Czege, 'Clausewitz: Historical Theories Remain Sound Compass References: The Catch Is Staying on Course', *Army*, 38/9 (September 1988), 42.
37. Eliot A. Cohen, 'Strategy: Causes, Conduct, and Termination of War,' in Richard H. Shultz, Jr, Roy Godson and George H. Quester (eds.), *Security Studies for the 21st Century* (Washington, DC: Brassey's, 1997), 364–6.

38. Michael Scheuer, 'Al-Qaeda's Insurgency Doctrine: Aiming for a "Long War"', *Terrorism Focus*, The Jamestown Foundation 3, no. 8, February 28, 2006; http://www.jamestown.org
39. Timothy Naftali, 'US Counterterrorism before bin Laden', *International Journal* (winter 2004–5), 25–34.
40. R. Craig Nation, *War in the Balkans, 1991–2002* (Carlisle, MA: Strategic Studies Institute, 2003); Ivo H. Daalder and Michael E. O'Hanlon, *Winning Ugly: NATO's War to Save Kosovo* (Washington, DC: Brookings, 2000); Tim Judah, *Kosovo: War and Revenge* (New Haven, CT: Yale University Press, 2000).
41. Stephen T. Hosmer, *Why Milosevic Decided to Settle When He Did* (Santa Monica CA: RAND, Project Air Force, 2001).
42. Sageman, *Understanding Terror Networks*, 178, which presents a 'structuralist' rather than an 'intentionalist' argument, sees 'social bonds' as more important than ideology, but on closer examination, the two seem inseparable.
43. Gerges, *Far Enemy*, 232–5.
44. Ed Blanche, 'Al-Qaeda Recruitment', *Janes Intelligence Review*, 14 (January 2002), 27–8; Paul J. Smith, 'Transnational Terrorism and the al Qaeda Model: Confronting New Realities', *Parameters*, 32/2 (summer 2002), 33–46.
45. Margaret Purdy, 'Countering Terrorism: The Missing Pillar', *International Journal* (winter 2004–5), 3–24; Karin von Hippel, 'The Root Causes of Terrorism: Probing the Myths', *Political Quarterly* (September 2002), 35; Brian Michael Jenkins, 'Strategy: Political Warfare Neglected', *San Diego Union-Tribune*, June 26, 2005; http://www.rand.org/commentary
46. Lee Harris, 'Al Qaeda's Fantasy Ideology: War without Clausewitz', *Policy Review* (August/September 2002), 19–36, illustrates how little we know about the relationship between ideas and war.
47. *Vom Kriege*, II/5, 324; *On War*, 163.

# Conclusion

By 1827, Clausewitz believed he had established the foundation for a revolution in military theory. He was, however, concerned with the form, or in some cases the lack thereof, in which his ideas were expressed, fearing, correctly as it turned out, that they would be endlessly misinterpreted. Perhaps no author's prediction has ever been more accurate. As one prominent historian noted, '*On War* obligingly reflects back the intellectual predispositions of whoever looks into it'.[1] Yet, its value certainly is more than that of 'poetry' or more than 'an expression of the intrinsic contradictions of the human condition', as some have claimed.[2] Instead, it is an indispensable part of our body of knowledge concerning war.

Readers who give as much attention to the book's form as they do its content will find it somewhat easier to understand. However, they will still need to set aside time to reflect on it. *On War* is and, regrettably, must remain an unfinished work. We need to resist the temptation to finish it, to rewrite the famous opus according to the values of liberal democracy. At the same time, we must refrain from erasing what revisions its author did make, and allow *On War* to be no less than what it is, even in its unfinished state: it is more than an argument for pursuing decisive battles in war.

As the opening discussions in this book have shown, *On War* is foremost a search for objective knowledge. Yet, it frequently transitions between objective and subjective knowledge, from what *war is* to how we *should* wage it. As illusory as the 'objective' nature of knowledge may be, it is an illusion with far-reaching implications. If Clausewitz could not arrive at 'the truth, the whole truth, and nothing but the truth', which he indicated was the aim of theory, neither can we. Nevertheless, we can benefit from the truths he did discover, however subjective they may be, by using them to test our own. His discovery of war's underlying laws—purpose, chance, and hostility, for—instance, remains as valid today as yesterday. These laws underpin the universe and the events of war, and we would do well to test our theories and principles against them. In other words, we should concern ourselves less with whether *On War* is still relevant, and more with whether its propositions are still valid.[3] This is not to say we should treat Clausewitz's work as if it were canon. However, if we wish to master the ever-growing body of knowledge on war, or just the part of it we find most urgent, at some point we have to master *On War*.

Unfortunately, while Clausewitz believed he was on the verge of achieving a revolution in military theory, he did not indicate precisely which of his ideas he considered revolutionary. His prefatory note of 1827 indicates those ideas were to be found in the first six books of *On War*. However, in these books we find many ideas, not all of which are wholly original to him. Clausewitz was not a plagiarist, but he did draw freely from others' ideas, sometimes nearly verbatim.

Much like *The Six Books of a Commonwealth* by the sixteenth-century political scientist Jean Bodin (1530–96), the Prussian's masterwork is also something of a critical commentary, bringing together many ideas from multiple sources, but on military rather than political subject matter.[4] Where Clausewitz is most original is in his discussion of the nature of war, in his examination of the breadth and depth of the relationship between war and policy, his analysis of friction, his inquiry into the nature of genius, and his exploration of strategy's role in unifying purpose and means, and of the validity of certain strategic principles or concepts, such as the center of gravity and the relative strength of the defense over the attack. These ideas formed the major themes of this book.

Clausewitz demonstrated that the nature of war, which he captured synthetically in the metaphor of a wondrous trinity, divisible and yet not, is complex and variable. It is complex in the sense that it involves manifold laws and tendencies, which are often at odds with one another. It varies according to the diverse societies which use it, the purposes they pursue, and the means they employ. In other words, Clausewitz came close to saying war has no nature of its own.

He ultimately avoided this conclusion, however, by discovering the principal laws that interact in war, every war, and thus form war's nature. In contrast, the essence of war is simply violence. Yet, violence, in truth, is rarely simple. It is a pulsation, practically a living force in its own right. Violence resides at the center of the trinity. It is, in a nutshell, the 'theory' that Clausewitz said must hover between three points of attraction. Just as war is an 'act of violence', so his theory of war addresses the application of that violence. As much as the magnitude and duration of violence may vary from war to war, violence is still the root means in every war.

Adding further specificity to the nature of war, Clausewitz argued that the laws of logical necessity do not apply to real war; they are reserved for the fiction that is war in the abstract. Instead, real war is governed by the laws of probability. That deceptively straightforward difference presents some weighty implications for the theorist and the practitioner. It means, above all, that war's ability to achieve the purposes of policy begins as a 50–50 proposition: war is a risky business, regardless of the stakes. We can, of course, take actions which will increase the odds in our favor, but so can our foe. The complexities of the larger political situation are generally such that rarely, if ever, can we expect the chances of success to be 100 percent. Rather than reducing war's probabilities to a series of algorithms, as in game or decision theory, Clausewitz maintained that courage and self-assurance, qualities which Enlightenment theorists marginalized, were indispensable. They balance the inhibiting influence of uncertainty.

Moreover, since war does not obey the laws of logical necessity, arguments advocating a particular course of action based on military or political necessity are specious. Such arguments are based on a logical imperative which, by definition, cannot exist.[5] What we tend to think of as military or political necessity is often merely a matter of subjective judgment on the part of the commander, or the policymaker. That does not mean those judgments are wrong, only that appeals to the inner logic of war are misleading.

Finally, accepting the laws of probability means we must reconsider any talk of cycles of war. Cycles would require the existence of a logical imperative, but all the theorist or the practitioner can count on are outcomes expressed in terms of likelihood: for every 100 battles we fight, we should expect to win 50. We can see such divided results do tend to occur historically, for instance, when we compare the wars between the French and the British, or the French and the Germans. Obviously, circumstances may skew the odds a bit from time to time. Nonetheless, the point is, probabilities trump cycles.

Clausewitz's reflections regarding war and policy are considered by many scholars as his most important contribution to military thinking. Whether he regarded them so highly is something we cannot verify. However, we do know that while they were not entirely original, they penetrated deeper than those of his contemporaries. By arguing that war is merely 'the continuation of political activity by other means', Clausewitz situated armed conflict within its proper milieu. It can never be separated from that milieu, not so much because war would become a thing devoid of sense, since even war stripped of political purpose can make sense from a purely logical standpoint, but because it simply would not occur.

Political activities, as Clausewitz broadly conceived them, are what, in any and all cases, give rise to strife. Even in situations where military aims appear to drive events, they actually do not. Military aims are shaped by politics, and can only be realized to the extent political conditions allow. Political influences either cause or allow military classes to cultivate certain values, to create particular means, and in effect to develop a particular style of warfare. Militaristic societies, for instance, are but a particular expression of political conditions; conversely, the same is true for societies in which militaries enjoy less influence, and perform primarily constabulary roles.[6] Nonetheless, the influence of this sort of political determinism on Clausewitz's thought has thus far gone unnoticed by his interpreters. This determinism does not, however, in any way diminish the validity his observation that war's proper milieu is politics.

Each historical era, so Clausewitz concluded, has its own 'theory', its own way of waging war. Unfortunately, his statement goes a bridge farther than history can support. Or, more precisely, history can defend this view only if we draw the lines between historical eras just right. Eras essentially have more than one theory of war. The pursuit of unlimited military aims on the battlefield for limited political purposes characterized European warfare throughout much of nineteenth-century, and into the twentieth. Yet the Cold War saw the use of limited military aims (though unlimited means were stockpiled on both sides) in support of virtually unlimited political purposes. And wars of limited means for limited ends, such as that waged by the Arabs and T. E. Lawrence in World War I, share space with those of limited means for unlimited ends, as carried out by Mao and others. Still, Clausewitz's point was more along the lines that there are many kinds of wars, and all of them are valid. When we regard contemporary wars in this light, their inner workings are more apparent, and not entirely different from those of the past.

Friction is perhaps Clausewitz's second most popular concept, and probably the easiest to understand. We find it in every field of endeavor, and its very ubiquity may make it less interesting. However, it is not on that account less important. While practitioners generally take friction into account, theorists often do not. Many contemporary RMA theories, in fact, assume that the right kind of technology can reduce or eliminate the influence of friction altogether. The right kind of technology is, of course, always just over the horizon. Although other works in Clausewitz's day, such as *Reflections on the Art of War* by the Prussian officer and diplomat Georg Heinrich von Berenhorst (1733–1814), stressed the importance of psychological factors and chance, Clausewitz was evidently the first to dissect friction.[7] He saw friction and psychological factors as the principal influences that separate practice from theory, and he believed correct knowledge could help commanders improve their judgment, and in effect close this gap.

As noted earlier, Clausewitz was also the first to attempt a scientific dissection of military genius. He believed genius was a balance of intellectual and emotional traits, adjusted so that each would aid rather than impair judgment. However, he also saw genius as an innate talent that established the rules, methods, and models for art, whether music, painting, sculpture, or military art. Genius was more than the proverbial soldier marching to a different beat. The rules genius established had to prove effective on a consistent basis, which would in turn lead others to emulate them. Otherwise, as Clausewitz acknowledged, we might mistake a lucky fool for a genius.

Clausewitz defined strategy as the use of engagements for the purpose of the war. This definition is admittedly limited in several critical respects, but it is one that many contemporary strategic theorists and practitioners still regard as valid. It does not address how economic power might be used in war, for instance, or how economic and military power might be integrated. However, it does connect purpose and means which, as we have seen, is the fundamental relationship that not only holds *On War* together, but also unifies activities at all levels of war. Moreover, this concept of strategy is an effective one for educating strategists and others.

*On War*'s strategic principles are closer to today's notion of operational art than to strategy. Yet contemporary military doctrine still considers the bulk of these principles valid, though some clearly pertain to linear rather than nonlinear combat environments. Furthermore, as Clausewitz admitted, he was less than satisfied with having been unable to discern principles for wars fought for negotiated settlements. In such wars, centers of gravity, as one example, may be present, but the physical and psychological forces of the belligerent parties will not likely be pronounced enough to cause such focal points to emerge.

The more war tends toward nonviolent observation, so Clausewitz reasoned, the less likely we would need the guiding help of principles and concepts. In a sense, this logic is valid, for when such operations occur today, rules of engagement (ROE) tend to take the place of doctrinal principles.[8]

Nonetheless, it seems Clausewitz was less than satisfied with having found no universal principles for such wars. Contemporary efforts to develop principles for so-called 'operations other than war' have not fared much better. The center of gravity concept is a classic example of reflecting back one's intellectual predispositions, as militaries worldwide have tended to interpret this concept in their own images. It is closer to a center of power than a source of power, but current definitions gravitate toward critical capabilities, which is a different concept altogether.

As this study has shown, Clausewitz's overall concern was to replace the artificial theories of his day with one that was grounded in the reality of war, that is, fighting or combat, which also included the threat of combat. Whether his expansion of this idea to include the threat of combat was deliberate or an afterthought hardly matters when we recall that *On War* is an unfinished work.[9] It is there, and it helps solidify the Copernican center of his entire theory.

Unfortunately, just as he predicted, his revolution has been largely misunderstood, not only in his own era, but for the better part of two centuries. His nineteenth-century heirs, for instance, inspired more by Napoleon's battlefield victories than the ideas in *On War*, tended to tie theory, which rested on the centrality of combat, directly to the pursuit of decisive victory on the battlefield.[10]

Perhaps no less surprising, scholars from the early twentieth century to the present, all too aware of war's growing apocalyptic potential, saw in Clausewitz's discussion of the relationship between war and policy the complete antithesis of the nineteenth-century view. Each also misread his observations concerning absolute war. The former saw it as a description of war's true nature, which strategies and war plans may not violate. The latter perceived it as a threat to the rational control of war by policy, and hence argued that strategies should be designed in ways that contained war's nature. Neither interpretation, however, put much effort into evaluating Clausewitz's revolution, or took seriously his attendant search for the best form for presenting his ideas. Both, in short, succumbed to the temptation to finish an unfinished symphony.

However, the fact that a revolution is misunderstood, or missed altogether, does not mean one did not occur. Copernicus' revolution had little effect until well after his death. Most scholars would agree that *On War* sits astride two diametrically opposed, and yet completely accurate, characterizations. On the one hand, it is the only 'truly great book' on war, and like 'Thucydides' *History* a 'work for all times'.[11] On the other hand, it is often quoted, 'but little read'. Just as one historian labeled Copernicus' *On the Revolutions* as *The Book Nobody Read*, we could say the same of Clausewitz's opus.[12] The purpose of this study was to show that knowledge of Clausewitz's purpose and method makes *On War* more accessible and easier to comprehend. *On War* is a work for all times because many of the ideas in it underpin much of our corpus of knowledge of armed conflict. The problem with any body of knowledge, however, is that it has to be read before it can truly exist.

## NOTES

1. Eric Alterman, 'The Uses and Abuses of Clausewitz', *Parameters*, 17/2 (summer 1987), 18–32.
2. Bruce Fleming, 'Can Reading Clausewitz Save Us from Future Mistakes?', *Parameters*, 34/1 (spring 2004), 62–77, maintains *On War* is too full of contradictions to be regarded as anything but poetry.

3. Ian Roxborough, 'Clausewitz and the Sociology of War', *British Journal of Sociology*, 45 (December 1994), 619–36, points out that 'as a discipline sociology has not been very successful in producing an integrated theory about the nature of warfare'. This underscores the importance of *On War* as a baseline.
4. Jean Bodin, *The Six Books of a Commonwealth*, trans. M. J. Tooley (Oxford: Blackwell, 1955).
5. This does not deny strategy's inner logic; whether that logic is actually paradoxical as Luttwak claims is another matter. Edward N. Luttwak, *Strategy: The Logic of War and Peace* (Cambridge, MA: Harvard University Press, 2001).
6. Morris Janowitz, *The Professional Soldier: A Social and Political Portrait* (New York: Free Press, 1971); Jan van der Meulen, 'Post-modern Societies and Future Support for Military Missions', in *The Clausewitzian Dictum*, 59–74, maintains that Janowitz's ideas have recently regained currency.
7. Georg Heinrich von Berenhorst, *Betrachtungen über die Kriegskunst*, 3 vols. (Osnabrück, Germany: Biblio Verlag, 1796–9); see Wilhelm Rüstow, *Feldherrnkunst des Neunzehnten Jahrhundert: Zum Selbststudium und für den Unterricht an hö̈heren Militärschulen*, 2nd edn. (Leipzig, Germany: F. Schultheiss, 1867), 181–7.
8. US Department of Defense defines ROE as 'Directives issued by competent military authority which delineate the circumstances and limitations under which United States forces will initiate and/or continue combat engagement with other forces encountered'. *Joint Doctrine Division, J-7, Joint Staff*, Dept. of Defense, December 17, 2003. In theory, they define when, where, how, and against whom military force can be used, but in practice they supercede doctrine; Scott D. Sagan, 'Rules of Engagement', in Alexander L. George (ed.), *Avoiding War: Problems of Crisis Management* (Boulder, CO: Westview, 1991), 443–70.
9. Like any author, Clausewitz moved back and forth between chapters, editing and refining his ideas, as he went. He wrote on the right half of the page, and reserved the left for corrections and alterations. The handwritten manuscript available at the Staatsbibliotek Preussischer Kulturbesitz in Berlin shows this quite clearly. *Vom Kriege*, esp. between 448–9, also reproduces a few pages from earlier drafts.
10. Martin Kitchen, 'The Political History of Clausewitz', *Journal of Strategic Studies*, 11/1 (March 1988), 27–50.
11. Bernard Brodie, 'Clausewitz: A Passion for War', *World Politics*, 25/2 (January 1973), 228–308, here 291; Rüstow, *Feldherrnkunst*, 536. A number of scholars have used Brodie's expression, with good reason; see Bassford, *Clausewitz in English*, 3; Smith, *On Clausewitz*, viii.
12. Rüstow, *Feldherrnkunst*, 536, again; Owen Gingerich, *The Book Nobody Read: Chasing the Revolutions of Nicolaus Copernicus* (New York: Walker, 2004).

# Selected Bibliography

Abegglen, Christoph M. V., 'The Influence of Clausewitz on Jomini's *Précis de l'Art de la Guerre*', Masters Dissertation, War Studies, King's College, London, 2003.

Alger, John I., *The Quest for Victory: The History of the Principles of War* (Westport, CT: Greenwood, 1982).

Aller, Chris van, 'Machiavelli and Clausewitz on the Political Determinants of National Security', *Defense Analysis*, 13 (1997), 5–18.

Alterman, Eric, 'The Uses and Abuses of Clausewitz', *Parameters*, 17 (summer 1987), 18–32.

Angstrom, John and Isabelle Duyveston (eds.), *Rethinking the Nature of War* (London: Frank Cass, 2005).

―― *The Nature of Modern War: Clausewitz and His Critics Revisited* (Stockholm: Department of War Studies, Swedish National Defence College, 2003).

Aron, Raymond, 'Reason, Passion, and Power in the Thought of Clausewitz', *Social Research* (winter 1972), 599–621.

―― 'Clausewitz' Conceptual System', *Armed Forces and Society*, 1 (November 1974), 49–59.

―― trans. Christine Booker and Norman Stone, *Clausewitz: Philosopher of War* (Englewood Cliffs, NJ: Prentice-Hall, 1985). [Originally *Penser la guerre, Clausewitz*. Paris: Editions Gallimard, 1976.]

Baldwin, P. M., 'Clausewitz in Nazi Germany', *Journal of Contemporary History*, 16 (1981), 5–26.

Bassford, Christopher, 'Jomini and Clausewitz: Their Interaction', paper presented to the 24th Meeting of the Consortium on Revolutionary Europe at Georgia State University, 26 February 1993. *Proceedings of the Consortium on Revolutionary Europe*, XX (1992). Tallahassee, FL: Florida State University, 1994.

―― *Clausewitz in English: The Reception of Clausewitz in Britain and America, 1815–1945* (New York: Oxford University Press, 1994).

―― 'John Keegan and the Grand Tradition of Trashing Clausewitz', *War in History* (November 1994), 319–36.

―― and Edward J. Villacres, 'Reclaiming the Clausewitzian Trinity', *Parameters* (autumn 1995).

Baucom, Donald R., *Clausewitz on Space War: An Essay on the Strategic Aspects of Military Operations in Space* (Maxwell Air Force Base, AL: Air University Press, 1992).

Beiser, Frederick C., *Enlightenment, Revolution, & Romanticism: The Genesis of Modern German Political Thought, 1790–1800* (Cambridge, MA: Harvard University Press, 1992).

Betts, Richard K., 'Is Strategy an Illusion?', *International Security*, 25 (fall 2002), 5–50.

Beyerchen, Alan D., 'Chance and Complexity in the Real World: Clausewitz on the Nonlinear Nature of War', *International Security* (winter [1992]1993), 59–90.

\_\_\_\_ 'Clausewitz, Nonlinearity, and the Importance of Imagery', David S. Alberts and Thomas J. Czerwinski (eds.), *Complexity, Global Politics, and National Security* (Washington, DC: National Defense University, 1997).

Black, Jeremy, *War and the New Disorder in the 21st Century* (New York: Continuum Press, 2004).

Brown, Robin, 'Clausewitz in the Age of Al-Jazeera: Rethinking the Military–Media Relationship', Paper, Harvard Symposium Restless Searchlight: The Media and Terrorism. (August 21, 2002).

Bubke, Otto, *Clausewitz and Naval Warfare* (Bergisch Gladbach: Amt fur Studien und Übungen der Bundeswehr, 1987).

[Bülow-Dietrich], A., *The Spirit of the Modern System of War* (London: T. Egerton, 1806).

Caraccilo, Dominic J. and John L. Pothin, 'Coup d'œil: The Commander's Intuition in Clauswitzian Terms', *Air & Space Power Chronicles* (February 16, 2000).

Carlyle, Robert, *Clausewitz's Contemporary Relevance*, Occasional Paper no. 16 (Camberley: The Strategic and Combat Studies Institute, 1995).

Cimbala, Stephen, *Clausewitz and Escalation: Classical Perspectives on Nuclear Strategy* (London: Frank Cass, 1991).

\_\_\_\_ *Clausewitz and Chaos: Friction in War and Military Policy* (Westport, CT: Praeger, 2001).

Clark, Mark T., 'The Continuing Relevance of Clausewitz', *Strategic Review*, 26 (winter 1998), 54–61.

Clausewitz, Carl von, *On War*, ed./trans. Michael Howard and Peter Paret (Princeton, NJ: Princeton University Press, 1976, Rev. 1984).

\_\_\_\_ *Historical and Political Writings*, eds./trans. Peter Paret and Daniel Moran. (Princeton, NJ: Princeton University Press, 1992).

\_\_\_\_ 'Bemerkungen über die reine und angewandte Strategie des Herrn von Bülow', *Neue Bellona*, IX (1805), no. 3.

\_\_\_\_ *Schriften–Aufsätze–Studien–Briefe*, Intro. Werner Hahlweg (Göttingen: Vandenhoeck & Ruprecht, 1966).

\_\_\_\_ *Politische Schriften und Briefe*, ed. Hans Rothfels (Munich: Drei Masken, 1922).

\_\_\_\_ *Vom Kriege. Hinterlassenes Werk des Carl von Clausewitz*, 19th edn. edited and introduced by Werner Halweg (Bonn: Ferd. Dümmlers Verlag, 1980).

\_\_\_\_ *Verstreute kleine Schriften*, Collected, Edited, and introduced by Werner Hahlweg (Osnabrück: Biblio Verlag, 1979).

Coats, W. J., 'Clausewitz's Theory of War: An Alternative View', *Comparative Strategy*, 5 (1988), 351–73.

Collins, John M., *Grand Strategy: Principles and Practices* (Annapolis, MD: US Naval Institute, 1973).

Coroalles, Anthony M., 'On War in the Information Age: A Conversation with Carl von Clausewitz', *Army*, 46 (May 1996), 24–6.

Cozette, Murielle, 'Realistic Realism? American Political Realism, Clausewitz and Raymond Aron on the Problem of Means and Ends in International Politics', *Journal of Strategic Studies*, 27 (2004), 428–53.

Creveld, Martin Van, '*The Transformation of War* Revisited', *Small Wars and Insurgencies*, 13 (summer 2002), 3–15.

―――― *The Transformation of War* (New York: Free Press, 1991).

―――― 'The Clausewitzian Universe and the Law of War', *Journal of Contemporary History*, 26 (1991), 403–29.

Daston, Lorraine, *Classical Probability in the Enlightenment* (Princeton, NJ: Princeton University Press, 1988).

Dill, Günther (ed.), *Clausewitz in Perspektive* (Frankfurt am Main: Ullstein, 1980).

Duyvesteyn, Isabelle, *Clausewitz and African War: Politics and Strategy in Liberia and Somalia* (London: Routledge, 2004).

Earle, Edward Mead (ed.), *Makers of Modern Strategy: Military Thought from Machiavelli to Hitler* (Princeton, NJ: Princeton University Press, 1944).

Eccles, Henry E., *Military Concepts and Philosophy* (New Brunswick, NJ: Rutgers University Press, 1965).

Echevarria II, Antulio J., 'Clausewitz: Toward a Theory of Applied Strategy', *Defense Analysis*, 11 (1995), 229–40.

―――― 'War, Politics, and RMA—The Legacy of Clausewitz', *Joint Forces Quarterly* (winter 1995–6), 76–82.

―――― 'A Wake for Clausewitz? Not Yet!', *Special Warfare*, 9 (August 1996), 30–5.

―――― *After Clausewitz: German Military Thinkers before the Great War* (Lawrence, KS: University Press of Kansas, 2000).

―――― 'Clausewitz's Center of Gravity: It's Not What We Thought', *Naval War College Review* (winter 2003).

Elting, John, 'Jomini: Disciple of Napoleon?', *Military Affairs* (spring 1964), 17–26.

Esposito, V. J. 'War as a Continuation of Politics', *Military Review*, 34 (February 1955), 54–62.

Etzold, T. H., 'Clausewitzian Lessons for Modern Strategists', *Air University Review* (May–June 1980), 24–8.

Feaver, Peter D. and Richard H. Kohn (eds.), *Soldiers and Civilians: The Civil–Military Gap and American National Security* (Cambridge, MA: Massachusetts Institute of Technology, 2001).

Fleming, Bruce, 'Can Reading Clausewitz Save Us from Future Mistakes?', *Parameters* (spring 2004), 62–76.

Freedman, Lawrence, *The Transformation of Strategic Affairs*, Adelphi Paper, no. 379, International Institute for Strategic Studies, London, 2006.

―――― (ed.), *Superterrorism: Policy Responses* (Oxford: Blackwell, 2002).

Freudenberg, G. F., 'A Conversation with General Clausewitz', *Military Review* (October 1977), 68–71.

Furlong, Raymond B., '*On War*, Political Objectives, and Military Strategy', *Parameters* (December 1983), 2–10.

Gallie, W. B., *Philosophers of Peace and War: Kant, Clausewitz, Marx, Engels and Tolstoy* (Cambridge: Cambridge University Press, 1978).
\_\_\_\_ 'Clausewitz Today', *European Journal of Sociology*, 19 (1978), 143–67.
Gat, Azar, 'Clausewitz on Defence and Attack', *Journal of Strategic Studies*, 11 (March 1988), 20–6.
\_\_\_\_ *The Origins of Military Thought: From the Enlightenment to Clausewitz* (Oxford: Oxford University Press, 1989).
\_\_\_\_ 'Clausewitz's Political and Ethical World View', *Political Studies*, 37 (1989), 97–106.
\_\_\_\_ *The Development of Military Thought: The Nineteenth Century* (Oxford: Clarendon Press, 1992).
Gerges, Fawaz A., *The Far Enemy: Why Jihad Went Global* (Cambridge: Cambridge University Press, 2005).
Gibbs, N. H., 'Clausewitz on the Moral Forces in War', *Naval War College Review* (January–February 1975), 15–22.
Gilbert, Felix, 'From Clausewitz to Delbrück and Hintze: Achievements and Failures of Military History', *Journal of Strategic Studies*, 3 (1980), 11–20.
Gillies, Donald, *Philosophical Theories of Probability* (London: Routledge, 2000).
Glenn, Russell W., 'The Clausewitz Posthumous Analysis of the Gulf War', *British Army Review*, 100 (April 1992), 21–23; *Australian Defence Force Journal*, 93 (March–April 1992), 7–9.
Gray, Colin S., 'How Has War Changed Since the End of the Cold War?', *Parameters*, 35 (spring 2005), 14–27.
\_\_\_\_ *Strategy for Chaos: Revolutions in Military Affairs and the Evidence of History* (London: Frank Cass, 2002).
\_\_\_\_ *Modern Strategy* (Oxford: Oxford University Press, 1999).
Gunaratna, Rohan, *Inside Al Qaeda* (Cambridge: Cambridge University Press, 2002).
Guyer, Paul (ed.), *The Cambridge Companion to Kant* (Cambridge: Cambridge University Press, 1999).
Hacking, Ian, *The Taming of Chance* (Cambridge: Cambridge University Press, 2002).
Handel, Michael I. (ed.), *Clausewitz and Modern Strategy* (London: Frank Cass 1986).
\_\_\_\_ *Masters of War: Classical Strategic Thought*. 2nd and 3rd edns. (Portland, OR: Frank Cass, [1996] 2001).
\_\_\_\_ 'Corbett, Clausewitz, and Sun Tzu', *Naval War College Review*, 53 (2000), 106–24.
\_\_\_\_ & Ferris, J., 'Clausewitz, Intelligence, Uncertainty and the Art of Command in Military Operations', *Intelligence and National Security* (January 1995), 1–58.
Hartmann, Uwe, *Carl von Clausewitz and the Making of Modern Strategy* (Potsdam: Miles, 2002).
\_\_\_\_ 'Dialektik bei Carl von Clausewitz', *Clausewitz-Studien*. no. 3. (winter 1996), 152–75.
Heer, Hannes and Klaus Naumann (eds.), *War of Extermination: The German Military in World War II, 1941–4* (New York: Berghahn, 2000).

Herberg-Rothe, Andreas, 'Primacy of Politics or Culture in a Modern World? Clausewitz Needs a Sophisticated Interpretation', *Defense Analysis*, 2 (August 2001).
\_\_\_\_ *Das Rätsel Clausewitz. Politische Theorie des Kriegs im Widerstreit* (Munich: Wilhelm Fink Verlag, 2001).
\_\_\_\_ 'Clausewitz und Hegel. Ein heuristischer Vergleich', in *Forschungen zur brandenburgischen und preußischen Geschichte*, Jahrgang 10, Heft 1/2000, pp. 49–84.
Heuser, Beatrice, *Reading Clausewitz* (London: Pimlico, 2002).
Holsti, Kalevi J., *The State, War and the State of War* (Cambridge: Cambridge University Press, 1997).
Honig, Jan Willem, 'Interpreting Clausewitz', *Security Studies* (spring 1994).
Hooker, Richard D., Jr, 'Beyond *Vom Kriege*: The Character and Conduct of Modern War', *Parameters* (summer 2005), 4–17.
Howard, Michael, *Clausewitz* (Oxford: Oxford University Press, 1983).
\_\_\_\_ *Clausewitz: A Very Short Introduction* (New York: Oxford University Press, 2002).
\_\_\_\_ (ed.), *The Theory and Practice of War* (New York: Praeger, 1966).
Huntington, Samuel P., *The Soldier and the State: The Theory and Politics of Civil–Military Relations* (Cambridge, MA: Harvard University Press, 1957).
Kahn, Hermann, *On Thermonuclear War* (Princeton, NJ: Princeton University Press, 1961); reprinted (Westport, CT: Greenwood Press, 1978).
Kaldor, Mary, *New & Old Wars: Organized Violence in a Global Era* (Stanford, CA: Stanford University Press, 1999).
Keegan, John, *A History of Warfare.* (New York: Knopf, 1993).
Kessel, Eberhard, 'Zur Entstehungsgeschichte von Clausewitz' Werk Vom Kriege', *Historische Zeitschrift*, 152 (1935), 97–100.
\_\_\_\_ 'Carl von Clausewitz: Herkunft und Persönlichkeit', *Wissen und Wehr*, 18 (1937), 763–74.
\_\_\_\_ 'Die doppelte Art des Krieges',*Wehrwissenschaftliche Rundschau Zeitschrift für die Europäische Sicherheit*, 4 (1954), 298–310.
\_\_\_\_ 'Zur Genesis der modernen Kriegslehre: Die Entstehungs geschichte von Clausewitz' Buch "Vom Kriege" ', *Wehrwissenschaftliche Rundschau Zeitschrift für die Europäische Sicherheit*, 3 (1953), 405–23.
Kiesewetter, Johann G. K., *Grundriss einer Allgemeinen Logik nach Kantischen Grundsätzen zum Gebrauch für Vorlesungen*, 2 vols. (Leipzig: H. A. Kochly, 1824–25).
\_\_\_\_ *Darstellung der Wichtigsten Wahrheiten der neueren Philosophie*, 4th edn., 2 vols. (Berlin: Flittner, 1824).
Killion, Thomas H., 'Clausewitz and Military Genius', *Military Review*, 75 (July–August 1995), 97–100.
King, James E., 'On Clausewitz: Master Theorist of War', *Naval War College Review* (fall 1977), 3–36.
Kinross, Stuart, 'Clausewitz and Low-Intensity Conflict', *The Journal of Strategic Studies*, 27 (March 2004), 35–58.
Kissinger, Henry A., *Nuclear Weapons and Foreign Policy* (New York: Harper and Brothers, 1957).

Kitchen, Martin, 'The Traditions of German Strategic Thought', *The International History Review*, 1 (1979), 163–90.

—— 'The Political History of Clausewitz', *Journal of Strategic Studies*, 11 (March 1988), 27–50.

Kuhn, Thomas S., *The Structure of Scientific Revolutions*, 2nd edn. (Chicago, IL: University of Chicago Press, 1970).

Laplace, Marquis de, *A Philosophical Essay on Probabilities*, Trans. Frederick Truscott and Frederick Emory (New York: Dover, [1951] 1995).

Laqueur, Walter, *Guerrilla Warfare: A Historical & Critical Study* (New Brunswick, NJ: Transaction, 1998).

Lawrence, T. E., *Seven Pillars of Wisdom* (New York: Doubleday, [1926] 1935).

Lebow, Richard Ned, 'Clausewitz and Nuclear Crisis Stability', *Political Science Quarterly* (spring 1988), 89–110.

Leonard, Roger Ashley, *A Short Guide to Clausewitz On War* (New York: G. P. Putnam's Sons, 1967).

Liddell Hart, Basil H. *The German Generals Talk* (New York: William Morrow and Company, 1948).

—— *Strategy*, Rev. eds. (New York: Praeger, [1954] 1967).

Lonsdale, David J., *The Nature of War in the Information Age: Clausewitzian Future* (London: Frank Cass, 2004).

Lynn, John A., 'War of Annihilation, War of Attrition, and War of Legitimacy: A Neo-Clausewitzian Approach to Twentieth-Century Conflicts', *Marine Corps Gazette*, (October 1996), 64–71.

McAleer, Kevin, *Dueling: The Cult of Honor in Fin-de-Siècle Germany* (Princeton, NJ: Princeton University Press, 1994).

McIvor, Anthony D. (ed.), *Rethinking the Principles of War* (Annapolis, MD: Naval Institute, 2005).

Maiziere, Ulrich de (ed.), *Freiheit ohne Krieg: Beitrage zur Strategie-Diskussion der Gegenwart im Spiegel der Theorie von Carl von Clausewitz* (Bonn: Ferdinand Dummlers Verlag, 1980).

Matthews, Lloyd J., 'On Clausewitz', *Army* (February 1988), 20–4.

Metz, Steven and Frederick M. Downey. 'Centers of Gravity and Strategic Planning', *Military Review* (April 1988), 22–33.

—— 'A Wake for Clausewitz: Toward a Philosophy of 21st Century Warfare', *Parameters* (winter 1994–5), 126–32.

Moody, Peter R., Jr, 'Clausewitz and the Fading Dialectic of War', *World Politics*, 31 (1979), 417–32.

Moran, Daniel, 'Clausewitz and the Revolution', *Central European History*, 22 (June 1989), 183–99.

Münkler, Herfried, *The New Wars* (Malden: Polity Press, 2005).

Murray, Penelope (ed.), *Genius: The History of an Idea* (Oxford: Blackwell, 1989).

Murray, Williamson, 'War, Theory, Clausewitz, and Thucydides: The Game May Change But the Rules Remain', *Marine Corps Gazette*, 81 (January 1997), 62–9.

Murray, Williamson, Macgregor Knox, and Alvin Bernstein (eds.), *The Making of Strategy: Rulers, States, and War* (Cambridge: Cambridge University Press, 1994).
Nardulli, Bruce R., 'Clausewitz and the Reorientation of Nuclear Strategy', *The Journal of Strategic Studies* (December 1982), 494–510.
New, Larry D., 'Clausewitz's Theory: *On War* and Its Application Today', *Airpower Journal*, 10 (fall 1996), 78–86.
Nielsen, Suzanne C., *Political Control over the Use of Force: A Clausewitzian Perspective* (Carlisle: Strategic Studies Institute, 2001).
Nooy, Gert de (ed.), *The Clausewitzian Dictum and the Future of Western Military Strategy* (The Hague: Kluwer Law International, 1997).
Osgood, Robert Endicott, *Limited War: The Challenge to American Strategy* (Chicago, IL: University of Chicago Press, 1957).
\_\_\_\_ *Limited War Revisited* (Boulder: Westview Press, 1979).
Otte, T. G., 'Educating Bellona: Carl von Clausewitz and Military Education', Keith Nelson and Greg Kennedy (eds.), *Military Education: Past, Present, Future* (New York: Praeger, 2002).
Owens, Admiral Bill, *Lifting the Fog of War* (New York: Farrar, Straus, Giroux, 2000).
Paquette L., 'Strategy in Time in Clausewitz's *On War* and in Sun-Tzu's *Art of War*', *Comparative Strategy*, 10 (1991), 37–51.
Paret, Peter, *Yorck and the Era of Prussian Reform, 1807–1815* (Princeton, NJ: Princeton University Press, 1966).
\_\_\_\_ 'Education, Politics, and War in the Life of Clausewitz', *Journal of the History of Ideas*, 29 (1968), 394–408.
\_\_\_\_ *Clausewitz and the State: The Man, His Theories, and His Times* (Princeton, NJ: Princeton University Press, 1976).
\_\_\_\_ *Understanding War: Essays on Clausewitz and the History of Military Power* (Princeton, NJ: Princeton University Press, 1992).
\_\_\_\_ 'From Ideal to Ambiguity: Johannes von Muller, Clausewitz, and the People in Arms', *Journal of the History of Ideas*, 65 (January 2004), 101–11.
\_\_\_\_ (ed.), *Makers of Modern Strategy: From Machiavelli to the Nuclear Age* (Princeton, NJ: Princeton University Press, 1986).
Parkinson, Roger, *Clausewitz: A Biography* (New York: Stein and Day, 1971).
Perlmutter, Amos, 'Carl von Clausewitz, Enlightenment Philosopher: A Comparative Analysis', *Journal of Strategic Studies*, 11 (March 1988), 8–19.
Popper, Karl R, *Objective Knowledge: An Evolutionary Approach* (Oxford: Clarendon Press, 1972).
Reid, Brian Holden (ed.), *The Science of War: Back to First Principles* (London: Routledge, 1993).
Reynolds, Charles, 'Carl von Clausewitz and Strategic Theory', *British Journal of International Studies*, 4 (1978), 178–90.
Rogers, Clifford J., 'Clausewitz, Genius, and the Rules', *The Journal of Military History*, 66 (October 2002), 1167–76.

Rosello, Victor M., 'Clausewitz's Contempt for Intelligence', *Parameters* (spring 1991), 103–14.

Rosen, Edward, *Copernicus and the Scientific Revolution* (Malabar: Robert E. Krieger, 1984).

Rosinski, Herbert, 'Scharnhorst to Schlieffen: The Rise and Decline of German Military Thought', *United States Naval War College Review* (summer 1976), 83–103.

Roth, Gunter, 'The Thought of Annihilation in the Military Doctrine of Carl von Clausewitz and Count Alfred von Schlieffen', Militärgeschichtliches Forschungsamt (ed.), *Operational Thinking in Clausewitz, Moltke, Schlieffen and Manstein* (Bonn: E. S. Mittler and Son, 1988).

Roxborough, Ian, 'Clausewitz and the Sociology of War', *British Journal of Sociology*, 45 (December 1994), 619–36.

Sageman, Marc, *Understanding Terror Networks* (Philadelphia, PA: University of Pennsylvania Press, 2004).

Schneider, James J. and Lawrence J. Izzo, 'Clausewitz's Elusive Center of Gravity', *Parameters*, 17 (September 1987), 46–57.

Shephard, John E., Jr, '*On War*: Is Clausewitz Still Relevant?', *Parameters* (September 1990), 85–99.

Sidoti, Capt Anthony F., 'The Relevance of Carl von Clausewitz in Operation Iraqi Freedom', *Air & Space Power Chronicles* (21 January 2004).

Simpson, B. M. III, 'The Essential Clausewitz', *Naval War College Review* (March–April 1982), 54–61.

Smith, Hugh, 'The Womb of War: Clausewitz and International Politics', *Review of International Studies*, 16 (1990), 39–58.

\_\_\_\_ *On Clausewitz: A Study of Military and Political Ideas* (New York: Palgrave-Macmillan, 2005).

Smith, James B., 'Some Thoughts on Clausewitz and Airplanes', *Air University Review*, 37 (May–June 1986), 52–9.

Speelman, Patrick J., *Henry Lloyd and the Military Enlightenment of Eighteenth-Century Europe* (Westport, CT: Greenwood Press, 2002).

\_\_\_\_ (ed.), *War, Society and Enlightenment: The Works of General Lloyd* (Boston, MA: Brill, 2005).

Staudenmaier, W. O., 'Vietnam, Mao and Clausewitz', *Parameters*, 7 (1977), 79–89.

Steiner, Barry H., 'Psychological and Psychoanalytical Interpretations of Clausewitz', in *Bernard Brodie and the Foundations of American Nuclear Strategy* (Lawrence, KS: University Press of Kansas, 1991), 217–25.

Stern, Jessica, *Terror in the Name of God: Why Religious Militants Kill* (New York: HarperCollins, 2003).

Strachan, Hew, *European Armies and the Conduct of War* (London: Unwin Hyman, 1983).

Strange, Joe, *Centers of Gravity & Critical Vulnerabilities: Building on the Clausewitzian Foundation So That We Can All Speak the Same Language* (Quantico, VA: Marine Corps University, 1996).

Stuart, Reginald C., 'Clausewitz and the Americans: Bernard Brodie and Others on War and Policy', in *War and Society: A Yearbook of Military History*, vol. 2 (New York: Holmes and Meier, 1977).

Sumida, Jon T., 'The Relationship between History and Theory in On War: the Clausewitzian Ideal and Its Implications', *Journal of Military History*, 65 (April 2001), 333–54.

Summers, Harry G., Jr, *On Strategy: A Critical Analysis of the Vietnam War* (Novato, CA: Presidio Press, 1982).

—— *On Strategy II: A Critical Analysis of the Gulf War* (New York: Dell, 1992).

Swain, Richard M., 'Clausewitz for the 20th Century: The Interpretation of Raymond Aron', *Military Review*, 66 (April 1986), 38–47.

—— 'Clausewitz, FM100-5, and the Center of Gravity', *Military Review* (February 1988), 83.

—— ' "The Hedgehog and the Fox": Jomini, Clausewitz, and History', *Naval War College Review* (autumn 1990), 98–109.

Tashjean, John E., 'Pious Arms: Clausewitz and the Right of War', *Military Affairs* (April 1980), 82–3.

—— 'The Trans-Atlantic Clausewitz, 1952–1982', *Naval War College Review*, 35 (1982), 69–86.

Taylor, Paul D., 'Clausewitz on Economic Sanctions: The Case of Iraq', *Strategic Review*, 23 (summer 1995), 49–58.

Vagts, Alfred, *A History of Militarism: Civilian and Military*, Rev. edn. (New York: Free Press, 1959).

Wallach, Jehuda L., *The Dogma of the Battle of Annihilation: The Theories of Clausewitz and Schlieffen and Their Impact on the German Conduct of Two World Wars* (Westport, CT: Greenwood Press, 1986).

Wass de Czege, Huba, 'Clausewitz: Historical Studies Remain Sound Compass References: The Catch is Staying on Course', *Army* (September 1988), 37–43.

Watts, Barry D., 'Friction in the Gulf War', *Naval War College Review* (autumn 1995), 93–109.

—— *Clausewitzian Friction and Future War* (Washington, DC: Institute for National Strategic Studies, 1996; Rev. edn., 2004).

Weiland, Karl F., 'Strategie und Taktik in der Theorie Carl von Clausewitz', http://www.carlvonclausewitz.de/weiland

White, Charles Edward, *The Enlightened Soldier: Scharnhorst and the Military Gesellschaft in Berlin, 1801–1805* (New York: Praeger, 1989).

Wilkinson, Philip, 'The Changing Nature of War: New Wine in Old Bottles—A New Paradigm or Paradigm Shift?', *The Royal Swedish Academy of War Sciences: Proceedings and Journal* 207/1 (2003), 25–35.

Wills, Gary, 'Critical Inquiry (*Kritik*) in Clausewitz', *Critical Inquiry* (December 1982), 281–302.

Windsor, Philip, 'The Clock, the Context and Clausewitz', *Millenium: Journal of International Studies*, 6 (1977), 190–96.

Wylie, J[oseph] C[aldwell], *Military Strategy: A General Theory of Power Control* (New Brunswick, NJ: Rutgers University Press, 1967).

Zedong, Mao, *Selected Military Writings* (Beijing: Foreign Languages Press, 1977).

Zhang, Yuan-Ling, 'Fortschreiten vom Einfachen zum Zusammengesetzten. Ein sonderbares methodisches Verfahren in Clausewitz' Werk "Vom Kriege" ', *Clausewitz-Studien*, no. 1 (spring 1996), 37–45.

Zimmer, Winfried, 'Clausewitz and the Human Dimension of War', *Military Review*, 74 (March 1994), 51–6.

# Index

absolute war  40, 67, 117, 196
al-Qaeda  74–5, 77, 118, 185–6

Beethoven, Ludwig van  7, 11 n 28
Berenhorst, Georg H. von  17 n 4, 194
Betts, Richard  144
*Bildung*  30
bin Laden, Osama  118
Bodin, Jean  192
Brodie, Bernard  1, 8 n 2, 86
Bülow, Heinrich Dietrich von  3, 31, 42, 73
   principal theories of  13–14, 16–17

center of gravity (defined)  177, 192, 195
   applied concept  180–1
   competing definitions  177–8
   pure concept of  179–80
Clausewitz, Carl von:
   centrality of combat  133–6, 145
   concept of war  64; pure  65, 134–5
   on contemporary military theory  15–16
   on genius  108–9, 113–14
   levels of war  140
   life and education  43–7
   method in *On War*  37–42
   on objective knowledge  23, 25–6
   and political determinism  84–5, 91–3
   *Politik* (definition of)  89
   prefatory notes to *On War*: (circa 1818)  31; (1827)  1, 5, 71, 192
   principle (of destruction)  135
   purpose of *On War*  13, 21
   revolution in military theory  1, 5–6
   strategic conditions (for success)  158
   strategic elements  139
   strategic principles  155; attack  161–2; boldness  155; cunning  155, 165; concentration of forces  155, 163–5; culminating point of victory  141, 167; defense  157–61; economy of force  155, 165; perseverance  155, 165; purpose  167–8; strategic reserve  164; superiority of numbers  155, 163; turning movements  166
   strategy (definition of)  125–6, 133, 144
   on theory  30–1
   on war's nature  55–6, 61

Cold War  68
Copernicus, Nicholas  2–3
   and Clausewitz  9 n 9, 17, 55
   and Clausewitzian revolution  6, 141, 195–6
   revolution of  2–3, 196
   unifying concept of heliocentric theory  24–5
Corbett, Julian  144
*coup d'oeil*  29, 109, 112
Creveld, Martin von  57, 76, 160

Delbrück, Hans  10 n 19, 71
duel  30, 62–3, 79 n 11

Fichte, Johann Gottlieb  112
friction  103, 107, 117
   chance  71, 103, 106
   danger  103–4
   exertion (physical)  103, 105
   uncertainty  41, 103, 105
Fuller, J. F. C.  156, 174 n 58

genius  58, 113, 119 n 2 and n 6, 139, 156, 194–5
   and H. D. von Bülow  14
   and Henry Lloyd  14, 28
   importance of  16
   military genius  5, 102; defined  108–9, 118, 119 n 4
Gneisenau, August von  45
Goethe, Johann Wolfgang von  112
Gray, Colin  144
guerrilla wars  76, 138
Gulf War (1990–1)  138, 184–5

Hahlweg, Werner  22
Hegel, Georg F. W.  38, 91
Herder, Johann Gottfried von  112
Horner (USAF General) Charles  184
Howard, Sir Michael  2, 8 n 1, 48, 89, 100 n 36
Hughes, Wayne  143
Huntington, Samuel  138
Hussein, Saddam  184

Jomini, Antoine-Henri  13, 17, 18 n 16, 31, 42
   principal theories of  15–16

# Index

Kahn, Herman 87
Kant, Immanuel 3
  *Critique of Judgment* 109
  definition of genius 102, 110–11, 113, 118
  doctrine of concepts 13, 39
  hierarchy of laws, principles, etc. 127
  general methodology 42
  system of logic 3, 22, 37, 49
Keegan, John 57
Kiesewetter, Johann 155
  as a lecturer (on Kant) 3–4, 9 n 14, 22–4, 37
  definition of critical inquiry (*Kritik*) 47
  definition of logic 38
  definition of a principle 155
  explication of genius 110
  explication of laws 127
Krepinevich, Andrew 178
Kuhn, Thomas 26

Laplace, Pierre Simon de 71, 80 n 24
Lawrence, T. E. 137–8, 194
laws (defined) 127–8
Liddell Hart, Sir Basil 15, 86, 115–16, 135, 144
Lilienstern, August Rühle von 90
Lloyd, Henry 3, 73
  and *coup d'oeil* 29
  and genius 28
  principal theories of 13–14, 16–17

MacArthur, Douglas 87, 166
Machiavelli, Niccolò 145
Mahan, Alfred Thayer 144
Manstein, Erich von 115–16

military operations (post-Cold War) 146
Moltke, Helmuth von (the elder) 114–15
  definition of strategy 142

Osgood, Robert 86

Paret, Peter 2, 8 n 1
Popper, Karl 23
principles (defined) 126–8
probability 40; laws of 66, 69, 145, 192

Ritter, Gerhard 88
Rommel, Erwin 115
rules (defined) 129–30
Rumsfeld, Donald 178

Scharnhorst, Gerhard von 43–5
Schelling, Thomas 86
Schlieffen, Count Alfred von 143
Schubert, Franz 7, 11 n 28, 96
Schwarzkopf, Norman 184

terrorism 76
trinity (wondrous) 69–70, 106, 192
  chance 71
  hostility 72–3
  purpose 73–5

Walzer, Michael 140
Warden, John 178
Weigley, Russell 56, 93
Weinberger/Powell doctrine 85, 98 n 6
Wylie, J. C. 139, 178

Zedong, Mao 7, 137, 194